CAMRA'S
South East
Pub Walks

CAMRA'S
South East

Pub Walks

BOB STEEL

Published by the Campaign for Real Ale Ltd.
230 Hatfield Road
St Albans
Hertfordshire AL1 4LW
www.camra.org.uk/books

Design and layout © Campaign for Real Ale Ltd. 2012
Text © Bob Steel

ISBN 978-1-85249-287-8

A CIP catalogue record for this book is available
from the British Library

Printed and bound in China by Latitude Press Ltd

Head of Publishing: Simon Hall
Project Editor: Katie Hunt
Editorial Assistance: Emma Haines
Design/Typography: Stephen Bere
Cover Design: Dale Tomlinson
Cartography: Stephen Bere
Walk locations map: John Plumer (JP Map Graphics Ltd)
Ordnance Survey mapping: The
National Map Centre, St Albans
Head of Marketing: Tony Jerome

Photographs: Bob Steel
Additional photography: Andrew and Annemarie (Flickr) p39(t);
Ian Ashdown (Flickr) p86(r); John Brice p21(tl); Andrew Bowden
(Flickr) p86(l); Fuller's p139; Gill Gibson p133, 138(r); Graham Hall
p51 (t), p52 (tr, b); Simon Hall p47, p48 (t), p50, p51 (b); Katie Hunt
p155-60; Jim Linwood (Flickr) p38(b); David Packham p172(l); Terry
Richards photography p154; Mick Slaughter p17; Robert Wicks p10

Cover photography: Top: Julia Gavin / Alamy; Left: Penelope
Fewster (Flickr) Right: Julian Elliott / Alamy

Acknowledgements

I'd like to thank those who have assisted in the production of this
book. Several individuals in local CAMRA branches came up with
suggestions for routes and/or pubs, and although they are too
numerous to name individually I thank them all. In particular, I would
mention James Whiteoak of Medway branch, and Les Middlewood of
South Herts branch for very detailed assistance, and also John Bishop, Phil DeFriez, Ivan Bullerwell, Brendan Sothcott and Kevin Travers.
I would also like to place on record my sincere thanks to Graham
Pritchard and to 'Hammerkop' for permission to use photographs, as
well as to several publicans and licensees who provided photos of
their pubs. Finally thanks to Tudor Hughes for proof-reading drafts
and to Katie at CAMRA for the usual patience and forebearance.
Bob Steel

Contents

How to use this guide

The walks in this guide have been divided by county into three groups: Kent & East Sussex, West Sussex & Surrey and North of the Thames. The walks are all possible to do as day trips from London, or elsewhere in the region, but you could combine several of the routes for a longer walking holiday.

Overview map
This map can be found on page 12. It shows the locations of all the walks and is useful when planning a longer trip that takes in several of the walks, or organising transport and accommodation. Transport information can be found on page 177.

Walk information
Located on first page of each walk, this tinted box will give you some general information needed to plan your route including the start point, public transport access, distance, recommended Ordnance Survey map, and pubs visited. Further information about the walk such as terrain and suggested start time can often be found in the opening paragraph.

KEY FOR WALK MAPS

🏃	Walk start point
▬ ▬	Walk route
• • • •	Detour/Alternative route
1	Featured pub
1	'Try also' pub
A	Corresponds to grid reference in the text
➤	Direction of walk
�‍⊙	Ordnance Survey grid reference
❶	Tourist Information Centre

Mapping
The routes are plotted on Ordnance Survey maps, with suggested detours clearly marked. The start (🏃), waypoints (**A**) and featured pubs (**1**) are marked on the map as shown. One grid square on the map equates to 1km (³/₅ mile) square.

The routes
Featured pubs are numbered as they appear in the route and written in red. Other recommended pubs are numbered and written in blue. All other pubs are written in italics. Ordnance Survey grid references are marked with a (�‍⊙) symbol, and those grid references shown on the map, labelled with the corresponding letter (waypoints).

Information boxes
Tinted boxes give you information about local history, geography and other features of note.

Pub information
A blue box at the end of each walk gives you information about the pubs featured in the route, with information such as the opening hours and contact details – it is recommended that you phone ahead to check times with the pubs, as these can be subject to change. The numbered icons correspond with those in the text and on the map. This box also includes information about 'try also' pubs.

Introduction

This is the fifth book in CAMRA's pub walks series and, in many ways, the most ambitious: selecting thirty routes from a region stretching from Buckinghamshire to Kent and from Essex to the Hampshire border was a challenge in itself, given the large number of good pubs and varied walking country to choose from. We're confident, however, that, given the challenge, we've arrived at a great selection.

The walks

Compared to the uplands of the Lake District and the Peak District, the landscape of South East England is gentler, often more wooded, and with more varied geology. It's a common misconception however that the South East is 'flat' for, although some of these walks don't get far over fifty feet above sea level, the terrain in parts of the High Weald of Kent, the Surrey Hills, or the Chilterns is far from level, and some walks involve some challenging climbs. As in previous books in the series we have avoided simplistic numerical grading systems of walk difficulty in favour of descriptive assessments of the degree of challenge, including the navigational difficulties (see below).

Most of the walks are between 5 and 12 miles in length, although in many cases it's possible to shorten, or lengthen, the walks to suit your circumstances. Although you will need a fair level of fitness, most of the routes in the book can be enjoyed by the leisure walker.

The pubs

CAMRA's first concern is with cask ale, and the quality of it. Members of local branches of the Campaign visit the region's pubs regularly, monitoring beer quality and other issues of concern to pub users. No other pub walks guide can draw upon the independent expertise and advice of thousands of individuals, whose collective research goes into the *Good Beer Guide* and CAMRA's numerous local campaign newsletters, which in turn helped to influence the selection of pubs for this guide.

CAMRA also encourages pubs to offer a warm welcome, serve good food, and maintain the convivial atmosphere which makes the British pub a unique institution. I'm a great believer in the adage that pubs are not restaurants, and that they should always welcome the casual drinker who is not dining. That said, the days of the uninspiring sandwich and the stale pork pie as the epitome of pub catering are, thankfully, well behind us; pub food is now something to be proud of, but it's a pity that in moving into the food market many places have lost their pubby character in the process. It doesn't have to be like this: visit, for example, the Salehurst Halt in East Sussex (p51) to see how a pub can simultaneously win a gastronomy award and remain a plain and simple local serving top quality ales.

Of course not all pubs are the same, which is one of the great strengths of the British pub: the 100 or so pubs featured in this volume range from classy and upmarket to basic and unspoilt. Each walk offers at least two recommended pubs, and usually more, to choose from; this way you can use the descriptions to go for the one(s) which suit(s) you.

Personally I believe the best place for a good pub on a walk is, all else being equal, at or towards the end – the prospect of several stiff miles to cover after leaving the pub ought to temper mid-walk drinking. Accordingly, whilst many of the walks here have a mid-route stop, nearly all of them offer a tempting pub at the finish of the day.

Finding your way

In general, and perhaps ironically, navigation in lowland agricultural land can be a bit trickier than on the uplands in our National Parks, although armed with the route descriptions here and the maps you ought not to go too far astray.

It's useful to recognise the signed waymarks which will guide you around the very good network of rights of way in the South East; footpaths (right of way on foot only) are indicated with yellow arrows, and bridleways (also right of way on cycle and on horseback) with blue arrows. In addition you may see some red waymarks which indicate a 'byway', some of which are open to all traffic although they are often unsurfaced. Since reference to these distinctions is frequently made in the text, recognising these on the map and in the landscape will assist correct navigation.

Although the routes are plotted using Ordnance Survey mapping, we recommend that you carry a copy of the recommended map with you too; this will assist enjoyment of the routes, help you to identify more distant points of interest and, for the stronger and more ambitious walkers, offer possibilities to lengthen some walks.

With the exception of the recently created South Downs National Park, the region does not enjoy National Park status but there are several designated Areas of Outstanding Natural Beauty (AONB); for example the North Downs, the Chilterns and the High Weald. In these areas paths are generally well-used and well-signed. In addition there are many long distance paths or trails with their own special waymarks and, once again, these routes in the main have good signage, so where our routes follow these you should have fewer navigational difficulties. Outside these areas some of the paths are more infrequently walked and not so obvious on the ground and greater care needs to be taken to avoid going astray.

Access, transport and timing

CAMRA has a commitment to supporting public transport as well as the pub and unlike most other pub walks books you can access all these walks by public transport; indeed, two thirds of them start and finish at railway stations. In some more inaccessible cases, use of taxis may ease access to and from the start. Traveline (www.traveline. info) is a useful resource for journey planning, and plotting door-to-door journeys using public transport. If relying on public transport, it is always worth checking the time of the last train or bus back to where you are staying before setting out on your day's walk, and noting down the number of a local taxi firm should you get into difficulties. Many route descriptions in this book have phone contacts and links to relevant websites.

Some of the routes are linear; that is, they start and finish at different places. Where this is the case public transport is always available to return to the start, if need be, so those arriving in the area by car should have no difficulty returning to their vehicle at the end of a walk. We do not assume that all walkers attempting these routes will be coming from London, but as many will, or will be travelling via the capital, rail access information from London is given in all cases. I have often found it frustrating using other pub walking guides that little thought is given to timing your walk so that the pub is actually open when one gets there! This is a particular issue in countryside areas where most pubs retain an afternoon closure. A new feature introduced into this guide is the 'timing tips' at the top of the walk which should assist you in planning your walk to make the most of the pub stops. Of course you don't have to visit all the pubs on each walk; there's almost always a choice of drinking options to suit your taste.

The countryside code

When walking in the countryside, it's always worth following a few simple, common-sense guidelines to help protect the countryside that you're enjoying and keep you safe.

• Plan ahead and be prepared for the unexpected. Bad weather and restricted access to land – for example, during breeding season – may force you to alter your plans, so follow local signs and advice and don't be afraid to turn back.
• Leave gates as you find them. The countryside is a working area and even well-intentioned

actions can affect people's livelihoods and the welfare of animals.

• Protect the appearance, flora and fauna of the countryside by taking your litter home.

• If you're walking with a dog, keep it under control. It's your responsibility to make sure your dog is not a nuisance or a danger to farm animals, wildlife or other people.

• Consider other people – other walkers, riders and cyclists and those who work and live in the countryside.

What to wear and what to take

Many readers will be experienced walkers and may not need any advice, but if you're relatively new to country walking the following tips may be useful. The walks in this book do not venture into remote country, but nonetheless you should be well equipped for comfort as well as safety. Many of the routes can be muddy so soles with a good grip are recommended, and walking boots should be used for more demanding terrain or when the going underfoot is likely to be wet or icy. They provide support for your ankles and keep your feet warm and dry. A thick pair of socks will make them more comfortable in cold weather too.

Always pack enough clothing to wear for any potential turn in the weather. It's a good idea to have layers of clothes so that you can take one off or put one on as you warm up or the weather cools down. A waterproof jacket will keep off both rain and wind, with hoods and pockets being particularly useful features. Fleeces are good to wear in between your 'base layer' and jacket, especially ones with zips as they allow you to cool off easily if necessary. Avoid jeans – they take a long time to dry if they get wet. Lightweight, loose-fitting trousers made from synthetic material are favoured by walkers. They dry quickly and have handy pockets for carrying maps. Waterproof over-trousers or gaiters will prevent trousers and socks from getting wet, but can be difficult to get on and off easily.

Wear sun hats and sun cream in summer, if need be, and take plenty of water to drink. It's a good idea to carry something to eat – even if it's only a couple of cereal bars.

A rucksack can be very useful – use it to carry any spare clothing and food as well as other essentials like a map, compass, mobile phone, emergency whistle, torch and simple first aid kit.

The maps and directions in this book will help you follow the walks, but if you want to venture off the beaten track to do a little more exploring on your own, or even connect sections of different walks from the book, you should carry a map and compass, and know how to use them. Each walk lists the relevant Ordnance Survey map in its introduction, as well as grid reference points along the route.

Saftey on the roads

Some of the routes include short stretches on rural lanes and roads. In general these are not very busy, but always take care as sometimes vehicles appear suddenly and travel quickly (especially on country roads with national speed limits). If there is not a footpath, walk in single file on the right-hand side (facing the traffic) except on corners and bends with poor visibility when you should cross (carefully) to get a better view.

Facilities for the disabled and children; and dogs

We have not included information on access for disabled visitors, as this changes all the time, and it's best to ring ahead and check.

Many pubs welcome children, especially before 9pm, either in the whole pub or in a designated area. Of course, if you're walking with young people, once again you may be well advised to ask ahead, especially if there are no alternative venues on the route.

Similarly dog owners will know that pub policy towards their pets varies considerably so once again the advice is, check ahead. Contact details for every pub are included in the relevant walks.

Enjoy the walks!
Bob Steel

SOUTH EAST PUB WALKS ON THE INTERNET

There is a forum online for owners of this book to share their experiences of the routes in the book – the walks themselves, the beer quality, suggestions for additions/deletions etc. Visit **www.aletrails.com** and follow the links to South East Pub Walks.

The South East brewing scene

The changing face of brewing in the South East of England has been the subject of much discussion: some delight in the increase in choice, while others bemoan increased competition. For beer drinkers it has mostly been a good news story. Looking back over the recent past we can see that the resurgence in brewing in the South East dates back to the foundation of the Society of Independent Brewers in 1980. SIBA was founded in response to the refusal of the Brewers' Society to allow small brewers to join their organisation as they could not admit members producing less than 200 barrels a week or 10,000 barrels a year. SIBA was started with these declared aims: to promote the interchange of technical knowledge between members; to promote in all ways the interests of smaller brewers; and to make attempts to ease constraints to free trade in the brewing industry. Thirty years on the membership of SIBA has grown from about 20 members to over 570.

SIBA's crowning achievement was the introduction of Small Brewers Relief in 2002. This tax relief system has provided the fiscal stimulus that has allowed the resurgence of brewing in the UK. In 2004 Small Brewer's Relief was extended to breweries producing up to 60,000 hectolitres.

The South East region of SIBA covers Greater London, Kent, East and West Sussex, Surrey, Berkshire and Hampshire. Since 1999 there has been a tripling in the number of breweries, both large and small. This rapid growth has been facilitated by Small Brewers Relief but driven by the demands of the marketplace for more flavour, provenance of ingredients and localism; there is a desire for people to know where the beer has been made, what has gone into it and that it is being made with loving care and attention.

Brewers who failed to wake up to this new reality have either failed or been taken over. A lack of innovation and investment in their cask beer

Oast house at Little Scotney Farm

offerings in favour of big brand products with little to differentiate them from the international brands has been the cause of a lack of growth in many regional breweries. Hardys & Hansons, Ridleys, King & Barnes and many other regional breweries have either succumbed in the last 15 years or are a shadow of their former selves. Bucking the trend are the likes of Harveys, Timothy Taylor and Moorhouses; these are brewers with a long history but the good sense to invest in their capital equipment, and producing award winning beers.

Driving innovation are the microbreweries. These are the trail-blazers who are packing flavour into their beers, trying out new brewing methods while focusing on their local markets. Demand for aroma hops from the microbrewers, and resurgent regional and local brewers, has helped arrest the decline in hop growing in the South East. New varieties of hops are tried and tested in a spirit of experimentation and innovation. Sales of Maris Otter barley for malting have grown as well, driven by the desire to use the best that British farmers can produce, despite the extra expense compared to more modern barley varieties.

Our own Westerham Brewery is a beneficiary of the resurgence of craft beer in the South East. We have reintroduced old recipes and styles from the Black Eagle Brewery that closed in 1965, using their yeast strains and water supply. We are not however mired in the past. We have developed the Hop Rocket, a late hopping device to extract more flavour and aroma from the Kent hops we use in most of our beers. We have recently experimented with first wort hopping, continuous hopping and new methods of dry hopping our beers. We have also produced a number of international-style beers and lagers. This experimentation is what real ale in the South East is all about.

Robert Wicks, Westerham Brewery

Beer styles

You can deepen your appreciation of cask ale with this run-down on the main styles available.

Bitter

Towards the end of the 19th century, brewers moved away from vatted beers stored for many months and developed 'running beers' that could be served after a few days' storage in pub cellars. Bitter was generally deep bronze to copper in colour due to the use of darker malts that give the beer fullness of palate. Best is a stronger version of Bitter but there is considerable crossover. Bitter falls into the 3.4% to 3.9% band, with Best Bitter 4% upwards, but a number of brewers label their ordinary Bitters 'Best'. A further development of Bitter comes in the shape of Extra or Special Strong Bitters of 5% or more. With ordinary Bitter, look for a spicy, peppery and grassy hop character, a powerful bitterness, tangy fruit and juicy and nutty malt. With Best and Strong Bitters, malt and fruit character will tend to dominate.

Golden Ales

This new style of pale, well-hopped and quenching beer developed in the 1980s as independent brewers attempted to win younger drinkers from heavily-promoted lager brands. Strengths will range from 3.5% to 5%. The hallmark will be the biscuity and juicy malt character derived from pale malts, underscored by tart citrus fruit and peppery hops, often with the addition of hints of vanilla and sweetcorn. Above all, such beers are quenching and served cool.

IPA and Pale Ale

India Pale Ale changed the face of brewing early in the 19th century. The new technologies of the Industrial Revolution enabled brewers to use pale malts to fashion beers that were genuinely golden or pale bronze in colour. First brewed in London and Burton-on-Trent for the colonial market, IPAs were strong in alcohol and high in hops: the preservative character of the hops helped keep the beers in good condition during long sea journeys. Beers with less alcohol and hops were developed for the domestic market and were known as Pale Ale. Look for juicy malt, citrus fruit and a big spicy, peppery, bitter hop character, with strengths of 4% upwards.

Mild

Mild was once the most popular style of beer, but was overtaken in popularity by Bitter from the 1950s. It was developed in the 18th and 19th centuries as a less aggressively bitter style of beer than porter and stout. Early Milds were much stronger that modern interpretations, which tend to fall in the 3% to 3.5% category. Look for rich malty aromas and flavours with hints of dark fruit, chocolate, coffee and caramel and a gentle underpinning of hop bitterness.

Old Ale

Old ale recalls the type of beer brewed before the Industrial Revolution, stored for months or even years in unlined wooden vessels known as tuns. The beer would pick up some lactic sourness as a result of wild yeasts, lactobacilli and tannins in the wood. The result was a beer dubbed 'stale' by drinkers: it was one of the components of the early, blended Porters. Old ales, contrary to expectation, do not have to be especially strong: they can be no more than 4% alcohol. Neither do they have to be dark: old ale can be pale and burst with lush sappy malt, tart fruit and spicy hop notes.

Porter and Stout

Porter was a London style that turned the brewing industry upside down early in the 18th century. It was a dark brown beer that was originally a blend of brown ale, pale ale and old ale. It acquired its name as a result of its popularity among London's market porters. The strongest versions of Porter were known as Stout Porter, or simply Stout. Such vast quantities of Porter and Stout flooded into Ireland from London and Bristol that a Dublin brewer named Arthur Guinness decided to fashion his own interpretation of the style. Guinness in Dublin blended some unmalted roasted barley and in so doing produced a style known as Dry Irish Stout. Look for profound dark and roasted malt character with raisin and sultana fruit, espresso or cappuccino coffee, liquorice and molasses.

With thanks to Roger Protz

South East overview map

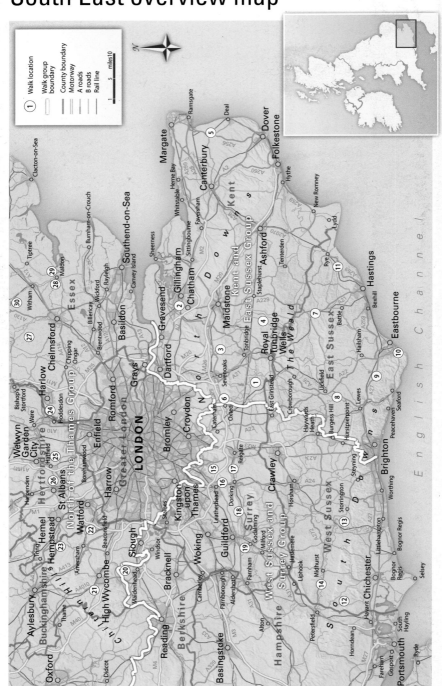

Kent & East Sussex Group

Queen's Head, Icklesham

The Kentish Weald

WALK INFORMATION

Start/Finish: Cowden station (option to finish at Hever)

Access: Trains from London Bridge and East Croydon

Distance: 5.2 miles (8.4km) for circuit returning to Cowden. Add 1.8 miles for return walk to Queen's Arms

OS map: OS Explorer OL147

Key attractions: Typical Wealden scenery: undulating, well-wooded and rural

The pubs: Rock, Chiddingstone Hoath; Kentish Horse, Markbeech. Try also: Queen's Arms, Cowden Pound; Greyhound, Hever

A very good walk in the fine countryside of the High Weald of Kent, easily accessible yet with a real rural feel to it. The few settlements you'll see are of typical cottages in the local vernacular style, sporting colourful cottage gardens, in summer at least! The pubs won't disappoint, the Rock in particular being a real unspoilt rural gem. Lovers of traditional pubs should also not miss the opportunity to visit the Queen's Arms at Cowden Pound, perhaps the most basic of all rural pubs in the South East. The terrain is undulating, especially in the first half. Navigation needs some care in places, and reference to the map will help route-finding. A nocturnal visit to the Queen's Arms needs forward planning in terms of transport home.

Exit from Cowden station and walk down to the road at the foot of the access drive. Head left, uphill, on the road for about 200 yards to turn right into Wickens Lane (look for a public footpath sign). Pass Rickwood's farm house, with great views out across the Weald, and take the signed path to the left, up a stony track, in a further 150 yards. Just before the cottage bear right over the stile and follow the path towards the lone telegraph pole.

The Rock at Chiddingstone Hoath

TIMING TIP

Doing this walk on a Sunday, when it is open at lunchtime, or in summer will enable you to visit the Queen's Arms in daylight.

Key

▬ ▬ ▬ ▬ ▬ Walk route

• • • • • • • • Alternative route

The next stretch needs a little care as there is no distinct path on the ground: once through another stile in the hedge bear right, but not quite at right angles, heading uphill towards a gap in the line of trees on the right. Bear left of the water trough when it comes into view, aiming downhill to another stile leading into the trees. Follow the path through here and emerge into a long narrow field flanked by thick tree cover to right and left, a

very pastoral scene. Hold broadly to the centre of this long field for a few hundred yards and, as it starts to narrow by a freestanding oak tree, look for a stile on the left-hand boundary of the field by some holly bushes. Drop down through the woody dingle to a little bridge over a tiny stream (A, ⊙, 494417), taking the obvious path doubling back uphill through the wood, levelling off as it joins another track merging from the right.

A pleasant stroll through the trees leads into another field surrounded by trees on all sides. Keep to the right-hand margin of the field, climbing steadily, with no habitation in sight. Exit the field by a new metal kissing gate and follow the track through the trees to the road via a couple more kissing gates.

Oast houses at Hever

The Queen's Arms, with its long-serving licensee Elsie

Go straight across and take a signed option, diverging slightly left after a minute or two, onto a clear track through a field. This is the highest point of the walk and has the extensive views to match, where the trees permit. Meet the road and bear left downhill to the quiet junction at the hamlet of Hoath Corner. Here, alongside a few cottages in the local vernacular, sits the **Rock** **1** . Named after a local sandstone outcrop, this is a classic unspoilt Kentish pub is pretty close to the imagined ideal of a 'typical' English pub of a quieter age. A wonderful main room welcomes you, brick floored with inglenook and stove. Regulars congregate around the bar stools, where you might find the odd dog stretched out lazily, the sort that look utterly at home furnishing a good country pub. Horses have to wait outside though, as they not infrequently do. There's even an old 'ring the bull' game in the bar.

Although there are new licensees and the place is no longer leased directly to Larkins brewery, it still majors on the excellent ales from the local micro, along with a guest or two. Moreover there are no plans to change the winning formula. Food is served from noon until 2.30 (longer on Sundays) and evenings 7-9; and there is a smarter (but not too smart!) separate room more suited to dining. However, this is primarily a pub for drinkers, and long may it remain so!

On departing from the Rock navigation is more straightforward: retrace your steps just a few yards to the road junction and turn right down the quiet lane, heading westwards. In some 200 yards bear right on the well-signed footpath, where you can enjoy one of the best views of the day, right across to the North Downs escarpment. Follow the clearly defined track through a wooded dell and up into a plantation of immature birch trees to join a T junction of paths (B, ⊙, 494438). Now walk to the left: it's about a mile along this path to the road, and muddy in places, but although it's a straight track it lacks neither in variety or interest, and there are plenty of good distant views too. Emerge on the road, and continue in the same direction, signed 'Markbeech'. There's no pavement, but it's not an excessively busy lane. It's about half a mile down to the centre of the hamlet, with the **Kentish Horse** **2** prominent at the junction.

The Kentish Horse presents an attractive appearance with a part-weatherboarded exterior. Unfortunately most of the internal character has been beaten out of the pub, save for the little snug on the right with some settles, which is my recommended spot if available. A large extension at the rear caters for diners, and there's a garden beyond that. The usual ales are Harveys Sussex Best Bitter and Larkins Traditional Bitter, two firm favourites in this part of the world. Food is served lunchtimes until 2.30, and of an evening from 7 until 9, and comes recommended.

LEFT: **The Kentish Horse, Markbeech** RIGHT: **The wonderful old bar in the Rock**

Leaving the pub there are three alternative finishes, depending on your mood and the time. Basically these are returning to Cowden station, a distance of under a mile; or to head up to Hever station, a little over a mile, with the option of visiting either the Queen's Arms at Cowden Pound (see opening hours) or the Greyhound en route.

In the first case, turn left into Cowden Pound Road past the church, and look for the footpath leading through the churchyard to a further stile on the right, then down, passing to the right of the small water company enclosure, and down the left hand side of the large field, over another stile, keeping in the same direction with the trees on your right. Reach yet another stile leading into the woodland, whereupon the track becomes larger and leads past a house. Keep straight ahead, ignoring the track on the left crossing the railway line. This stretch is very shady and will be quite dark unless the sun is streaming through the trees. Reach the road just by the railway bridge; the station entrance is immediately left under the bridge.

An alternative to the finish above is a visit to the **Queen's Arms 3**, better known as Elsie's after the long-serving licensee. It is almost mandatory if you like unspoilt old pubs, for they simply don't get much more basic than this. To get there, continue up Cowden Pound Road from the Kentish Horse to the road junction, the best part of a mile. There's a spartan public bar and a larger but scarcely more elaborate saloon, and nothing but quiet conversation and well-kept Adnams ale to enjoy, unless you hit upon one of the convivial

music nights when the place may be very busy. Be warned that in the evening, unless you fix up a cab or your own transport, it's over a mile on unlit roads to Hever station (see map). You'll need a good torch and, ideally, a reflective jacket to walk down in the dark. Don't miss the last train!

The second option from the Kentish Horse is to detour to Hever station via the Greyhound. Walk along the road, beyond the footpath off to Cowden station, for about 250 yards, looking for and taking the path on the right by Bramsells Farm. It's a delight all the way, mainly downhill, starting with good views, dropping into woodland, under the railway and up to the lane. Here it's not far back to the right to reach the **Greyhound 4**, whilst for Hever station, take the lane in the opposite direction bearing left at the first junction and straight ahead for about 600 yards.

The Greyhound is a heavily modernised old roadside pub catering primarily for diners, but has up to four real ales on the bar – Harveys and Young's Bitters; Wells Bombardier, and Taylor Landlord. Allow fifteen minutes to walk back to the station, to be on the safe side.

PUB INFORMATION

1 Rock
Chiddingstone Hoath, TN8 7BS
01892 870296
Opening Hours: 12-4 Mon; 12-3, 6-11; 12-11 Fri & Sat; 12-5 Sun

2 Kentish Horse
Cow Lane, Markbeech, TN8 5NT
01342 850493
www.kentishhorse.co.uk
Opening Hours: 12-11 (midnight Fri & Sat)

TRY ALSO:

3 Queen's Arms
Hartfield Road, Cowden Pound, TN8 5NP
01727 855669
Opening Hours: 5-10.30 (9 Wed & Fri, 9.30 Sat); 12-2 Sun

4 Greyhound
Uckfield Lane, Hever, TN8 7LJ
01732 862221
www.greyhoundhever.co.uk
Opening Hours: 11-10.30 (11 Fri & Sat)

Historic Rochester & Chatham

WALK INFORMATION

Start: Strood station

Finish: Gillingham station

Access: Frequent trains to/ from London Charing Cross and Victoria

Distance: 5.5 miles (8.7km)

OS map: OS Explorer OL136

Key attractions: Rochester Cathedral & Castle; historic old town; Chatham naval dockyard

The pubs: Coopers Arms; Good Intent; Man of Kent; Britannia Bar Café, all Rochester; King George V, Brompton; Will Adams, Gillingham. Try also: Cannon, Brompton

The Medway towns surely offer one of the best urban strolls in the South East, with plenty of varied interest throughout. Rochester boats England's second oldest cathedral, founded in AD 604 by Bishop Justus. The adjacent castle defended the strategic Medway crossing halfway between London and Dover. Nearby Chatham is more workaday but nonetheless has its own proud history centred around the naval dockyard, now a major visitor attraction. Culture vultures will want to make at least a full day of it, to allow a morning's sightseeing in Rochester before sampling the well-spaced and varied pubs. Better still, make a weekend of it and take your time. Starting at Strood, across the Medway, allows you to enter Rochester in the most appropriate way, via the river bridge on foot with fine views of cathedral and castle.

Cannons stand guard over the cathedral across the Medway

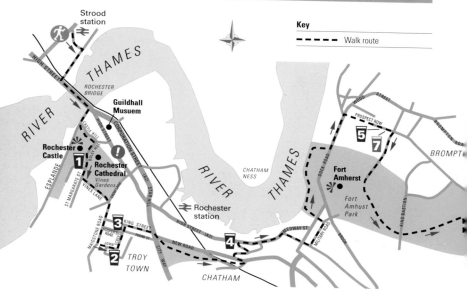

Leave Strood station and walk down to the river and Canal Road, joining the Saxon Shore Way. Pass under the railway bridge and join the A2 road which leads over the Medway and directly into the centre of Rochester. The town is dominated by the castle and cathedral, and although the immediate riverside is not a pretty place, the setting is dramatic. Away to your right you can see the bridge carrying traffic on the M2 across the Medway. Once across the river carefully cross the road. Ahead of you is the pedestrianised high street where, if you have arrived sufficiently early, there are plenty of cultural opportunities (see below), but the best view of the castle is obtained by turning right onto the Esplanade immediately after crossing the bridge, and then left straight away onto Castle Hill. Steps lead up into the Castle Gardens from where there are good views all around but particularly of the river and the bridge, and the handsome terraced houses of Castle Hill.

One can leave the gardens by the exit at the top left where Castle Hill meets Boley Hill. Here the cathedral is directly ahead, and is well worth a visit. Although the foundation dates back to AD 604, which makes it England's second oldest site of continuous worship behind Canterbury, what we see today is a confection of building styles from different periods, with the oldest surviving parts the work of the French monk Gundulf in 1080. Since that time there has been continuous remodelling, refurbishment and restoration, mainly due to fires and other damage over the years. Renovation and restoration continued well into the 20th century following war damage.

If you want to visit the High Street, dropping down the few yards to the left on Boley Hill brings one to the junction with the *King's Head*. In addition to the sundry coffee shops and eateries, cultural attractions include the Baggins Book Bazaar, England's largest secondhand bookshop, and the Guildhall Museum (left, beyond the handsome old Corn Exchange with its projecting clock). Beyond the tourist office to the right, stands the Six Poor Travellers' House. This wonderful building, now a free museum, was a charity house founded by the Elizabethan MP Richard Watts to provide board and lodgings for six poor travellers for one night; it continued to do so right up to the Second World War. The house and charity are

LEFT: **Morris men at the King George V** RIGHT: **Rochester is the heart of 'Dickens Country'**

immortalised in Dickens' Christmas short story 'The Seven [sic] Poor Travellers'. At the rear, a courtyard and herb garden is a delightful oasis.

By now the day will be well advanced and it's time to remember that this is first and foremost a pub walk. From the junction of Castle Hill and Boley Hill, walk uphill between castle and cathedral to merge to the left with St Margaret's Street where, a few yards along on the right, is the first port of call for the day, the weatherboarded **Coopers Arms 1**. This listed pub very much looks the part for this historic part of town, and shouldn't disappoint within either: there are still two largely separate bars, front and back, and the furnishing

and décor convey a traditional atmosphere. Up to four ales (Courage Best, Young's Special and a couple of guests, often one from local micro Nelson) are available, which you can enjoy, weather permitting, in the pleasant beer garden once you have drunk in the internal pleasures of the building. Lunchtime food is obtainable until 2pm (2.30 Sundays); and it's worth bearing in mind that the next two pubs don't serve food…

From the Coopers, continue up as far as Vines Lane, the first turning left, and walk down, flanked by some veritable old walls on the right, behind which lies King's School, claiming to be the world's second oldest school. The listed buildings are certainly very handsome. On the left are the Vines Gardens, where monks from Rochester's Priory grew grapes for their wine. The statue of a monk in the gardens, carved from the

The Coopers Arms

LEFT: **Inside the Man of Kent** RIGHT: **Rochester's historic High Street**

stump of a plane tree damaged in the 1987 storm, is a reminder of that time. Note the good view of the cathedral tower through the trees. At the end turn right into Maidstone Road, walking up under the avenue of trees, with some good brick terraced houses across the street. Devotees of pub heritage will enjoy the tiled panels advertising Mews brewery on the exterior of the *Granville Arms*, but further on, by the Watts Charity Almshouses, turn left down the dead-end road and through an alley and suddenly you're a world away from the tourist's Rochester and stop number two is ahead. The **Good Intent 2** presents a rather uninspiring face to the world but inside it's a different story, not least on account of the gravity-dispensed beers available. The spacious public bar in this unpretentious local has a definite 1970s feel about it, and sports a large screen TV and pool table. The quieter back bar and the garden offer alternative venues to enjoy one of up to three changing beers and a cider. The garden hosts occasional beer festivals too. The pub won the local CAMRA branch's gong for Pub of the Year in 2008.

All you need to do to reach the next pub is to head down to the bottom end of John Street and, checking your watch (see opening times), ensure that the **Man of Kent 3** is open when you arrive, for this is arguably the best beer drinker's pub on the route. The exterior of this street-corner alehouse carries a splendid faience in favour of

Style and Winch, the now defunct Maidstone brewery. Doorways from a former multi-roomed exterior survive along with some etched glass windows. Inside, the L-shaped bar has a very traditional feel, but the best news is the array of no less than 11 beer engines dispensing the wares of all of Kent's microbreweries. In addition you can choose from a lengthy menu of ciders, Kentish wines and continental beers by draught and bottle, making the Man of Kent a permanent beer festival. No wonder then that it has gathered accolades from the local CAMRA branch.

It's a hard pub to leave, but there is a walk to do! If you do want to divide the route up, this is a good place to break however, since Rochester station is only some five minutes walk away at the foot of Star Hill. Continue the walk by turning right into King Street and walk up the hill to join the main road at Star Hill by the *Rising Sun*. Turn uphill to the roundabout and, crossing carefully, enter the park straight ahead. Walking between the tennis courts and the children's playground, keep on the path aiming to the left of the rather ugly brick building (the University for the Creative Arts!), above the road below, joining the road just below the UCA, close to a curious wooden whalebone structure in the parkland above. Now, joining the main road, use the controlled crossing and aim for Gundulph Road opposite, and zig-zag down here, taking the left fork, to join the eastern end of

Rochester's long High Street. It's a few yards left now to arrive at the **Britannia Bar Café** . In fact it's more a smart pub than café bar, retaining a fairly traditional feel as befits a pub rather than a shop conversion. Catering for a business as well as residential clientele, the Britannia offers a wide food menu to complement its three ales. As for the latter, expect Goachers Light plus two rotating guests. In good weather the little walled rear garden is a pleasant sun trap.

It's a short walk now into Chatham, reached by walking east on the High Street for a few minutes, crossing the busy new(ish) road which is part of Chatham's gyratory road system, and reaching the quieter crossroads of the shopping axis fifty yards later. Here turn left into pedestrianised Military Road, and walk down to the green entrance gates. Turn left here and make your way across the new bus stands to the riverside and pick up the waterside walkway. Pass the *Command House*. This was the official residence of the officer in charge of the gun wharf, but for the past thirty years or so it has been a pub and (in the basement) a music venue. It does at least offer Fuller's London Pride if you want a quick pit-stop.

Walk through the gates (they are normally open during daylight hours: if not, walk back up to Dock Road and turn left) and along the waterfront past the modern offices of Medway Council towards the wonderful facades of Chatham's old naval dockyard. When you reach the dockyard boundary the riverside path ends abruptly so rejoin Dock Road, passing a heritage trail information board, and turn left down the main road towards the dockyard entrance. In about 250 yards, by the gateway entrance to the dockyard with its splendid coat of arms, use the subway to cross the road and climb the steps (Saxon Shore Way sign), keeping the residential tower block on your right, and you're suddenly in the old maritime district of Brompton, which, despite falling on hard times with the dock closure, still has plenty of its old character. The old High Street is off to the left, whilst the smarter houses in Prospect Row and Mansion Row off to the right are former officers' homes. Stout defences and ditches, known as the Chatham Lines, once encircled this area, taking advantage of the natural vantage point above the vital naval base, and some of the defences survive (see below). The area is littered with the bodies of dead pubs, but fortunately there are some survivors. The best of these is immediately ahead: the **King George V** . The 'KG Five' as it's affectionately known is a characterful building with a comfortable interior, retaining much evidence of its former layout, including fine etched glass windows advertising Public and Private bars, and Parlour. Perhaps the best survivor is the pair of old doors which once led to the Jug Department, the entrance for those buying drinks to take away. Back in the present the pub is a real community focus, festooned with naval memorabilia. Expect Adnams Bitter plus a range of guest ales including a dark mild, usually from Goachers. Food is available, including all-day pizza, so you can top up on calories if the tank is running low.

A couple of doors along the street your eye will be drawn to the striking green tiled frontage of the **Cannon** . This former Trumans house, which retains the former brewery's branding on its frontage faience and in a pretty light fitting, is worth a visit as it retains its two bar layout and, like the King George V, is a real locals' pub. It doesn't claim to offer the same range of ales as its neighbour but you can expect Fuller's London Pride.

Leaving the Cannon walk further up and take the first left into Maxwell Street, into a surprisingly wooded area, up to the garrison church at the top. It's dedicated, unsurprisingly, to St Barbara, the patron saint of Artillerymen and Engineers. Fork left immediately beyond into Amherst Redoubt. Straight ahead a new gateway leads into the Fort Amherst Park. Fort Amherst was one of Britain's largest fortresses, built in the mid eighteenth century as part of the network of redoubts which encircled Brompton and the naval dockyard, to protect against a French invasion. Today it's a visitor attraction set in acres of parkland, with

LEFT: **Man of Kent, with its fine Style**   RIGHT: **Interior detail from the 'KG Five'**

the extensive network of hand-hewn tunnels a particular draw. It's also reputed to be one of Kent's most haunted places. Before taking the path through the site I recommend making your way around the terrace on the right to the viewpoint, which offers a wide vista across the twin towns and the meandering river. Double back to continue over the footbridge, which gives a good view of the remains of the fort, before continuing along the path along the high ground towards the prominent stone Royal Naval War Memorial ahead, with its distinctive green spherical cap. Here bear left to keep the memorial on your right. Follow the obvious path towards Gillingham until it leaves the park via a narrow fenced alley to reach the road. Use the zebra crossing and, turning left for a few yards, head down Stafford Street. First left into

Saxton Street, a terrace of old houses some of which have had gruesome 'improvements' foisted upon the frontages. No matter, for some way down we arrive at the **Will Adams** 6 on the corner of Lock Street. It's a slightly tatty street corner local, which retains one or two decent architectural features such as etched glass outside. Named after a famous local son who was reputedly the first sailor to make it to Japan, the long narrow pub is now a single bar and is your best bet for real ale in Gillingham. Expect up to three changing ales plus draught cider and perry. As warned above, hours are limited so let's assume you have planned ahead! A mural inside depicts Will's adventures.

Leaving the pub, turn right into Lock Street, then first left and first right brings you into Gillingham's High Street. The rail station is at the far end.

PUB INFORMATION

1 Coopers Arms
10 St Margaret Street,
Rochester, ME1 1TL
01634 404298
Opening Hours: 12-11.30
(10.30 Sun)

2 Good Intent
83 John Street, Rochester,
ME1 1YL
01634 843118
Opening Hours: 12-midnight
(11 Sun)

3 Man of Kent
6-8 John Street, Rochester,
ME1 1YN
07772 214315
www.themanofkent.com
Opening Hours: 2 (12 Sun)-11;
12-midnight Fri & Sat

4 Britannia Bar Café
376 High Street, Rochester,
ME1 1DJ
01634 815204
www.britannia-bar-cafe.co.uk
Opening Hours: 10-11 (2am Fri
& Sat); 12-11 Sun

5 King George V
1 Prospect Row, Brompton,
ME7 5AL
01634 842418
www.kgvpub.com
Opening Hours: 11.45-11;
12-10.30 Sun

6 Will Adams
73 Saxton Street, Gillingham,
ME7 5EG
01634 575902
www.thewilladams.co.uk
Opening Hours: 7-11; 12.30-4
Sat; 12-3, 8-11 Sun

TRY ALSO:

7 Cannon
15 Garden Street, Brompton,
ME7 5AS
01634 841006
Opening Hours: 11-midnight

Ightham & Plaxtol

WALK INFORMATION

Start/Finish: Borough Green station

Access: Trains from London Victoria via Bromley South

Distance: 10.1 miles (16.2km)

OS map: OS Explorer OL147

Key attractions: Ightham Mote (National Trust); Knole House, garden & orangery (National Trust, 7 miles)

The pubs: Golding Hop, Plaxtol; Padwell, Stone Street; Old House, Ightham Common

A stretch of the attractive countryside of Kent's Greensand Ridge, a couple of characterful old pubs, and a good choice of beers make this an appealing walk. Views are good, with a lot of orchards as well as woodland and open vistas; the pubs are well spaced, but the limited hours at the Old House mean that some careful time planning (and possibly a shorter version of the route) will be needed to take it in. Culture vultures can build in a visit to Ightham Mote which is right on the route. Navigation is fairly straightforward and the terrain moderate, but it can be muddy in places. There is quite a bit of road walking, but most of it is on quiet lanes with very little traffic. Carry a torch and/or reflective clothing if there's any risk of finishing the route in poor light.

Kentish orchards abound on this walk

Arriving at Borough Green station, exit through the car park and cross the bridge heading south, continuing ahead on the High Street to the road junction by the fish & chip shop when the main road curves right after a few yards. Cross straight over and then take the public path about fifty yards up on the left into The Landway. This is an older part of Borough Green, and has some interesting old cottages, in contrast to the area around the railway station. The path is easy to follow, and quickly leaves the houses behind and plunges into pleasant woodland, crossing a stream at one point.

Emerge onto a tarmac lane by a picnic area and the start of some woodland walks. Turn left and walk alongside the lane in a wooded valley cut by the tiny River Bourne. Just ahead is the old mill pond to Basted Mill; this old paper mill was one of several mills which stood on the Bourne, which later joins the Medway near East Peckham. The heavily modernised mill buildings here at Basted are now private residences.

Continue beyond here, past a number of cottages, ignoring the bridleways right and left until the road (now called Plough Lane) starts to climb and a wide track forks off to the right by Orchard Cottage. Take this bridleway, past

TIMING TIP

Watch out for the limited opening hours at the Old House; as a visit to this wonderful old pub is a must on this walk. I recommend saving the walk for a weekend and ensuring you get there either at lunchtime or after 7 when it re-opens. It may be advisable to book a cab to return you to Borough Green station in this case, which will save nearly two miles of walking.

Key

- - - - - Walk route

The Golding Hop – stepping back in time...

some agreeable old houses in big gardens, before plunging into another area of woodland, with overhanging trees, while the Bourne accompanies you on the left all the way to the junction with the road (A, ⊙, 606550). This section may well be rather muddy.

When you get to the quiet lane turn right and walk uphill, disregarding the first footpath off to the left into the orchards, but looking for a second a few minutes further on, beyond

A bosky path near Borough Green

atmospheric old **Golding Hop** 1 . The setting is pretty idyllic and the building clings to the roadside right on this seemingly off-the-beaten-track lane, despite its proximity to nearby 'civilisation'. The pub's small but interesting interior is made up of a main bar with a room off at the far end, and a tiny two storey extension into an adjacent outbuilding as you enter. It's as quirky as it sounds, and the character owes a lot to Eddie & Sonia, licensees for the past 25 years or so. The beers, Adnams plus guests, are served by gravity from casks stillaged behind the bar. Cider drinkers are also well catered for notably in the home produced 'rough stuff'… The home-cooked food is simple and filling, at very reasonable prices, with the home-made pizzas the only concession to foreign fare! Outside, the little terrace catches the sun during the first half of the day and is a great spot although there is a garden across the road too.

This is not a pub that's easy to leave, especially as the onward walk, continuing on the lane to the south, entails a steady climb uphill before reaching the pretty cottages on Yopps Green Lane. Pass Jordans on your right, a half-timbered house with a lovely garden and stone tiled roof, and look out for the bridleway on the right, beyond Yopps Green Cottage. There's a stone waymark at ground level and a sign for Grove Cottage. Head up on this wide track through some orchards, turning left, and then, at a T junction with another

the line of pylons. Cross the stile (with a good view to the left) and head in the direction of the pointing sign, that is, diagonally through the orchard on a clear track between the fruit trees. Reach another waymark, at the far edge of the field, leading to the right past an old house and joining a farm track, with first a right and then a left turn (look for the waymark), bringing you out onto an even narrower lane. It's now only the shortest of strolls up to the left to reach the

LEFT: **Pub sign at the Golding Hop** RIGHT: **The Old House, Ightham Common**

path by a small telegraph post, right. The good track continues to climb gently uphill through the next field, with good views out to the south.

At the path junction ahead, with a confusing array of waymarks, take the obvious and wide bridleway right, following it up along the edge of the tree belt to reach the busy A227 road in about 500 yards. Here cross over and take the signed bridleway, opposite, through the gate and through the Fairlawn estate. Head slightly right in a couple of hundred yards, keeping in the trees

and bracken, and then following the bridleway straight downhill, with wide views especially to the right, to join another bridleway at the foot of the hill. Here turn right and walk down towards Ightham Mote at the foot of the valley. This moated medieval manor house, dating in part to the early fourteenth century, is Grade I listed and was hailed by Pevsner as 'the most complete small medieval manor house in the country'. It includes surely the only Grade I-listed dog kennel in the land, and has been the site of one of the National Trust's most lengthy and comprehensive restoration projects, over fifteen years since they were bequeathed the place in 1985. If you don't wish to visit, or time is short, it's nonetheless

Ightham Mote

worth knowing as you pass that the toilets and café are open to the public without having to pay to go in. Moreover, your route passes the house and moat just before you reach the public road, and after turning right and walking up the lane there's a good view over the garden and lake too.

Some 250 yards beyond the lake and garden there's a clearly signed bridleway off to the left opposite a cottage; take this path, running gently uphill for about ten minutes until, on reaching a bar gate, the bridleway bears right and begins a steeper and quite sustained climb for some minutes, so take your time on this stretch.

Emerge from the woodland and cross a wide field with views towards the houses of Stone Street nestling under the steep woodland hangers of the Greensand ridge ahead. When you reach the road at a junction, look for the signed bridleway directly opposite and take this route, which continues in the same north westerly direction, for another 500 yards to reach another road. Arriving here you'll find the next pub just a few yards along on the right. The **Padwell** 2 has undergone a remarkable transformation under its new owners, from what by all accounts was a very run-down and unexciting pub, and a great deal has been achieved in transforming the place into a bit of a beer and food destination. It's certainly been heavily modernised inside, although there are still two open fires and some remains of the former separate rooms at the front. To the rear is an extensive dining area and food reports are very favourable. What is striking is the beer range which, although a work in progress, was pretty impressive on my visit: six ales on draught, mostly guests from local and regional micros like Hopdaemon or Tonbridge, but expect Larkins Bitter as a regular.

Leaving the Padwell, head left (east) along the road for a very short distance, taking the entry on the left (public footpath sign) towards the vicarage. The path narrows into an atmospheric earthen track heading up onto the ridge ahead. Gird your loins for a fairly stiff climb through the beech woodland, which is one of the highlights of the walk. At the top of the hill bear right onto another path and join Church Road at Seal Chart Common (B, ⊙, 572553). The church and primary school stand in succession on the roadside ahead.

Chimneyscape at Ightham Mote

Another fine stretch of bridleway beckons: take the signed path, just beyond the school, on the left. It runs along the top of the ridge, which is quite narrow in places with steep drops on both sides, with the views through the trees to the south being particularly wide-ranging.

It's over half a mile along this path (ignore side paths) until you emerge on a minor road. The stretch from here to the final pub is all on road, albeit lightly trafficked. Turn left onto the road and walk down to the junction in 250 yards or so. Go straight over (signed Ightham) onto what becomes a narrow, sunken lane, where the lack of a pavement shouldn't cause too many problems. At the next road junction turn left into Common Road which is a bit more suburban, fronted with large houses, and walk down to the next junction by the *Harrow* pub. Here bear right into Redwell Lane, and it's just a few minutes further down to reach the **Old House** 3 on a bend in the lane. This pub, which deserves its place in CAMRA's National Inventory of Historic Pub Interiors, was first licensed as a beerhouse in 1872 and didn't obtain a full licence until 1953. The homely bar room with its parquet flooring has a Victorian panelled counter and bar back, and a massive brick inglenook fireplace

LEFT: **The Golding Hop** RIGHT: **Plenty of choice at the Padwell, Stone Street**

which has been rediscovered by the present owners. The room to the right with its bay window has a front room feeling with its armchairs and chaise longue. Don't miss the old cash register with its notice 'retired after 28 years faithful service'.

At present there is no food here, but the beer range is very good, with up to six available at any time and all served by gravity. Loddon Gravesend Shrimpers Bitter is a regular, with a tempting list from around the country in supportive attendance. In addition to all this there is a wonderful whisky list of some 200, which must surely make it one of the best ranges south of the border. All in all, this is a real rural gem, the sort of pub we have been losing because of lack of patronage. So make sure you don't miss this wonderful old place and help to keep it in business!

If you're walking back to Borough Green station from here, it's about a mile and a half, but with a few twists and turns to negotiate, so stay sober! Start by walking up to the end of Redwell Lane and turn left to join the main road, the A227, in a few yards. Unfortunately there's nothing for it now but a 300 yard walk along the main road which has no pavement, only a very

narrow verge on the left. A few yards after the entrance to Ightham Warren, on the right, look out for a narrow opening which is the public footpath leading into the cricket field. Walk clockwise around the field to the far left corner, where a path leads into the field and through another orchard lower down.

Reaching a tiny lane, turn right and walk along for about a hundred yards, then take a clear path on the left. Walk downhill with views across to Borough Green and beyond, taking a right-then-left dogleg in the path halfway down, to reach a metal gate fifty yards short of the main road. Swing right on an obvious path at the foot of another field with a large laurel hedge on the left. Cross a lane and continue, reaching the suburban outskirts of town at C (605572). Turn left onto the residential road, then almost immediately right on another footpath (before the T junction), crossing a further cul-de-sac to join an older lane by some attractive old cottages.

Here bear right for the few yards to the junction, turning left by the accountants' office, which brings you back onto the road we started out on, leading straight down to Borough Green station, over the crossroads, in 150 yards.

PUB INFORMATION

1 Golding Hop
Sheet Hill, Topps Hill, Plaxtol, TN15 0PT
01732 882150
Opening Hours: 11-3 (2.30 Mon), 6-11 (5.30-11 Fri); 11-11 Sat; 12-3.30, 7-10.30 Sun

2 Padwell
Stone Street, TN15 0LQ
01732 761532
www.thepadwell.com
Opening Hours: 11-11; 12-10.30 Sun

3 Old House
Redwell, Redwell Lane, Ightham Common, TN15 9EE
01732 886077
Opening Hours: 7-11; 12-3, 7-10.30 Sat & Sun

Orchards of the High Weald: Brenchley & Horsmonden

WALK INFORMATION

Start/Finish: Matfield

Access: Trains to Paddock Wood from London Charing Cross/London Bridge or from Victoria/East Croydon via Tonbridge, then local buses 6/6A to and from Matfield

Distance: (full route) 6 miles (9.5km)

OS map: OS Explorer OL136

Key attractions: Kentish orchards; remains of iron industry

The pubs: Hopbine, Petteridge; Gun & Spitroast, Horsmonden; Halfway House, Brenchley

A sortie into the High Weald, with some fine pubs. Much of the route follows sections of the High Weald Landscape Trail, a 90 mile route which meanders around the Area of Outstanding Natural Beauty (AONB) of the same name. Access is a little difficult for the non car-driver and forward planning will help the logistics of the walk: the walk starts at Matfield since there is a bus connection here to/from Paddock Wood town centre, close to the station. Bus 297 links the villages of Horsmonden, Benchley and Matfield with Tunbridge Wells, which could be an alternative starting point. Using these connections will enable one to visit the pubs at a preferred time, depending upon your arrival time in the area.

The High Weald Landscape Trail (HWLT) leaves Maidstone Road in Matfield just south of the junction with Maycotts Lane, close to the Post Office. The path keeps to the left of the field, striking across to the far left corner. Then it's a simple walk along the next field boundary to emerge on the road at the western end of Brenchley village. Now bear almost immediately

The attractive exterior of the Hopbine at Petteridge

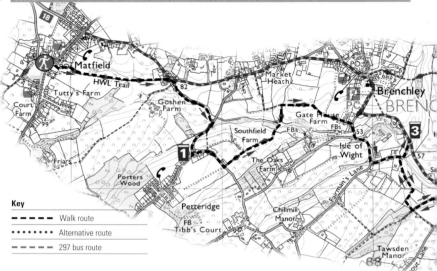

Key

- – – – – Walk route
- • • • • • • • Alternative route
- – – – – 297 bus route

right down the lane towards Goshen Farm, and left at the first house in a few yards.

This very good bridleway, still on the HWLT, offers a ribbon of woodland and brings one down to join the quiet Petteridge Lane at the bottom of a small wooded valley. Turn left here and walk up the hill, and after very little distance you'll come to pub number one, the **Hopbine** 1. Depending upon the season and the time of day, and bearing in mind that the Hopbine closes between 2.30 and 6pm, one can either call in now or save this pub for early evening.

Set in this idyllic little hamlet, which feels as close as one can probably get in the South East to the middle of nowhere, the pub blends in well with its tile-hung and weatherboarded exterior. Inside, the smart but atmospheric bar is beamed and wood-panelled, with a central log fire. Hops adorn the top of the servery as befits the name. The three beers are from the Hall & Woodhouse stable, including their take on the old King & Barnes Sussex Bitter: this was a former K&B pub. Impressively, the Hopbine has appeared in over 25 consecutive editions of the *Good Beer Guide*, nearly all under the same landlady, so they know what they're doing here! Food is available lunchtimes and evenings. Finally, one ought to mention the impressive bosky garden which runs down the slope at the back of the pub; and note approvingly the survival of the outside gents!

LEFT: **Brenchley village green** RIGHT: **The Halfway House is an extended old cottage**

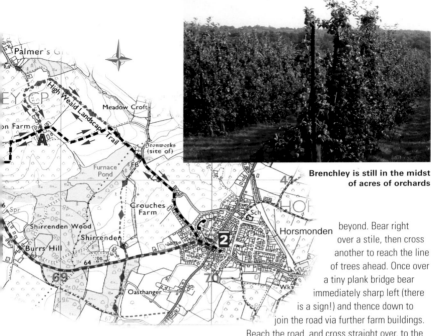

Brenchley is still in the midst of acres of orchards

beyond. Bear right over a stile, then cross another to reach the line of trees ahead. Once over a tiny plank bridge bear immediately sharp left (there is a sign!) and thence down to join the road via further farm buildings.

Reach the road, and cross straight over, to the edge of the field which has been newly planted with dwarf fruit trees, with a waymark close to the tall beech hedge.

Climb up around the edge of the field along the hedge, looking out carefully for the footpath sign (leading to the right) about halfway up the field. Take this path on a stony track with fine far-reaching views across the Weald, a typical Kentish scene, towards the new farm sheds ahead. Here (A, ⊙ 688413) you'll see a footpath sign pointing left, but if you're going to Horsmonden it will save time to continue ahead on the private farm road leading downhill towards the public road. You're unlikely to be challenged, it's a surfaced lane, but if you are you'll need to head up to the left and look for the waymark just before the tarmac lane resumes by the cottages in about 300 yards (see map). Otherwise walk down the lane and look out for the public path (waymarks) first merging from the left and then shortly afterwards, heading off to the right, some 150 yards before reaching another road at the foot of the hill. Take the path to the right, down the edge of a field to the valley bottom where there's an interesting short stretch along the side of a pond.

Leaving the Hopbine, bear hard left and pass the row of attractive cottages opposite. A short way along the lane a HWLT sign points left down a track. Follow this down, round to the right and, shortly, through some neglected orchards. The good track crosses a wooded valley and small stream further down, climbing up and turning 90 degrees right before long, offering views across to Brenchley and its parish church.

Join the road at Brenchley by Gate House Farm. If you are planning on taking the bus to Horsmonden, your best bet is to head uphill (left) and straight into the village, little more than five minutes' walk. Otherwise head right here, following the road round to the left at the foot of the hill, and then left again into narrow Short Lane a little further on. You're very close to the Halfway House at this point but I recommend leaving this until later.

Look for a metal gate on the right after some 200 yards, just before the lane climbs uphill. It looks like a private entrance at first, but there is a note stating that the footpath runs through the farm on the track; yellow waymarks lead one past the farm buildings (note the attractive pond down below on the left), and the route is well demarcated

LEFT: **The Gun & Spitroast, Horsmonden** RIGHT: **Halfway House, Brenchley**

This is the furnace pond to the once significant Brenchley ironworks, famous as the furnace owned by John Browne who was the first holder of the post of King's Gunfounder in 1615. He developed a lighter cannon, enabling ships to carry more armaments. In 1613 as many as 200 men were employed at the furnace which was working to at least 1667 and later became a mill. There's little to see today apart from the large pond, but as the path crosses the dam just before reaching the road one can appreciate the significant head of water which was available here.

Join narrow Furnace Lane and walk to the right, uphill, with care (no pavement) for about 600 yards to enter the village of Horsmonden. Bear left and ahead, on the pleasant village green, is the **Gun & Spitroast 2** , surely the only pub in the country to carry this name. It's a rambling building with a long frontage to the road, and retains a good deal of character, as one would hope for a building that has seen a few hundred years, although obviously not without significant alteration. There's a separate dining room and secluded garden. You'll find a good range of up to six ales available, with two from Ringwood, and rotating guests with a local emphasis: for example Rolvenden micro Old Dairy. Buses run nearby (ask in the pub if you can't see the bus stop) back to Brenchley via the Halfway House, and will stop outside on request!

If you want to walk back, retrace your route to Short Lane, but this time head up the hill to the right, and the pub is just a few yards further up on the left at the road junction. Check the map.

The **Halfway House 3** is one of Kent's classic pubs. An eighteenth century house with later additions, it's been opened out in an atmospheric and quirky manner which needs to be seen to be appreciated, but there's lots of very old timber almost everywhere and plenty of agreeable nooks and crannies to sit in, whatever the size of your group. The servery is actually in the weatherboarded building at the top end of the pub, and what a servery it is: around ten ales dispensed by gravity straight from the cask, and ditto the local Chiddingstone cider. The Whitsun and August beer festivals can see up to 70 beers available. The food attracts wide praise and can only be recommended.

There are outside seats and an extensive garden catering for all ages, if the weather permits; locals and visitors seem to mix sociably and in the best traditions of the pub, and it's a testament to its popularity that they can turn over so much beer in a relatively out-of-the-way location like this.

The 297 bus will take you from outside the pub back into Matfield, but be warned, the last service passes the pub at 6.05, so if you're intending to stay later make sure you make alternative arrangements.

PUB INFORMATION

1 Hopbine
Petteridge Lane, Petteridge,
TN12 7NE
01892 722561
Opening Hours: 12-2.30, 6-11;
12-3, 7-10.30 Sun

2 Gun & Spitroast
The Heath, Horsmonden,
TN12 8HT
01892 722925
www.gunandspitroast.co.uk
Opening Hours: 12-2, 5-11;
12-11 Sat & Sun

3 Halfway House
Horsmonden Road, Brenchley,
TN12 7AX
01892 722526
Opening Hours: 12-11.30
(11 Sun)

**CAMRA awards adorn the
walls of the Halfway House**

Sandwich & the coastal golf links

This is one for lovers of old towns, for Sandwich is one of the prettiest in Kent, and Canterbury is only ten miles distant. The walking is pleasant but easy, for the most part across coastal sands and shingle with big skies overhead. There's a stretch along the sea just for good measure. Navigation is pretty simple and helped by good waymarking. Drinking options in and around Sandwich are good and improving. You can extend the walk to the Roman fort at Richborough; and if you're really keen to step out a bit, and have your own map, it's an easy extension to the route in the other direction across the links down to Deal, which itself is one of the very best of the Kent coast towns and has a couple of excellent pubs as well as a Tudor castle to draw you along.

Sandwich harbour

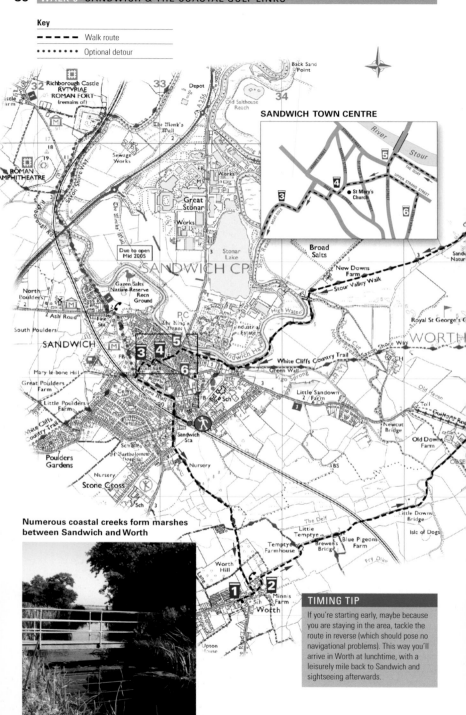

Key

– – – – Walk route

••••••• Optional detour

Numerous coastal creeks form marshes between Sandwich and Worth

TIMING TIP

If you're starting early, maybe because you are staying in the area, tackle the route in reverse (which should pose no navigational problems). This way you'll arrive in Worth at lunchtime, with a leisurely mile back to Sandwich and sightseeing afterwards.

LEFT: **A shady path by the golf links** RIGHT: **A backwater on the marshes near Sandwich**

From Sandwich station make your way out to the main Dover Road by the level crossing. Unless you are heading out to Richborough for some Roman cultural sightseeing (see box and dotted route on map) from here head south, away from town, passing St Bartholom-ew's Hospital on the opposite side of the road. St Bart's is one of two ancient almshouse foundations still extant in Sandwich. It was founded in 1190, initially for itiner-ants but later providing a permanent home for sixteen elderly people. The nearby hospital chapel, built in 1217 as part of the original foundation, is still used for its original purpose and is occasionally open to the public.

As the road swings right after about 300 yards a signed path leads off left. Taking this, one is almost immediately in a very flat rural landscape, with wide views taking in the club-house at Sandwich's Royal golf course and the spire of Worth church. Pass a nursery, and later a pleasant drainage ditch on a footbridge, then through an area of reeds. Keep ahead, ignoring side paths, through some orchards to arrive at Worth village, with the St Crispin Inn alongside and the church opposite.

Now a couple of miles inland, Worth grew up taking advantage of fertile soil surrounding the coastal creeks; local legend also claims that Henry V, or more plausibly one of his courtiers, returning from his St Crispin's Day (25th October) victory at Agincourt, disembarked at Worth and there met and fell in love with a village ale-wife, hence the name of the inn. Worth is fortunate to have retained two pubs, and both merit a visit. Head to the right down the village street for a couple of minutes to get to the **Blue Pigeons 1**. Housed in an unusual (for a village at least) three storey brick building, the place has a distinctive bar room which they describe as 'shabbily chic'. Hmmm… There's a separate restaurant, and games/TV room, leaving, one hopes, the main bar for the enjoyment of drinks, including four hand-pulled ales (Black Sheep, Wells Bombardier, Taylor Landlord and Harveys Sussex Best Bitter). Service is cheery and attentive.

Return down the road, having left some capacity to visit the **St Crispin Inn 2**. From the outside it's a fairly plain, traditional white-rendered building; the interior is opened out and modernised but with some taste, with plenty of timber and some respect for the building. The floorboarded bar room wraps around the servery, and the rear opens out into a modern conservatory which overlooks the semi-enclosed garden. There's also a patio area with a

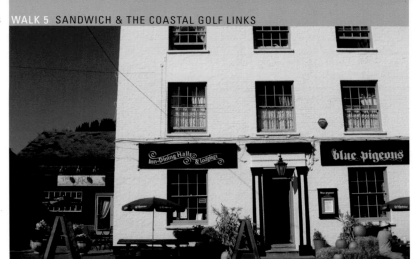

Blue Pigeons, Worth

SANDWICH: ONE OF THE ORIGINAL CINQUE PORTS

Sandwich was, and still is, a principal Cinque Port. Originally the Cinque Ports were a confederation of five harbours: Sandwich, Dover, Hythe, Romney and Hastings; and additionally, the two ancient towns of Winchelsea and Rye. Edward the Confessor was largely responsible for this defensive confederation which also arose from the frequent need to convey people and supplies to the continent to progress the frequent wars and battles. The towns supplied the Crown with ships and men, and in return received many privileges, financial and otherwise. Between the eleventh and thirteenth centuries, Sandwich was regarded as England's major port, but the Kentish coastline has changed considerably over the centuries. A combination of furious storms like that in 1287 and coastal processes have resulted in the silting up of harbours. This is what did for Richborough in earlier times. Sandwich itself is now 2 miles inland and only Dover retains its major port status.

The River Stour in Sandwich

slightly French-style glass screen, so plenty of choice about where to sit! Beers are from the Enterprise Inns list: expect Sharp's Doom Bar, Young's Bitter, and Draught Bass.

Leaving the Crispin turn left and walk down the quiet lane, bearing right at the Temptye Farm bridleway in a few minutes. Across to the left are the distinctive cooling towers of Richborough power station, although these may not be part of the local scenery for much longer. Constructed in 1962, Richborough utilised coal from the Kent coalfield. In 1971 the station was converted to run on oil, but soon after the price of oil rose, rendering the whole enterprise uneconomic. It had a brief flirtation with an experimental fuel known as Orimulsion, an emulsion from natural bitumen, but this was an environmental disaster and the plant eventually closed in 1996. Current plans are to demolish the towers and convert the site to a 'green' energy park with biomass and gasification plants and anaerobic digester. Watch this space...

Continue down the lane to the railway line, and cross. Now the path changes character, with tall hedges enclosing the narrow lane, a good spot for collecting brambles and sloes in season. Emerge from the shady path by a bridge over a drainage ditch, bearing half left on the obvious path and keeping close to the watercourse. Join a signed earthen track towards the white farmhouse. Reach the road by the bird observatory, and cross directly,

RICHBOROUGH ROMAN FORT

A detour to visit Richborough, about a mile north of Sandwich (see map) is highly recommended, although there are no pubs! Rutupiae, as the Romans called it, preceded Dover as the gateway of entry to Britain. It is here that Plautius assembled his legions after landing in Britain during the invasion of AD 43; and Watling Street left by its West Gate straight for Canterbury and London. At this time Thanet was a true island and the channel separating it from the mainland was the Wantsum; the fort guarded the channel. Excavated evidence suggests a large settlement grew up here, but this too fell victim to huge floods and storms, and changes to the coastal geography put paid to the once mighty fort itself. The ruins are still significant however and well worth a visit. Ironically the port assumed a modern significance in both World Wars when Richborough became a transit camp, both for troops going to the continent in the Great War; and for refugees arriving from Nazi persecution in the Second.

Richborough Castle still has Roman walls and extensive earthworks

through a couple of kissing gates, heading out towards the sea via the Royal St George's Golf course, host of the 2011 Open Championship. Reach the shingle beach, a good spot on a sunny day for a rest. The Isle of Thanet stretches out to the left (north) with Ramsgate prominent, while to the south the shingle runs straight towards Deal.

Head left and walk towards the large building about three quarters of a mile distant. Approach the buildings on the lane and, passing through the gate, bear left on the waymarked path just before reaching the large buildings. This is the Stour Valley Walk, which then holds the same bearing across the links (look for the waymarks when the Land Rover track veers right after a while). You're heading directly inland with the golf course on your immediate left. You arrive on a small lane close to the river. Cross the lane and take the signed path a little to the left, running up onto an embankment and following the river, with all its activity. It's a straightforward walk

now into town, joining the Saxon Shore Way path a little further on, and veering right here, then through a small park to reach the historic quayside of Sandwich with its handsome buildings, and the town bridge just beyond.

Sandwich is well-pubbed and most, if not all, offer real ale in some shape. Check the town map for the respective pub locations. Your best

The walk follows the beach for a mile or so

LEFT: **Inside the Red Cow, Sandwich** RIGHT: **Fleur-de-Lis, Sandwich**

bet if you are pressed for time and can only do one or two is to first head for the **Red Cow** 3️⃣ on Moat Sole, near the old Guildhall. Here, in a venerable old building replete with beams and timber flooring, the enthusiastic landlord serves up some interesting local brews as well as national brands, and keeps them well. There's a large enclosed garden and you'll get food here at most times. Not far away, the **Fleur-de-Lis** 4️⃣ in Delf Street opposite the *Market Inn* is a popular and friendly old inn, with plenty of character. The unusually long bar fronts distinct areas and, although it's increasingly food-oriented, the drinker is welcome and well catered for; Greene King IPA and Black Sheep Bitter are augmented by a rotating guest. The inn at one time was the coach office for the town, where you could book journeys

to all parts. Bus freaks should know that just along the street its 1922 successor still stands, erected by the East Kent Road Car Company. The handsome office and waiting room is now a listed building retaining many of its original features.

If you're looking for further drinking options in town try the **Crispin** 5️⃣, by the bridge, with plenty of timber panelling creating a pubby atmosphere; and offering four ales; and/or the **George & Dragon** 6️⃣ in Fisher Street, close to the old quayside, where at least one local guest should be on offer among the three beers, and recent quality reports are favourable. If you're venturing down the railway/road to the historic town of Deal, take your *Good Beer Guide* and seek out the excellent *Ship*, or in neighbouring Walmer, the *Berry*. Both are highly recommended.

PUB INFORMATION

1️⃣ Blue Pigeons
The Street, Worth, CT14 0DE
01304 613245
www.bluepigeonsatworth.co.uk
Opening Hours: 12-3, 5-11
Mon-Thu ; 12-11 Fri-Sun

2️⃣ St Crispin Inn
The Street, Worth, CT14 0DF
01304 612081
www.stcrispininn.com
Opening Hours: 12-2.30, 6-11;
12-9 (4.30 winter) Sun

3️⃣ Red Cow
12 Moat Sole, Sandwich, CT13 9AU
01304 613243
Opening Hours: 11-11

4️⃣ Fleur-de-Lis
6-8 Delf Street, Sandwich,
CT13 9BZ
01304 611131
www.thefleur-sandwich.co.uk
Opening Hours: 10-11 (10.30 Sun)

TRY ALSO:

5️⃣ Crispin
High Street, Sandwich, CT13 9EA
01304 621967
www.sandwichpubs.co.uk
Opening Hours: 11-11 (midnight
Fri & Sat)

6️⃣ George & Dragon
24 Fisher Street, Sandwich,
CT13 9EJ
01304 613106
www.georgeanddragon-sandwich.
co.uk
Opening Hours: 11-3, 6-11;
11-11 Sat; 12-4 Sun

The garden of the St Crispin

Westerham & Chartwell

WALK INFORMATION

Start/Finish: Westerham Green

Access: Trains from London to Oxted, then bus 594/5 via Limpsfield Chart to Westerham

Distance: 7.3 miles (11.8km)

OS map: OS Explorer OL147

Key attractions: Chartwell (National Trust); Westerham village

The pubs: Carpenters Arms, Limpsfield Chart; Royal Oak, Crockham Hill; Grasshopper on the Green, Westerham. Try also: General Wolfe, Westerham

This is one of the more hilly routes in the book, weaving its way up and down the Greensand escarpment but, as a compensation, offering fine views both north to the Downs and southwards across the Weald. The landscape here is well-wooded, and the woodlands are criss-crossed by a dense network of paths, so in places the navigation needs some care. Some sections are likely to be muddy, even in summer, so wear suitable footwear. The drinking highlight is probably the first and flagship pub of the Westerham brewery, the Royal Oak at Crockham Hill. In Westerham town itself, there's a greater variety of beers on offer. To assist planning, allow about an hour from Westerham to Limpsfield Chart.

Rural affluence at French Street

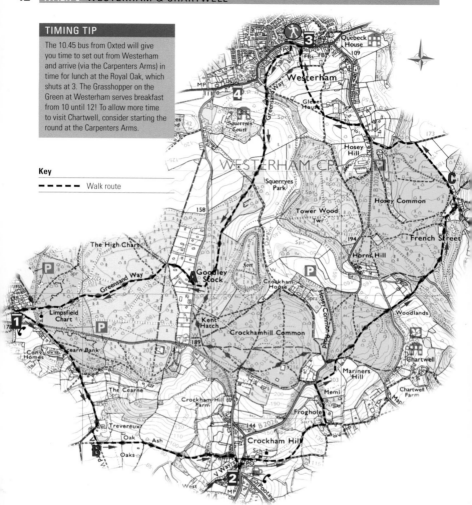

TIMING TIP

The 10.45 bus from Oxted will give you time to set out from Westerham and arrive (via the Carpenters Arms) in time for lunch at the Royal Oak, which shuts at 3. The Grasshopper on the Green at Westerham serves breakfast from 10 until 12! To allow more time to visit Chartwell, consider starting the round at the Carpenters Arms.

Key

— — — — Walk route

Westerham Green is, if you mentally remove the traffic, a very pretty spot even today: there are plenty of attractive buildings around the centre, and it is host to two statues representing famous men with Westerham connections, for different reasons. General Wolfe (1727-1759) was born here, and is remembered chiefly for his victory over the French in Canada. Winston Churchill, who presides over the Green in typical bulldog fashion, moved to the nearby house of Chartwell in 1922.

Start the walk by heading west (from the General Wolfe statue) to the *Kings Arms*, where the public path leaves town through the archway of this old coaching inn. Towards the rear of the car park the path is signed to the right along an alley, leading to and past some handsome old cottages, continuing west between the houses, and merging into a wider track by a pond. Pass Park Lodge, a small stream keeping you company for a short way, then fork right uphill on the Greensand Way. Behind the trees on the right lies the Squerryes, a 17th-century manor house which has been in the same family for almost three hundred years. There are good views behind over to the North Downs.

Kentish oasts

Navigation is very straightforward on this section, though it's a pity about the drone of the M25, which is quite intrusive. Passing through a couple of metal gates, the path plunges into woodland. If you can catch the morning sunshine with birdsong here, you'll be in the right mood. Pass a couple of waymarks, and at an obvious junction of paths, just beyond a point where the track swings left a little, turn right onto the wide stony track for 100 yards to join the road by a wooden gate at Goodley Stock (A, 439521). If you're in the correct spot, you're opposite a private road with our route, the signed Greensand Way, heading right immediately by the entrance opposite. It's easy going underfoot and gently downhill, with thick woodland cover again, until a five-way path junction some 10 minutes into the wood, with a plaque marking the halfway point of the 110-mile Greensand Way. Continue along the Greensand Way itself, bearing left on a wide track, simply looking for and follow the signs through the network of paths, more or less on the same bearing, to emerge on the little green at Limpsfield Chart.

Our first watering hole of the day, the **Carpenters Arms 1** occupies an enviable location fronting directly onto the green, whose immediate vicinity is, unlike Westerham, quiet and largely traffic-free. Recently bought by

Westerham brewery, the pub has great potential by virtue of its location. Opened out inside, there are nonetheless distinct eating and drinking ends, with a couple of traditional benches outside to enjoy the green and (one hopes) the sunshine. Westerham Bulldog and a seasonal beer from the brewery are the beers currently on tap.

The bridleway to Crockham Hill sets out directly opposite the pub: walk across the green to the road junction by the church, and head across downhill on the same bearing, down Trevereux Hill. This is now part of the Vanguard Way, another long distance path, from Croydon

The Grasshopper on the Green lies at the heart of Westerham village

Churchill, on Westerham's village green

It looks as if you are trespassing when you enter the driveway alongside a locked gate across the lane, but the public bridleway now veers around right, following the road, and a few yards later, right opposite the pretty Trevereux Cottages, take the signed Vanguard Way over a stile into the field, walking downhill towards a pair of oasts. After 100 yards, where the fence of Trevereux ends, turn 90 degrees left on what is (although unsigned here) a right of way running along the southern boundary of the house (B, 431508). It feels very rural here, and very peaceful. Keep to this line, heading towards some large houses on the hill ahead. Cross over a couple of stiles, into the woodland over a small stream and uphill to join a tarred path at Crockham Hill by a very modernistic house. Bear right, and walk along to join the public lane, whereupon it's a short distance downhill to the centre, such as it is, of Crockham Hill, by the village sign on a tiny green and, importantly, the next stop of the day, the **Royal Oak 2**

to Newhaven. Although a tarmac lane, you won't encounter much traffic as you drop steadily downhill past enviably-sited houses which take full advantage of stunning views out across the Weald. Ignore tempting-looking paths to right and left, instead following the lane right down to its foot by Trevereux, a large and imposing mansion.

The Royal Oak was the first acquisition of the Westerham brewery, whose small but modern plant is half a mile away. It's a handsome building

Westerham nestles in the Vale of Holmesdale sheltered by the North Downs

LEFT: **Beers at the Royal Oak** RIGHT: **General Wolfe joins Churchill on Westerham Green**

with striking windows. Inside, it's bright and clean, with smart floorboards, and rather formal in layout with tables and chairs, although there's a soft sofa in one corner by the wood-burning stove. The bar counter has survived several refurbishments, by the look of it, and remains a simple but attractive period piece. Expect to find the *Telegraph* and *Daily Mail* in the paper rack, while the well-heeled more mature local populace tuck into the very good food. As you'd expect, Westerham's beers (Bulldog, SPA/Summer Perle and Finchcocks), plus the occasional guest, are on offer at the bar, and are very good too. There's a small patio garden.

From the Royal Oak, cross the road and walk uphill for about 200 yards, past a row of houses, and turn right into the lane signed to the school and church. Pass the primary school, and beyond, close to the parish church, enter a field via a kissing gate. Cross this and enter a much larger field via a stile at the bottom corner. Work your way up around the right-hand margin of this field, with good views opening out to your right across the well-wooded High Weald, until you reach a wooden kissing gate leading to a small wooden plank bridge over a tiny stream.

In the next field keep left this time, uphill for some 100 yards, looking for a stile and waymark leading into the woods. Cross this stile and a walkboard. Ahead is a lengthy set of steps, which are quite steep, so take your time! At the top, emerge onto a tiny lane by a converted oast house and, whilst regaining your breath, take time to admire the vista.

When you're ready to carry on bear left along the lane, passing the attractive Froghole Farm, still climbing steadily. At the junction with the main road take the steep but short stone staircase and keep to the path straight ahead, with mature woodland on your left. In some 200 yards fork left to stay in the woodland, joining another track coming in from the left, swinging round the back of a house on your right, on a waymarked track. Twenty yards later bear off left on a track waymarked with the yellow sign of the Greensand Way. Now follow this path, crossing a wider track after 50 yards, through pretty woodland.

Descending steeply at the end, this path has the additional merit of emerging right opposite the entrance to Chartwell. Churchill and his wife Clementine bought Chartwell in 1922 for its wonderful views over the Weald, sitting as it does on the southern edge of the Greensand escarpment. They modernised and transformed the place, adding lakes and gardens outside. On the death of Churchill in 1965, Clementine immediately gave the house to the National Trust. Needless to say a visit is recommended; and if you're a member of the Trust you could just drop in for tea before continuing to Westerham.

The route continues directly opposite the path you emerged on, marked French Street, skirting the northern boundary of Chartwell. The half mile or so to French Street is in two parts, the first uphill and narrow, the second, once over a quiet lane, downhill, wider, and prone to mud. French Street is a tiny, rather attractive little

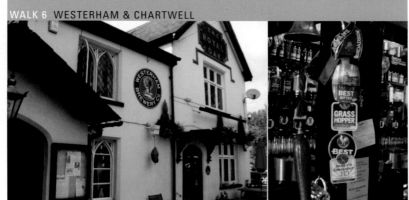

LEFT: **The Royal Oak at Crockham Hill** RIGHT: **Beer range in the Grasshopper**

hamlet, with some chocolate-box cottages, some of which have probably been slightly over-beautified. Bear left onto the quiet lane and walk up past a little private burial ground with its vernerable old yew tree. Beyond this bear right onto a footpath by the entrance to Gilhams Farm (C, 🧭 458529).

This is for the most part an easy pleasant downhill stroll through more woodland, with open country to your right. Bear left lower down and re-emerge on the French Street lane, close to its junction with the busier main road, which we join. Now turn right and walk down, the last 100 yards with no footway or margin so take care, and take a signed footpath opposite on the left (the drone of the M25 being very audible once again now). Walk down this path through a gate leading into an open field, with fine views suddenly emerging right down to Westerham itself nestling in the Vale of Holmesdale, and the North Downs escarpment beyond. Walk 20 yards across to the waymarker, and bear right on the broad open grass path running downhill, broadly towards the spire of Westerham church. Drop down the grassy bank closer to the village, through a short dark tree-lined alley and across a tiny stream and then, satisfyingly, the last few yards lead between buildings to emerge directly onto the village green, and the **Grasshopper on the Green** 🕄 .

This place has happily remained a pub serving food rather than becoming a restaurant, as has, arguably, the other *Grasshopper*, the big roadhouse out to the west on the A25. The name Grasshopper, incidentally, which also adorns one of Westerham brewery's beers, derives from the heraldic crest of the Greshams, a notable old local family whose country pile lay nearby at Titsey. As to the pub, there are three distinct areas set around the central servery; it's smart but not overpoweringly so. The pub offers the widest choice of ales in town, up to six, including Harveys Sussex Best Bitter and a couple from Westerham.

If you fancy another pint on leaving the Grasshopper, I'd recommend the **General Wolfe** 🕄, a handsome weatherboarded pub on the main road on the western outskirts of town. A *Good Beer Guide* regular, it serves beers from the Greene King stable

PUB INFORMATION

1 Carpenters Arms
12 Tally Road, Limpsfield Chart,
RH8 0TG
01883 722209
Opening Hours: 11-3 (not Mon),
5-10.30; 11-11 Sat; 12-10.30 Sun

2 Royal Oak
Main Road, Crockham Hill,
TN8 6RD
01732 866335
Opening Hours: 12-3, 6-11
(midnight Fri); 12-11 Sun

3 Grasshopper on the Green
The Green, Westerham,
TN16 1AS
01959 562926
www.grasshopperonthegreen.com
Opening Hours: 10-11.30 (12.30
Fri & Sat)

TRY ALSO:

4 General Wolfe
High Street, Westerham,
TN16 1RQ
01959 562104
Opening Hours: 12-11 (midnight
Fri & Sat); 12-10.30 Sun

Etchingham & Robertsbridge

WALK INFORMATION

Start/Finish: Etchingham station

Access: Trains from London Charing Cross/London Bridge/Waterloo

Distance: 7.2 miles (11.5km)

OS map: OS Explorer OL124

Key attractions: Rother Valley Railway; Robertsbridge village; Bodiam Castle (2 miles)

The pubs: Seven Stars; George; Salehurst Halt, all Robersbridge

To make matters complicated there are two Rother rivers in Sussex, and both feature in this book. This walk follows the upper part of the East Sussex Rother Valley through pretty countryside near the village of Robertsbridge. The village is large and still retains a good community feel and a couple of decent pubs. Nearby, the hamlet of Salehurst features an award-winning pub which has been given a new lease of life by enthusiastic licensees. This is hop country, around Salehurst in particular, and from the garden of the Halt pub you'll see them growing. The route, following the river as it does, can be muddy in places, particularly near the end. Navigation, as is usual through farmland, needs care if you are to avoid minor errors, although in general the signage is reasonable.

The attractive exterior of the George at Robertsbridge

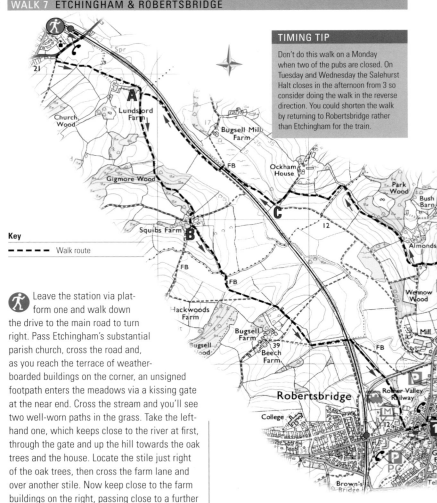

TIMING TIP

Don't do this walk on a Monday when two of the pubs are closed. On Tuesday and Wednesday the Salehurst Halt closes in the afternoon from 3 so consider doing the walk in the reverse direction. You could shorten the walk by returning to Robertsbridge rather than Etchingham for the train.

Key

- - - - Walk route

Leave the station via platform one and walk down the drive to the main road to turn right. Pass Etchingham's substantial parish church, cross the road and, as you reach the terrace of weatherboarded buildings on the corner, an unsigned footpath enters the meadows via a kissing gate at the near end. Cross the stream and you'll see two well-worn paths in the grass. Take the left-hand one, which keeps close to the river at first, through the gate and up hill towards the oak trees and the house. Locate the stile just right of the oak trees, then cross the farm lane and over another stile. Now keep close to the farm buildings on the right, passing close to a further clump of oaks and keeping close to the fence, walk round to the double stile with waymarks at the bottom of the hill (A, 💿, 719259). Don't take the left hand option across the stream: we'll be returning this way later.

Now keep ahead along the bottom of the field, with the stream on the left, towards distant trees. The path enters woodland after a few minutes, and is easy to follow, before it emerges into another field whereupon the right of way, less distinct here, follows the edge of the woodland and leads to a pair of semi-detached cottages at the end of a farm lane. Swing right here and walk up the few yards to Squibs Farm with several

The listed Seven Stars, Robertsbridge

Typical scenery of the route along the Rother Valley

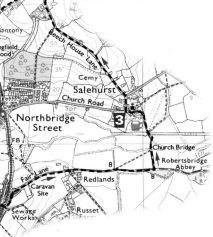

buildings and a kennels (B, ⊙, 722250). Here there are several waymarks. Head more or less straight ahead to the oast house, and take the good, unsigned track to the immediate left of the oast. If you're on the right path a wide view opens out to the left across the Rother Valley, whilst on your right is a tall hedge.

The grassy track reaches the foot of the hill; swing slightly to the left into an adjacent field. With luck, after 100 yards or so, you'll spot the parapets of a brick bridge. Cross this and you're into another field fringed with trees and running uphill. The right of way heads more or less directly across, slightly left, to exit at the far left corner. If the field has been ploughed or planted it may be easier to follow the boundary clockwise. Either way the exit is clear: at the

top left edge of the field, down to a stile on an earthern track by a large oak tree to a stile and small plank bridge. Now it's plain sailing: up and over the small spur and down to exit the field in the bottom left hand corner, then swing left along a wide avenue of trees towards the railway embankment: a pleasant spot. It can be very marshy close to the railway however, so let's hope you're suitably shod!

Pass under the railway via a brick bridge and then hold to the right hand of the two fairly obvious tracks across the meadow, following the line of the telegraph posts. You'll then pass under a bridge on the line of the former Robertsbridge to Tenterden railway, which is being restored by enthusiastic volunteers from the Rother Valley Railway. This line opened in 1900 and became the Kent & East Sussex Light Railway, later extended to Headcorn. The railway closed to regular passenger services in January 1954, although freight services continued between Robertsbridge and Tenterden until June 1961, when the line was closed completely, except for the short section between the main line and Hodsons Mill at Robertsbridge, which survived as a private siding until 1969. It is this latter section that you are passing under here.

The path passes a wood yard and emerges on the public road at Robertsbridge. Turn left for the village centre, and at the T junction, a short way to the left again, is the **Seven Stars 1** . This listed building is in fact a disguised 14th-century Wealden 'hall house' which has undergone alterations, including

LEFT: **On the way to Robertsbridge** RIGHT: **The Salehurst Halt**

a re-faced nineteenth century frontage in brick and tile. Inside, there's an atmospheric timbered main bar with a large fireplace, with a smaller room given over mainly to eating off to the right. Off the main bar to the far left is a smaller games room and access to the garden. It's in the estate of Harveys, so expect at least two of their beers. The pub has connections to the Hawkhurst gang (see box).

There are other pubs in Robertsbridge, although none should take precedence over the Halt at Salehurst (below). From a beer quality point of view perhaps the best bet (and the nearest) is the **George** 🮲 , a short distance to the south down the village street (so retrace

your steps to the T junction, and beyond). It's a smartened-up food oriented place these days but they offer three ales, Harveys Sussex Best Bitter, Fuller's London Pride and Taylor Landlord.

Either way you'll need to return to the Seven Stars, and take Fair Lane to the right. An attractive street of vernacular cottages is severed further along by the bypass, which you cross on a footbridge. Turn left once across and down to the quiet lane, followed by half a mile of very easy walking on this dead end road. Carry on straight ahead at the oast onto the 'private road' (but public path), beyond which you'll see on both sides of the lane a relatively rare sight these days: hop fields.

Oasts in the landscape, near Etchingham

The little hamlet of Salehurst, marked by its church tower, comes into view across the Rother Valley to the left. We reach the place via an excellent track signed left a short distance further on. Cross the river, and pass the track bed of the old railway line. There was a tiny halt here on the railway but it could never have prospered. Despite this the way up into Salehurst is surprisingly grand, a wide track segregated into two by a railing; a bit of a mystery. Salehurst is a pretty tiny place these days and you won't have any trouble finding, just beyond the church, the star of the show here, the **Salehurst Halt 3**.

The current owners have turned this out-of-the-way unpretentious little local into something of a destination. The homely, L-shaped bar with

plenty of wood and an open fire caters equally well for drinker and diner; the cosy little area left as one enters is a favourite of the drinking-only fraternity. Food is served until 2.30 at lunchtimes. There are usually three ales to choose from (as well as at least one draught cider) – from Harveys and Dark Star, and a (usually local) guest.

The Halt takes its locally-sourced food very seriously indeed (it's on the *Independent's* top 50 gastropub list) and it's a compliment to the place that it doesn't look or feel like a gastropub, but more a well-loved rural hostelry. The rear garden with its al fresco pizza oven offers great views over the Rother to the hop garden we saw earlier.

Leaving the pub walk back to the church and turn up the hill past the churchyard, and then take

ROBERTSBRIDGE AND THE 'HAWKHUST GANG'

Robertsbridge is a sizeable village which owes its origin and name to the Cistercian monks who founded an abbey here in the twelfth century. The bridge was probably built to improve on the river crossing at Salehurst, the original settlement and now a hamlet. Robertsbridge has a fine collection of timber framed buildings, which suggests a prosperous settlement. Its position in the river valley, in a well-wooded region and en route from the Sussex coast to London, would have contributed to its wealth. It didn't escape the attention of highly-

organised gangs who operated in this area inland from the smuggling beaches of East Sussex. One of the most notorious was based in Hawkshurst, not far from Robertsbridge. The steep hill outside Robertsbridge was the scene of a bloody battle in which an armed convoy of nearly a ton of tea was ambushed by the gang and a customs officer shot dead. Today the bypass has left the village street as something of a backwater enabling one to enjoy the ambience of the place without too much noise and pollution.

Half-timbered cottages on Robertsbridge's main street

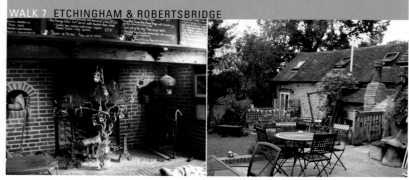

LEFT: **Large ingelnook in the George** RIGHT: **The attractive garden at the Halt, Salehurst**

the lane signed 'Hurst Green' in about 100 yards. It's a very quiet road and you won't encounter much traffic, but it is a steady climb. The reward for this is the fine view which you'll enjoy out to the west (left) across the Weald. Reach and pass Beech House Farm with its converted oast and, a little further on opposite Brushwood House, look for a signed footpath heading off to the left. Keep to the left hand side of the field (it's not exactly a yellow brick road). Pass a small pond, over a stile, and then down to the A21 road, crossing a private road just before reaching it. About 50 yards to the right there's an entry on the opposite side of the road which we want – but cross the busy road with great care as sight lines to the right are limited. Once across the road, follow the tarred lane (footpath sign) and the path continues in the same direction (across a stile) when the roadway bears left. Follow the field boundary to the right, enjoying the very fine views, perhaps the best of the day, across the valley.

Navigation on this next stretch needs some care. Follow the contours along and into a very nice stretch of woodland via another stile. At the foot of the slope bear right through the hedge on a path, and in ten yards cross a stile, bearing round sharp left down the field along the left hand boundary. At the foot of this field don't continue into the lower field but bear right along the tree line (the trees on your left now), until you reach and cross an earthen Land Rover track, to look for a stile in the scrub about twenty yards beyond. Cross over, bearing left onto a good track running downhill between the trees, to reach a small stream by a bridge (C, 727251). Cross over the stream and, although unsigned, bear sharp right into a narrow field between the river and the railway embankment. This narrow (and narrowing) field is very lumpy so watch where you put your feet.

Follow this field until the end, over a stile into an even narrower field. Halfway down, there's a signed path left which crosses the railway line. Take this, bearing sharp right once across, and follow the field margin at the foot of the railway embankment for about 600 yards, as far as a marshy section when you'll spot, with luck, the gate at the foot of the wooded slope which we passed a few minutes into the walk. You may get wet feet crossing this boggy area as you bear left to the gate and stile (A, 719259) to rejoin the outward route and retrace your steps in a few minutes further to reach Etchingham station.

PUB INFORMATION

1 Seven Stars
High Steet, Robertsbridge,
TN32 5AJ
01580 880333
www.seven7stars.co.uk
Opening Hours: 11-11

2 George
High Street, Robertsbridge,
TN32 5AW
01580 880315
www.thegeorgerobertsbridge.co.uk
Opening Hours: 11-11; closed Mon

3 Salehurst Halt
Church Lane, Robertsbridge,
TN32 5PH
01580 880620
www.salehursthalt.co.uk
Opening Hours: 12-3, 6-11; closed Mon

Isfield & the Ouse Valley

WALK INFORMATION

Start/Finish: Laughing Fish, Isfield

Access: Trains from London to Lewes or Uckfield, then frequent bus 29 (which runs between the two towns)

Distance: 7.2 miles (11.5km)

OS map: OS Explorer OL122

Key attractions: Idyllic riverside path; Lavender Line preserved railway; Lewes town and Castle (4 miles)

The pubs: Royal Oak, Barcombe; Anchor Inn, Barcombe Mills; Laughing Fish, Isfield

Between the Weald and the South Downs the landscape is more subdued and the hills smaller and less frequent. This is a straightforward, undemanding and above all very good walk, especially the return section along the attractive River Ouse. The plans to re-open the 'lost' railway between Lewes and Uckfield seem to be off the agenda for the moment, but for now the preserved Lavender Line acts as steward for about a mile of it. Expect the riverside Anchor Inn to be thronged on sunny summer weekends, but otherwise it's a quiet area. Being so close to Lewes, it would be commercial suicide for any pub not to offer at least one beer from the Harveys brewery; to try others, you'll need to wait until the last pub.

From Isfield station, with well-preserved old livery and signage, pass the Laughing Fish (to which we will return) and walk north west down the lane for about 300 yards. Where the road bends around to the right the Wealden Walks bridleway heads off to the left on a tarred lane fringed by tall hedges. Follow this for about half a mile to reach the river by White Bridge.

The Anchor Inn is right on the riverside

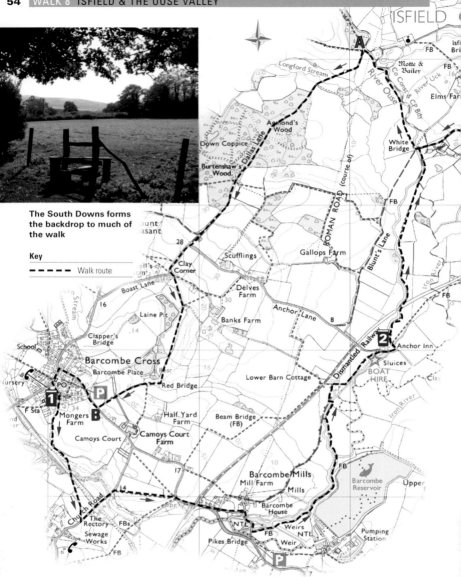

The South Downs forms the backdrop to much of the walk

Key

- - - - Walk route

Cross the bridge and bear right on a good grassy path through the riverside meadows. Cross into a second field over a double stile, and reach a narrow lane by a further stile (A, ⊙ 441181). Reference to the map here shows that there is a motte and bailey earthwork on the eastern side of the river around this point — and if the vegetation has died back in winter you should have better view of

it. The second point of interest is the parish church, set a little way back from the river, but standing in isolation some distance from the modern village. The answer lies partly in the line of an old Roman road, Ermine Street, also visible on the map, which crossed the river by a ford here just north of the confluence with the smaller River Uck. Isfield was founded at this site, and was defended by what is believed to be an old fortified manor house. The church was located in the middle of the village, but after the Black Death in 1348 the village was relocated away from the church, a common occurrence believed to be due to the survivors not wanting to live near the graves of so many plague victims.

Isfield

The walk bears left up the lane, away from the river, on an old carriage road which once linked the villages of Isfield and Barcombe. You pass a substantial pond on the right which in early summer is a colourful oasis of wild flowers. The small bridge takes you over the Longford Stream, a nursery for sea trout. Continue through the wood on the pleasant path (marked Dallas Lane on the map) bordered by many mature deciduous and coniferous trees including some Scots pines. Exit the estate after about a mile, via an unusual stile in a six-bar metal gate, onto an estate driveway. Pass a couple of lodges and then a rather imposing three storey group of estate dwellings.

Merge with a public road 50 yards further on, keeping in the same direction. At the next junction, by the entrance to Banks Farm on the left, start down the driveway but in 20 yards or so tackle the stile on the right leading into the field. Look for the metal gate in the far, lowest, corner of the field. This stile leads you onto a pleasant path along the river floodplain with some mature oaks to the left of the field. Follow the waymarked track across this field keeping the river on your right, and after another stile look for the path ducking into the trees and crossing the narrow stream. Cross the field ahead to the next stile, and take the earthen track leading gently uphill away from the river valley. This reaches the public road at B (424156).

Turn right, and walk into the village centre at Barcombe. Upon reaching the junction turn left onto the Lewes road where the first pub of the day, the **Royal Oak 1**, awaits. This handsome brick-built Harveys house has been modernised to provide a light, airy interior. Two beers from the Harveys range are available. The pub is open all day, and food is served lunchtimes and evenings; service is reputedly very efficient.

Turn right out of the pub and take the narrow lane immediately right again, following it to the end where you'll pick up a signed public footpath. Follow this round to the right down a narrow alleyway to come upon a great and slightly unexpected view across to the South Downs. Follow the path down to the lower part of the field and take the obvious stile, turning immediately left once over it so that you're walking along a shelf above a wooded dale below; actually this is a cutting on the former railway (another one) which once ran up to East Grinstead. This is the line which hosts, further north, the famous 'Bluebell Railway', one of the earliest preserved lines in the country.

LEFT: **At Barcombe Mills** RIGHT: **The Laughing Fish**

Inside the Laughing Fish

Shortly the path descends onto the old line, through a kissing gate and up through a bosky stretch, and across a couple a fields (note the very impressive old oak tree) to join a quiet lane. Here, bear left and cross on the old rail bridge, taking a well-signed track on the right just beyond. Head across the field, more or less along the contour, towards the trees at the far side, and you should emerge onto another lane by an old wartime pill box. Walk down to the right to reach once more the track bed of the former Uckfield to Lewes line, by the remains of Barcombe Mills station and the old station master's lodge. Currently the trackbed here is a permissive bridleway, but disregard this and carry on a wee bit further, taking a wide driveway peeling off the road to the left as the main road veers right towards the river bridge.

Down this driveway and, by the entrance to Barcombe House ahead, the public path bears 90 degrees right and crosses the complex of watercourses here by an old toll house with the restored charge board affixed. The mill was close by. It was first mentioned in the 16th century and by 1706 it was a combined corn and paper mill. Following improvements to the river, making it navigable, the mill was greatly enlarged in 1870 to four floors and two waterwheels. It closed in 1918 and met the fate which befell so many timber mills, finally being destroyed by fire in 1939.

Follow the lane round to the left and then right across another bridge, looking for the Ouse Valley Way waymark pointing left (upstream) along the riverside. There now follows one of the pleasantest miles in the book, easy riverside walking through grassy parkland. Cross the river by a waymark then keep right at a path junction ahead and, as you walk through the trees, you should see the **Anchor Inn 2** about 400 yards ahead of you. It lies just above a weir in a rural spot with almost no other habitation visible. Pleasant riverside tables and an extensive lawned garden with flowers are the highlights of this popular honeypot, which offers boats for hire. The interior isn't exciting but it does have a roof and heating if that's what you need. There's only one cask ale, and you don't need me to tell you whose it is…

There now follows another mile of very agreeable walking along the river (cross to the opposite bank upon leaving the Anchor) to reach White Bridge which we crossed earlier. This time, don't cross again, but simply retrace your steps along the cinder track and the public road to reach Isfield station and the **Laughing Fish 3** . Being a cynic I confidently assumed the name to be a recent one in the same genre as recent abominations such as the *Slug & Cucumber* and the *Sir Loyne of Beef*, but it turns out that it dates back to 1957 when the new guv'nor decided that the 'Station Hotel' was rather boring and this was, after all, the HQ of the local angling club. The current licensees have turned this place into a bit of a destination and a regular entrant in the *Good Beer Guide* by a combination of keeping their beer well and running a friendly and welcoming house. Expect three beers from the Greene King stable including their ersatz Kimberley Ale (speaking as someone who drank the original stuff as a student) and one or two guests, with Dark Star beers putting in regular appearances. Bus 29 stops across the road…

PUB INFORMATION

1 Royal Oak
High Street, Barcombe, BN8 5BA
01273 400418
www.royaloakbarcombe.co.uk
Opening Hours: 10-11; 12-11
Sun

2 Anchor Inn
Anchor Lane, Barcombe Mills,
BN8 5EA
01273 400414
www.anchorinnandboating.co.uk
Opening Hours: 11-3 (5 Sat
& Sun)

3 Laughing Fish
Station Road, Isfield, TN22 5XB
01825 750349
www.laughingfishonline.co.uk
Opening Hours: 11.30-11

The Cuckmere Valley & Alfriston

WALK INFORMATION

Start/Finish: Berwick station

Access: Trains from London Victoria/London Bridge via Lewes. Motorists could park at Alfriston and walk out to Berwick at low level, and this would shorten the return from the Sussex Ox.

Distance: 11.5 miles (18.5km)

OS map: OS Explorer OL123

Key attractions: Drusilla's Zoo, Alfriston; Lullington Tea Gardens; Long Man of Wilmington (chalk figure); Alfriston village and Clergy House; South Downs Way path

The pubs: Cricketers, Berwick; Plough & Harrow, Litlington; Sussex Ox, Milton Street

Riverside, downland and farmland are all represented in this easy walk in a very popular part of the South Downs. Well-heeled villages with pretty cottages nestle under the rolling grassy chalk hills, and we visit some of the best pubs close by the Cuckmere Valley. Although quite a long walk the miles go by fairly easily; the couple of hill climbs are on good tracks where the fine views compensate for any effort expended. Some sections may be muddy, especially after rain. It's a walk deep in the core territory of Harveys, the Lewes brewery, whose distinctive ales are available in all the pubs; but in the unlikely event you don't like them, two of the three featured pubs offer alternatives. A taxi booked ahead could be used to cut out the final three miles back to the station from the last pub.

The Sussex Ox

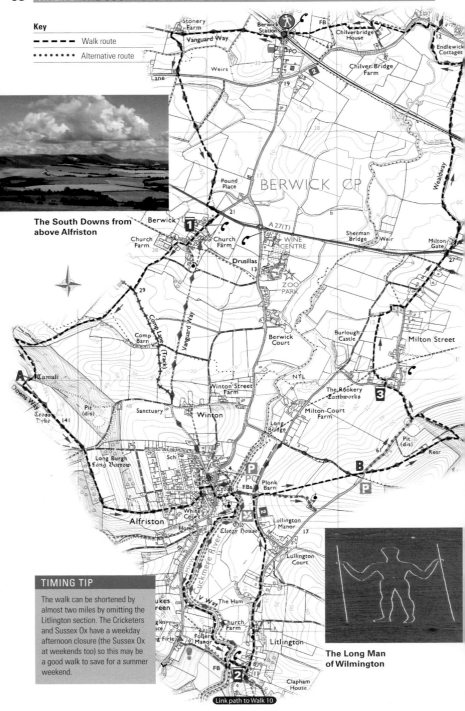

Key

– – – – Walk route

•••••••• Alternative route

The South Downs from above Alfriston

The Long Man of Wilmington

The Cricketers, Berwick, which serves beer straight from the cask

Leaving the station, cross to the southern side of the railway, by the Berwick Inn. Opposite, a bridleway leaves the road, by the side of the warehouse, marked 'Vanguard Way'. Immediately, you're treated to a classic view of the South Downs, falling away into the Cuckmere Valley on the left. The walk reaches a farm lane in about half a mile; here, follow the Vanguard Way to the left, down the farm track to the public road. The footpath continues opposite, over a plank bridge and then diagonally left through agricultural land. The right of way is rather indistinct on this stretch, partly depending on what is growing in the fields: keep on broadly the same bearing for a good half a mile, via a stile after a few hundred yards. If you look keenly ahead you may be able to pick out the chalk figure of the Long Man of Wilmington on the downland ahead. With his poles, he looks like an ancient skier. Also look out for the church spire of Berwick village, visible through the trees.

On reaching a line of telegraph poles, by a waymark and with a house some 200 yards across to your left, bear right along the field boundary (a hedge on your immediate right), and follow this path to reach the busy A27. Here take great care crossing as traffic is heavy. Once across, the turning to Berwick village is just a few yards to the left. Rurality quickly resumes and a few yards along on the left by way of reward stands the first pub of the day, the **Cricketers 1**. This Harveys house, once a pair of cottages, has a traditional flint and brick exterior with beautiful cottage gardens to front and rear. The interior still retains character although modernisation has occurred. The most authentic room is the central one with a terracotta tiled floor and wooden wainscot panelling. From here you can also see through to the stillage behind the bar where the ales (expect a good range of Harveys beers) are racked up for cask service – there are no handpumps on the bar. Well-regarded food is served all day, but don't forget the miles ahead…!

Continue up the pleasant village street which being a dead end is unlikely to be busy; you can detour to the attractive church by bearing left at the fork in about 200 yards, otherwise the track bears right, then left by Church Farm, making for the steep slope of the downs ahead. The ascent of this scarp slope is easier than it looks thanks to a good zig-zag track swinging first right and later left, to reach the summit of the South Downs ridge (A, ⊙ 505040). Views are predictably very good, looking across the Vale of Sussex to the Weald.

Berwick church

The South Downs Way path can be picked up by walking downhill away from the crest of the ridge for about thirty yards – its' a wide chalky bridleway which turns left, and heads towards Alfriston, the large village in the valley ahead of you. Cross a bridleway and continue downhill (with hedges either side now) and enter the village via a street of very large houses running down the hill. Reach Alfriston's pretty main street at the *George Inn*, although if you are gasping for further refreshment you might try the *Olde Smugglers Inne*, left, which has a more interesting beer range. Be warned that Alfriston can get packed with trippers in season and at weekends... Our route turns right at the George and then left opposite shortly down a path to the parish church.

At the corner of the church green by the National Trust sign, the path down to the river leads between flint walls (if you wish to visit the Clergy House, however, now is the time to detour: it's beyond the church. This 14th-century thatched and timber-framed Wealden 'hall house' was the

LINK TO WALK 10
From the Plough & Harrow, there is the option of linking to the extended Walk 10. Simply follow the eastern riverside path down the Cuckmere Valley for 2 miles (3km) to Exceat Bridge (see map).

first building to be acquired by the National Trust, in 1896). Reach the river by a white bridge, but don't cross. Bear right through the kissing gate to take the river bank path; the Cuckmere is a small river although this stretch is still tidal so depending upon the time of day you may encounter a decent width of stream or a rather disappointing little trickle, little more than a ditch! It does mean however that some sections of the riverside path can be muddy. The landscape compensates though, and close by there's the churchyard followed by the attractive cottage garden of the Clergy House beyond the church. The path meanders for about a mile of pleasant walking; reach the next bridge and cross, doubling back for a few yards to then bear right up into the village of Litlington. On emerging onto the village street, a few yards to your right is the **Plough & Harrow** 2 . It's a flint and tile-hung free house with a spacious interior: a main L-shaped bar, a small inglenook snug and a separate dining area towards the rear. Beers are from Dark Star and (of course) Harveys, with a guest.

The next section of the walk follows the village street northwards, passing the popular Litlington Tea Gardens on your right, and the parish church on the left. Beyond here there's no footway so take care as you walk along the lane, which could be busy at weekends. When the road bears a little

to the right by The Ham, the path resumes, on a margin segregated from the road by trees and shrubs. Then over a stile, and follow the right-hand edge of the field (with views back to Alfriston) over a couple of stiles and then through a small woodland area and back into a field where again keep to the right-hand margin and thence up to the road by the Great Meadow Barn at Lullington. The footpath continues almost opposite, climbing the chalk spur on the valley side. At the point where the hedge ends about 300 yards along, there's a fork in the paths. The walk route forks left here, through the trees and then diagonally up the neighbouring field towards a gap in the hedge 100 yards or so up from the corner to the immediate right (but in wet weather and/or if the field is ploughed it may be better to keep to the field margin). Keep the same diagonal bearing through the open downland, towards some trees, over a stile and a section of sunken path to emerge on the lane with a South Downs way marker pointing straight across (B, ⊙ 532033).

It's a small cultural detour to visit little Lullington church by continuing on the path straight ahead at the fork (see map). This tiny church, standing in splendid isolation, is in fact just a portion of the chancel of a much larger church, whose remains may be traced in the churchyard west of the entrance. Of the settlement of Lullington, little remains; it has shrunk to become something of a lost village. This detour path joins the same quiet lane skirting the downs towards Wilmington; you'll need to head left for five minutes to rejoin at point B.

Cross the lane and continue uphill on the South Downs Way (if you're in a hurry or tired, you can cut out the next hill, and the fine views, by continuing up the road). The path steepens for a while to climb past a covered reservoir on the left but the real draw of this section is the fine chalk coombe (dry valley) on the right.

Where the fence ends by a gate close to the top of the hill, and the track starts to veer right, cut the corner left across the grass to drop down to another track cutting back sharp left and dropping steadily downhill (don't go through the gate leading to another path contouring along the hillside). This downhill path offers views to the village of Milton Street below, and to the Arlington reservoir close to Berwick station a couple of miles distant.

When you meet the lane again, continue almost opposite on another track down to the village street; the sign of the **Sussex Ox** ⑥ is visible now down the street to the left. This cleverly modernised pub still feels welcoming to the drinker with its atmospheric bar area offering a wide range of seating. The Ox is a LocAle accredited pub so expect the beer menu to feature

Small villages nestle in the shadow of the South Downs

LEFT: **The Cricketers** RIGHT: **The historic back streets of Alfriston**

Sussex breweries, particularly Harveys and Dark Star. There's a separate, upmarket dining room at the front of the building but bar meals are available, and the food is good here.

The Ox is still about three miles from Berwick station so bear this in mind before you get too settled, unless you have arranged transport back. Leave the pub and walk past the car park to find the stile at the far edge, (footpath sign). The path zig-zags around following the field boundaries, then down the left hand edge of a larger field, past a plantation of saplings (ignore a path to the left going through the hedge after a few yards). Through another field, and around the boundary, and as you approach a small copse you'll see a waymark leading the path over a rickety-looking wooden bridge and around the edge of the copse, bearing right at the back of it and straight down to the lane. Now ignore the path continuing opposite; instead, just walk down this quiet lane to reach the anything-but-quiet A27 once again. This road is not called the 'South Coast stealth motorway' by critics for nothing; it's very busy here and you may have to wait patiently for a safe time to cross. Opposite, head straight away from the road on the 'Wealdway', bearing left at the fork in about 100 yards. Don't be deterred by the 'dead end bridleway' sign on the gate: the right of way continues later on as a footpath only. The pretty well-signed route heads down

the field edge towards the railway line which it crosses via a gate, continuing uphill towards some cottages coming into view ahead. Just before reaching them a path leads off left and down to the riverside which it parallels for the last short stretch to emerge on the lane. If you miss this path you'll simply reach the lane further east. Bear left, cross the river and then look for a path heading left down into the shrubbery. Take this since it will prevent you walking along the road around the bend ahead: the path parallels the road and emerges on the said lane opposite its continuation, via a stile. The reservoir installations are on the right. Completed in 1971, the 49 hectare Arlington Reservoir supplies water to the local area as well as functioning as a trout fishery. The reservoir supports diverse habitats, with over 150 recorded bird species; and harbours a wintering population of up to 10,000 wildfowl. Crossing a couple of stiles but staying to the right of the Chilver Bridge House grounds on the left, reach the lane-cum-bridleway beyond the house, and double back for a few yards to take a clear path to the right, via a metal kissing gate. Walk up the side of the field towards to the telegraph post. At the top of the rise, the last section of the path should be visible, heading back downhill to the houses and the lane by Berwick station, where if you have missed your train, the pub should be open.

PUB INFORMATION

1 Cricketers
Berwick, BN26 6SP
01323 870469
www.cricketersberwick.co.uk
Opening Hours: 11-3, 6-11; 11-11 Sat & summer; 12-10.30 Sun

2 Plough & Harrow
The Street, Litlington, BN26 5RE
01323 870632
www.ploughandharrowlitlington.co.uk
Opening Hours: 11-11; 12-10.30 Sun

3 Sussex Ox
Milton Street, BN26 5RL
01323 870840
www.thesussexox.co.uk
Opening Hours: 11.30-3, 6-11; 12-3, 6-10.30 (12-5 winter) Sun

Beachy Head circuit via East Dean, & Eastbourne town trail

WALK INFORMATION

Start: St Bede's School, Duke's Drive, Eastbourne

Finish: Eastbourne rail station

Access: Rail to Eastbourne. Regular bus 3 from Terminus Road bus/rail interchange to St Bede's School. For extended route: buses 12/12A/12X/13X from Exceat Bridge to Eastbourne Terminus Road

Distance: 11.5 miles (18.5km) including town trail (3.5 miles/5.5km). Extended route from St Bede's School to Exceat Bridge: 8 miles (13km)

OS map: OS Explorer 123

Key attractions: Eastbourne town and seafront; Beachy Head; Belle Tout lighthouse; Birling Gap beach; East Dean village; Seven Sisters; Cuckmere Haven

The pubs: Tiger Inn, East Dean; Ship; Eagle; Counting House, all Eastbourne. Try also: Dew Drop Inn, Eastbourne; Golden Galleon, Exceat Bridge

Located at the eastern end of the newly formed South Downs National Park, this impressive coastal walk from Eastbourne is in two parts: the main section is a bracing, circular route with cliff-top drama and expansive views of the rolling South Downs and the sea. The second part of the walk is a town trail around some of Eastbourne's best watering holes. Although the total distance might seem ambitious, once you've walked the main circuit the town trail is easily covered at leisure, with plenty of refreshment stops. If that's not enough variety for you, there is the option to extend the walk from Birling Gap across the famous Seven Sisters cliffs to Exceat Bridge, with a bus back to Eastbourne; or even to link from Exceat Bridge, up the Cuckmere Valley, to Walk 9. To make the most of it all, you'll need a weekend at least.

⬥ Start at the western end of Eastbourne seafront, at the kiosk by St Bede's School on a sharp bend in the road. Summon your energies and head straight up the first hill of the day, on a well-worn chalky path. As the slope levels out you will come to a marker post and three wide grassy paths. Take the lower, left-hand path and follow it around the top of a large tree-lined hollow to your left, with playing fields below and views out to sea.

Cliff tops beyond Beachy Head, with Belle Tout lighthouse in the distance

At the finger post follow the sign, left, towards Beachy Head, through a patch of trees and out into the open again, where you'll arrive at a lookout point and, undoubtedly, a freshening blast of sea air. Continue on the main path around the top of the cliffs and you'll see the *Beachy Head* pub and the Beachy Head Countryside Centre across the road to your right. The Countryside Centre is worth a quick stop, with well-presented information about the local downland environment.

The next part of the route is very straightforward, and is simply a case of following the cliff-top path (South Downs Way) towards Belle Tout lighthouse in the distance. Views unfold on your right to the iconic Seven Sisters cliffs beyond, kept gleaming white by constant erosion, and the downland countryside also begins to open out. The rolling chalk grassland and scrub is a surprisingly rich habitat, with an abundance of butterflies, birds and wild flora and its importance is reflected by the formation of the South Downs National Park in April 2011.

Belle Tout lighthouse is well known after the whole structure was dramatically moved 17 metres (56 feet) inland in 1999, due to threatening erosion of the cliff face. The lighthouse was built in 1832 and has had a fascinating and varied history. In 1902, it was replaced as a lighthouse

The Tiger Inn, East Dean

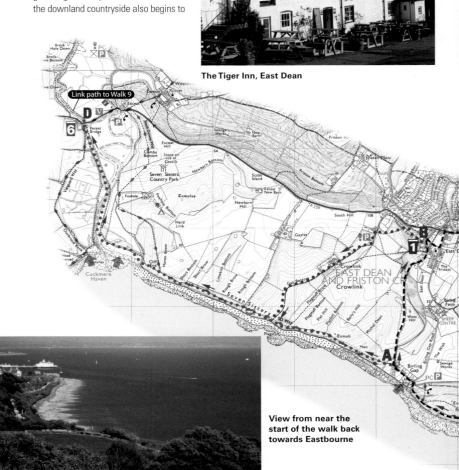

View from near the start of the walk back towards Eastbourne

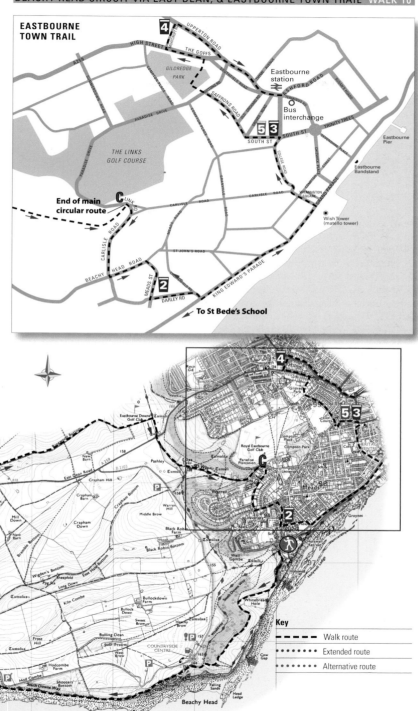

EASTBOURNE TOWN TRAIL

UPPERTON ROAD
HIGH STREET
THE GOFFS
A259
GILDREDGE PARK
Eastbourne station
ASHFORD ROAD
PARADISE DRIVE
SAFFRONS ROAD
Bus interchange
THE LINKS GOLF COURSE
SOUTH ST
COLLEGE ROAD
Eastbourne Pier
Eastbourne Bandstand
End of main circular route
C
LINK RD
CARLISLE ROAD
CARLISLE ROAD
GRAND PARADE
Wish Tower (matello tower)
CARLISLE ROAD
ST JOHN'S ROAD
BEACHY HEAD ROAD
MEADS ST
KING EDWARD'S PARADE
DARLEY RD
To St Bede's School

Key

— — — Walk route

•••••• Extended route

•••••• Alternative route

LEFT: **Beachy Head lighthouse** RIGHT: **Village green at East Dean**

by the current, more effective one, at the bottom of the cliffs and, today, is open to guests as an impressive B&B.

From Belle Tout, the path drops down towards Birling Gap where there is a staircase down to a beach, once popular with local smugglers. The beach is part of a marine nature reserve and with its rock pools and areas of pebbles and sand is good for seaside picnics in fine weather and certainly worth exploring. At this point, you might well be feeling quite windswept, in which case a quick tea stop could be in order. Conveniently, there is a café, shop and interpretation room run by the National Trust, who own land around Birling Gap.

On leaving Birling Gap, take the paved residential track to the right of the café and car park, just beyond the bend in the road. At the top of the track follow the path through a wooden gate, where it turns sharply right. In just a few yards you will come to a junction marked with a finger post (A, 552963). Left, is the optional extended route across the Seven Sisters to Exceat Bridge, from where you can catch a bus back to Eastbourne (see box). A further option is to continue on the main route to our stop at the Tiger Inn at East Dean, and then take the lane from the top left (NW) corner of the village green (B, 556978) and follow an alternative route back to the Seven Sisters via Crowlink (cutting out three Sisters on the way).

Our path, however, heads straight on from A, through one gate and along a field boundary then through a second gate to join a well-worn chalky track. Continue along this track for about 500 yards until you reach (the very!) Red Barn. Just beyond, the track bears left towards a gate but ignore this and continue northwards on a much fainter path towards the narrow corner of the field in the trees ahead. Before you reach the corner of the field, after about 200 yards, follow a path that veers off to your right through a gap in the trees and scrub, downhill through some trees and into Went Way. Follow this road all the way to the end, where you will come upon the delightful village green of East Dean. The **Tiger Inn** 1 faces you, enticingly, from the other

OPTIONAL EXTENDED ROUTE FROM BIRLING GAP TO EXCEAT BRIDGE (4 MILES/6.5KM)

Continuing along the cliff-top path from A (552963) it is simply, but strenuously, a case of traversing the Seven Sisters and eventually heading down the last one, and a steep final section, to reach the beach at Cuckmere Haven. The path continues along the back of the beach and then up the river's edge, crossing a bypassed section of the river halfway up to reach Exceat Bridge and the **Golden Galleon** 5 (D, 514994). Popular with the many visitors to the beautiful Cuckmere Valley, this Vintage Inns pub is large and comfortable with a wide range of food and a modest but decent beer offer. It will no doubt make for a welcome stop. There are frequent buses from outside the pub back to Eastbourne (see Walk Information), where you can pick up on the town trail. If you have time to spare, the Seven Sisters Country Park Visitor Centre across the estuary is worth a visit (buses also stop there). Or, if you are continuing along the Cuckmere River path to connect with Walk 9, it's another 2 miles (3km) or so upstream (see box and refer to your own map).

side. This quaint, 15th-century flint cottage was once the haunt of smugglers and wreckers and is now a magnet for walkers and cyclists. The cosy main bar has low beams, an inglenook and wood-burner and there are two other, smaller rooms. The pub is the brewery tap for Beachy Head brewery and offers a couple of their beers – usually Original and Legless Rambler – alongside the ubiquitous but delicious Harveys Sussex Best Bitter. The food is good and diners and drinkers invariably spill out onto the tables outside and often onto the village green.

Having satisfied your thirst and hunger, leave the Tiger past the Hikers Rest shop and café (which sells bottles of Beachy Head beer) and down the lane to the road at the bottom. Turn left here, cross the road and head towards the main A259. Crossing this road, bear right (where there is an Eastbourne-bound bus stop if you want a ride back to town) and then, a short way up the rise, take Downs View Lane on your left. The end of the lane joins with a footpath which you now follow for about a mile and a half (2.5km), onto a wide track through a golf course, until it ends on top of a ridge by a clubhouse. Turn right here, cross the busy road ahead and continue on the path to your right (now a branch of the South Downs Way). After 500 yards, veer left where the path diverges just past a marker post and before a triangulation point and dew pond and continue downhill in this direction, along the grassy ridge, to end up at the junction of Link Road and Paradise Drive (C, ◉, 598982).

The country walking now complete, you can set your sights on some serious refreshment. Turn right into Link Road and using the town trail map for detailed guidance, find your way via Carlisle Road and Beachy Head Road to Meads Village – an old and affluent part of the town whose Victorian and Edwardian history is clear to see in the elegant surrounding buildings. Indeed, with the advent of the railways, the Victorian and Edwardian eras were boom times for the town as a whole and many of the streets on our trail display architectural styles from those periods. The **Ship** **2**, on Meads Street, is a comfortable, well-furnished pub with a large bar with separate drinking areas, a dining area, conservatory and rear garden. A wide range of good food is available to satisfy any post-walk hunger and the beer range includes offerings from Beachy Head, Harveys, Flowers and guests.

Leaving the Ship to the left, turn left into Darley Road and head for the seafront. A sobering stroll along the front eventually brings you to a martello tower – one of a series of defensive towers built along the south coast in the early 1800s to resist a potential invasion by Napoleon. We turn left here into Wilmington Square and on into Wilmington Gardens, left and then right into College Road, then right and first left into South Street (whew!) where the **Eagle** **3** faces you from across the road. The Eagle is a lively town-centre pub catering for a mixed crowd, but with a definite focus on good beer, offering perhaps the best selection in town. There are five regularly

Walkers on the cliff-top path to Birling Gap

LEFT: **Eastbourne seafront and pier**   RIGHT: **The historic Counting House focuses on local beers**

changing guest beers from local breweries, and a real cider. The food also comes recommended and CAMRA members receive a discount.

South Street is spoilt for pubs and you could well spend the rest of your time here. Further along to the right is the **Dew Drop Inn** 5, a *Good Beer Guide* pub (like the other recommended pubs on this walk) – slightly worn, with a young vibe, but welcoming – and the *Dolphin* which is another good town pub. If you've thirst for a final destination, however, it's worth the walk to the Counting House. Head to the end of South Street, across into Saffrons Road, then cut to the right across Gildredge Park to The Goffs and then left and first right into Moatcroft Road.

The **Counting House** 4 looks for all the world like a country pub dropped in a town. Set in a large, sunken garden, this 16th-century flint-stone building with leaded windows is quintessentially Sussex. Inside, there are low beamed ceilings and wood panelling and a small galleried room to one side. Local artwork hangs on the walls and the local emphasis extends to the beers, with Hammer Pot, Rother and 1648 available on my visit. A varied menu is also served all day. On leaving the pub via the far end of Moatcroft Road, the last leg of our trail, to the station, is simply a case of following Upperton Road a few hundred yards downhill.

LINK (SEE MAP) TO WALK 9

From the end of the extended route at Exceat Bridge, there is the further option of linking to Walk 9. Simply follow the riverside path up the Cuckmere Valley for 2 miles (3km) to join Walk 9 at Litlington.

PUB INFORMATION

1 Tiger Inn
The Green, East Dean, BN20 0DA
01323 423209
www.beachyhead.org.uk
Opening Hours: 11-11

2 Ship
Meads Street, Eastbourne,
BN20 7RH
01323 733815
Opening Hours: 10-11 (midnight Fri); 10-10.30 Sun

3 Eagle
South Street, Eastbourne, BN21 4UT
01323 417799
www.theeagleeastbourne.co.uk
Opening Hours: 11-11 (midnight Fri & Sat)

4 Counting House
Moatcroft Road, Eastbourne,
BN21 1NB
01323 731158
www.pleisure.com/pubs-counting-house.html
Opening Hours: 12-11 (midnight Fri & Sat); 12-10.30 Sun

TRY ALSO:

5 Dew Drop Inn
South Street, Eastbourne,
BN21 4UP
01323 723313
Opening Hours: 12-midnight (1.30am Fri & Sat)

Dew Drop Inn

6 Golden Galleon
Exceat Bridge, Seaford, BN25 4AB
01323 892247
www.vintageinn.co.uk/
thegoldengalleonseaford
Opening Hours: 12-11; 12-10.30 Sun

Historic Winchelsea & the Brede Levels

WALK INFORMATION

Start/Finish: Winchelsea station

Access: Trains from London Charing Cross/Victoria via Hastings, or from St Pancras via Ashford

Distance: 7.6 miles (12.2km)

OS map: OS Explorer OL125

Key attractions: Winchelsea, 'Antient Town'; Romney Marsh; Rye (2 miles); Camber Sands & Castle (4 miles)

The pubs: Queen's Head; Robin Hood, both Icklesham; Plough, Cock Marling

This walk is a gentle stroll taking in the wide valley of the Brede and some of the hills on each side which were, in Roman times, either islands or peninsulas in a wide complex delta. The nearby village of Icklesham is fortunate enough to retain two pubs, both of which are of high quality and attract very favourable reviews. There are options for stronger walkers to extend the walk, either by taking in a longer loop via Udimore (and the Kings Head), and/or to continue into Rye along the valley at the end of the walk, where there are several options for further drinking. In both cases refer to your own copy of the OS map. Motorists could start and finish in the town rather than at the station.

Wickham Manor

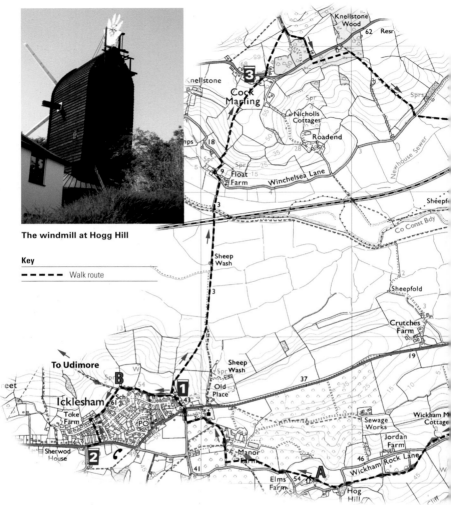

The windmill at Hogg Hill

Key

- - - - Walk route

It is difficult to imagine that the 'Antient town of Winchelsea', whose population and appearance are now that of a small village, was once a leading town of England, and Sussex's major port. Its importance was such that, when Old Winchelsea was destroyed by the sea, King Edward I personally provided the new site for the town on the hill of Iham. This explains why present-day Winchelsea with its grid-iron layout is clearly a planned settlement.

Start at Winchelsea station, where you might be forgiven for thinking there is no town at all,

for the little single track platform sits in splendid isolation, albeit in the midst of wonderful countryside. The village sits up in the trees on the hill half a mile to the south. Walk over the level crossing and head up the lane which, on a sunny morning, is a pleasure all the way; but prepare for a culture shock on reaching a hairpin bend in the main road as it starts to climb up into the old town. There's no pavement so only a masochist would want to walk up the side of this often busy route. Instead, take the signed path on the corner to the right, past a small water treatment

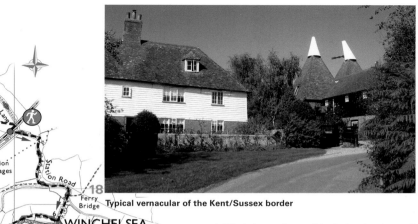

Typical vernacular of the Kent/Sussex border

works. This is a pleasant detour around the foot of the slope.

As you swing left to climb up onto the town ramparts on the obvious track further along, fine views open out across the valley.

Just before reaching the main road, look for the even wider view across towards Rye with its distinctive church tower, across levels that were once marsh and open water. On reaching the road cross straight over onto a quiet lane then take the first right, leading up to the centre of the town by the *New Inn* and the church of St Thomas the Martyr.

The original Winchelsea was probably a Saxon fishing village, built on a shingle bank or (in Saxon) chesil, (hence the suffix -chelsea, and of course the famous Chesil Beach in Dorset). It was about three miles east, well out to sea today. After it was lost to the waves, the new town was laid out between 1288 and 1294. St. Thomas's, here on the left, was the principal church of New

Winchelsea and was originally the size of a small cathedral. It's not entirely clear when and why it was shrunk, but all that remains of St Thomas's today is the chancel (which has become the nave) and the ruined transepts. Look for the 'Wesley Tree' along the churchyard wall as you walk down the street. This is the site where John Wesley preached his last outdoor sermon, six months before his death, on October 7, 1790. This is not the original tree but a new sapling planted in 1931.

Continue down the street, quickly leaving the buildings behind until, just beyond the sharp right bend at the bottom, the 1066 Country

Handsome exterior at the Plough

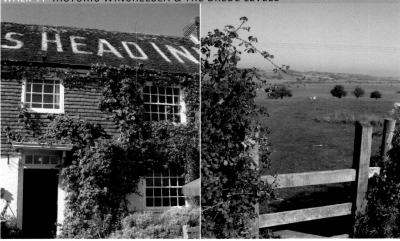

LEFT: **The Queen's Head** RIGHT: **Leaving Icklesham the path drops into the Brede Levels**

Walk path points diagonally out across a valley. A sign by the side of the road gives information about the decline of the town which once extended out to here; and on the St John's Hospital almshouses, the west wall of which survives a few yards to your left.

Follow the path downhill, across a green lane halfway down, and carry on down, keeping the small woodland on your right, towards the single tree at the foot of the valley. As you pass through the field boundary and head uphill towards Wickham Manor, above, look for the ruins below (to the left) of the New Gate, built about 1330 to guard the southern entrance into the town. The right of way leads over a stile to the left of the tiled outbuilding on the left of the main manor buildings.

Wickham Manor is a lovely old 16th century farm once owned by the Quaker William Penn, founder of Pennsylvania. Over to your left, there are fine views to the coast and across the Brede Levels. The well-signed route keeps more or less to the crest of the ridge ahead, crossing a narrow lane, once through a couple more stiles. Once

across the lane and into the field to the left of it aim for the end of the tree belt ahead, passing a well-sited pill box, then keep straight ahead. Soon, the Hogg Hill post windmill (A, ⊙ 887161) comes into view. Erected here in 1790 it has been much restored and apparently houses the recording studios of Sir Paul McCartney. The footpath passes right underneath it, after re-joining and quickly leaving the same lane crossed earlier.

Now the way is fairly clear down to Icklesham below, following the 1066 Country Walk signs, crossing or skirting a large field and then picking out the path by a converted oast to reach Icklesham's interesting parish church via the churchyard. In fact, just before entering the churchyard, a path to the left along the field margin avoids your having to walk along the main road for the 200 yards or so; and taking this path one emerges opposite the narrow Parsonage Lane that leads down to our first pub stop of the day, the **Queen's Head** 🔳. In a quiet location tucked well away from sight and sound of traffic, this previous local CAMRA Pub of the Year offers

OPTIONAL UDIMORE EXTENSION

Leave the route at B and follow the 1066 Country Walk until you meet a T junction after the buildings of Brook Farm. Turn right and follow the marked footpath down into the valley, ignoring a path branching to the right along the River Brede, then up to Udimore, taking the left-hand path after St

Mary's church and following it up to the junction with the main road. Cross the road onto the pavement, and the *Kings Head* is a short way down to the right. To return to the route, follow the footpath you have just taken back down to the valley floor and the path along the Brede.

at least five beers, often more, with several ciders. In both cases there's a strong emphasis on the local, in addition to the flagship Harveys Sussex Best Bitter which is of course de rigeur in these parts. The rambling interior with several distinct areas is comfortable and interesting, festooned with all manner of memorabilia and decoration; but a real draw here, given the right weather, is the lovely garden with great views across the Levels towards Rye. Both pubs in Icklesham offer food, and plenty of it, day and night. To reach the Robin Hood, turn right up Parsonage Lane, following the 1066 Country Walk. Continue for several minutes, swinging left by a converted thatched barn, and when the 1066 walk veers off to the right at B (🧭 875166), carry on for a few more minutes to emerge onto a street of bungalows. Bear left up to a T junction and then almost opposite, to the right of number 13, up another alleyway and so to the main road once again. The **Robin Hood** 🄁 is across the street, a little

way down on the right. It offers a contrast in style and décor to the Queen's Head, with a welcoming but dark interior, divided into two main rooms. Hops in profusion are suspended from the ceiling, almost obscuring the large collection of copper kettles. Five real ales (and Westons Old Rosie cider) are available from a changing list, with once again a strong local emphasis. There's a separate and very attractive room for diners on the way to the rear, which (not to be outdone by their rivals up the road) opens out onto a small garden at the back with more great views, this time in the other direction. Each July the pub hosts a popular beer festival.

Return via the same route to the Queen's Head; note that the longer route to Udimore if you decide to tackle it leaves on the 1066 Country Walk route halfway back at B.

The footpath across the Levels to Cock Marling exits via a stile from the rear of the Queen's Head car park, dropping down to the valley floor and offering a 180 degree panorama. Stay on the right

LEFT: **The idyllic garden at the Queen's Head** RIGHT: **The eclectic interior at the Robin Hood**

hand side of the little ditch as you cross the mast, keeping a double oast in your sights ahead. Cross the railway and two drainage ditches in quick succession on new footbridges (this is the point where those detouring to Udimore will rejoin), and then up to the lane close to the oasts. Walk up to and past these and, 100 yards beyond, a well-marked footpath on the right climbs up onto the northern side of the valley with more fine views. In a few minutes the path will disgorge onto the road just twenty yards to the right of the **Plough 3** . A solid traditional pub sign welcomes one to this attractive roadside pub in the tiny hamlet of Cock Marling. Inside the layout is open plan around the bar with, once again, a very pretty garden to the rear offering extensive views. Two beers from Harveys are joined by a guest, which was changing on my last visit from Hog's Back HBB to Woodforde's Wherry.

Walk back to the point where you emerged onto the road, crossing over when and where it's safe to do so. Almost opposite (by the 'Tuckaway' bungalow) a signed path leads into an area of parkland dotted with mature trees and good views beyond to the north. Aim left of the oak trees down the hill to the far corner of the field at the edge of trees, there cross a gravel driveway via two stiles onto a parallel drive with a clear bridleway sign. Here simply turn to the

right and follow this good track back to the main road. Here, right opposite, although not a right of way, a permitted conservation path offers the chance to avoid walking 300 yards down the main road to the left. Cross over and head down the track to bear left in just a few yards on an attractive route through the trees, emerging soon into a field (keep to the left hand margin, by the trees), with good views over the Levels once more. The public path merges from the left, look for the stile and yellow waymark, and then look diagonally to the right and you'll see the stile and waymark of the route we need to take downhill towards the station. It leads obliquely downhill, over a second stile, then continues broadly in the same direction to the field bottom (keep the copse of trees ahead well to your left). If the field has been ploughed over it may be easier after the second stile to head down the field edge to the foot of the field and then along. Either way you should reach another stile and, shortly after that, the quiet lane beyond. The signed right of way continues almost opposite over a plank bridge, (if you wish to detour to nearby Rye keep on the lane to rejoin the 1066 Country Walk – consult your map). Cross the lower field diagonally on a faint track down to the railway line and, via the exit onto another lane, Winchelsea station.

PUB INFORMATION

1 **Queen's Head**
Parsonage Lane, Icklesham, TN36 4BL
01424 814552
www.queenshead.com
Opening Hours: 11-11; 12-10.30 Sun

2 **Robin Hood**
Main Road, Icklesham, TN36 4BD
01424 814277
Opening Hours: 11-3, 7-11; 11-11 Fri & Sat; 12-5, 7-10.30 Sun

3 **Plough**
Udimore, TN31 6AL
01797 223381
www.theploughatcockmarling.co.uk
Opening Hours: 12-11; 12-4 Sun

West Sussex & Surrey Group

Royal Oak, Brockham

Stoughton & Compton

WALK INFORMATION

Start/Finish: Walderton

Access: Train from London Waterloo to Petersfield or London Victoria to Chichester, then frequent Countryliner bus 54. Car drivers can park in Walderton at junction of B2146 and Stoughton Road (GR 787106)

Distance: 8.6 miles (14km)

OS map: OS Explorer OL120

Key attractions: Uppark House (3 miles); Chichester and cathedral (8 miles); Weald & Downland museum (10 miles)

The pubs: Coach & Horses, Compton; Hare & Hounds, Stoughton

In the context of South East England, the valleys of the West Sussex chalk downland still have a relatively remote and rural feel to them, and the landscape is more wooded than it is further east in the new South Downs National Park. This circular walk traverses some of the dry valleys dissecting the dip slope of the Downs, with open views interspersed with shady tree-lined paths. Both pubs offer a good range of well-kept beers and locally-sourced food. Navigation is generally straightforward, but there are a few steep climbs before you finish. If you're relying on the bus you can save a bit of time by walking straight down the road back to Walderton from the Hare & Hounds, about a mile to the bus stop on the main road.

Start at the bus shelter, close to the small car park, at the junction of the B2146 with the lane to Stoughton and Walderton (787106). Walk north up the B2146 a short way, to a little loop road and green on the left of the main road. A small lane peels off to the left here; take this lane, ignoring the footpath heading left in thirty yards. Head steadily up the hill on this

A steady climb to Up Marden in the heart of the Downs

TIMING TIP

From the London region it's a long day trip; if you're relying on the 54 bus check times and connections carefully since it's a two hourly service. An early start on a summer's day is advised!

Key

– – – – – Walk route

lane, with fine views opening out over the valley below, until you reach a bridleway sign where the lane bends to the left. Keep ahead on the bridleway and, in another hundred yards, take the left fork where another bridleway returns to the valley floor. This flinty track leads you along the edge of a field, with the woodland hanger immediately right. The gradient levels off and it's easy and pleasant walking towards a prominent flint house ahead.

Here take the signed bridleway to the right and then, at the fingerboard almost immediately, continue straight ahead on a good track which

now starts to descend once more gently downhill, through the attractive woodland of Watergate Hanger. Reach and cross a private lane and, in a further fifteen yards, join another lane where the route becomes a public footpath (yellow waymark). Head on (uphill again briefly) on this route, keeping close to the wire fence on the right; it becomes a

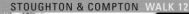

LEFT: **An autumn carpet along the bridleway out of Walderton** RIGHT: **Coach & Horses, Compton**

pleasant sunken track following a line of beech and other trees. The path leaves the woodland briefly as you near West Marden, and keeps to the left margin of a field; but in a few yards head over another stile and back into the woods rather than striking across the field to the road (A, ⊙ 774133). Now skirt around the edge of the small village of West Marden, crossing the lane via a stile (the path continuation is just a few yards to the left, by 'Marden Down'. There's a distant view of Uppark, the fine big house sitting high up on the down two miles ahead.

The path, climbing gently, leads through more pleasant woodland; when you reach a stile and three fingered waymark under the line of telegraph pylons, turn right on the wide earthen track up a short rise to another fingerboard. Here divert onto the footpath running some fifteen degrees left of straight ahead, through a field. Good views open up to the right, down towards Walderton, and there's a clearer view of Uppark in the other direction. Pass through a line of trees and gate, and follow the obvious line across the next field down towards the outskirts of Compton village below. Reach the lane by the old post office and, bearing left down the leafy lane past some attractive cottages (although the window police could do with paying a visit to some of them!), the first pub stop of the day is just around the corner. The **Coach & Horses** [1] sits right in the centre of the village and, judging by reviews, this excellent local makes a good impression on all who visit. There are a fine set of etched windows advertising what at one time would have been separate rooms, although most of the place is now a single bar (with a venerable old dining room at the rear) wrapped

around the servery. The interior is comfortable but tastefully decorated and furnished, and traditional features like a good wainscot around the walls and a lovely open fireplace have been retained. You can have a choice of parquet tiles, floorboards or carpet depending on where you sit. Service is efficient and friendly, but best of all is the quality of the beers which has made the pub a *Good Beer Guide* fixture in recent years. Dark Star Hophead is pretty much permanent, joined by up to three other guests from independent brewers (with a strong local emphasis) and a traditional cider. Tempting food from an adventurous menu is locally sourced. In summer you can sit outside and watch life go by, at a leisurely pace, on the square.

On leaving the pub, be warned that the climb out of the village is the steepest of the day. Turn sharp right, passing the village shop and tea room, and take the lane striking up the hill past the churchyard and new school hall. After two or three minutes there's a fingerboard: leave the lane and take the footpath (yellow waymark) slightly to the left, up to and through a six bar metal gate where there's a stile and a further waymark. If you're on the right path there'll be a steep hill ahead! Taking your time, head uphill, pausing to enjoy the rewarding views behind you from time to time. Higher up, look out for the Isle of Wight, visible for the first time on the horizon.

Cross a bridleway close to the top of the hill and continue on the same bearing, starting to drop down into the next dry valley. Look out for the little tower of remote Up Marden church ahead. The climb out the valley floor is again quite steep but not so painful as the last; moreover it's on a delightful sunken earthen lane which in autumn is

LEFT: **Window glass at the Coach & Horses** RIGHT: **Hare & Hounds, Stoughton**

covered with a carpet of colourful leaves. Walk up past the church to the lane junction where we turn right: it's possible to pop in and visit the churchyard and church a few yards further along here.

The path leaves the lane about 200 yards on the left, past some cottages. Follow it down into the woods and, shortly afterwards, join a wide track by a farmstead and turn left, following it gently down-hill. At the valley bottom look for the signed path heading off to the right, running pleasantly down the valley towards the hanger of woodland ahead. At an isolated-looking fingerboard, short of the wooded slope, bear right towards what looks like a clump of trees to your right. Follow this on the pathway to the left-hand margin of what turns out to be a linear hedge. Reach the tiny farm hamlet of Pitlands and, at the far end of the buildings and yard (opposite the metal gates), look for the signed path bearing left directly up towards the wooded ridge. There's a steady climb up through the trees to gain the ridge, and then start downhill, follow-ing the waymarks where the path doglegs slightly as it reaches the lower edge of the woods, with a view across to the steep and thickly-wooded ridge of Bow Hill and Kingly Vale opposite and below, in the valley, the linear village of Stoughton.

The path leads you right to the side door of the **Hare & Hounds 2**. Occupy-ing a tremendous location in a remote dry valley, the brick-and-flint Hare & Hounds is deservedly popular with walkers and cyclists. It seems to be aiming more towards the upmarket foodies with a smart dining room at the front and (in my humble opinion) a truly

awful new pub sign, but there's a very good little basic public bar. In here, rustic benches and tables sit on floorboards around a fireplace; and you can enjoy the pub's tempting range of well-kept beers. Expect Harveys Best, Taylor Landlord, a beer from Otter and a guest, alongside a traditional cider. The menu looks good with everything from sandwiches upwards. You may be tempted by the rear garden or the front tables, both with pleasant views.

On leaving the pub turn right down the lane to the green by the parish church. If you're pushed for time it's quicker to carry straight down the road to Walderton, which you'll reach in about 15-20 minutes. For the leisurely off-road finish, take the signed bridleway bearing off to the right by the telephone box, which regains the ridge via a tree-lined track. Carry straight up to the summit of the path, enjoying increasingly wide views across the valley and again to Hayling Island and the Isle of Wight. As the track starts to descend, take the signed path (yellow waymark) to the left, heading gently downhill under the telegraph wires. The cottages of Walderton come into view, nestling at the foot of the hill, and there's a log seat halfway down for a summer siesta or to simply enjoy the view. Cross a lane and continue for another 300 yards, ignoring the path striking across the field to the right, and following the track left, just beyond, into an alleyway which brings you out onto Walderton's upper lane. Bear right, then left at the main street, through the hamlet and past the *Barley Mow*, which you might wish to visit. The car park, and bus stop, isn't much more than 200 yards further on.

PUB INFORMATION

1 Coach & Horses
The Square, Compton, PO18 9HA
023 9263 1228
Opening Hours: 12-3, 6-11; 12-4, 6-10.30 Sun

2 Hare & Hounds
Stoughton, PO18 9JQ
023 9263 1433
www.hareandhoundspub.co.uk
Opening Hours: 11-3, 6-11; 11-11 Fri & Sat; 12-10.30 Sun

From Pulborough to Arundel via Amberley & the Wild Brooks

WALK INFORMATION

Start: Pulborough station

Finish: Amberley station or Arundel station

Access: Trains from London via Horsham

Distance: To the Sportsman, 5.9 miles (9.4km); to Amberley 8.5 miles (13.6km); to Arundel, 13.5 miles (21.7km)

OS map: OS Explorer OL121

Key attractions: Amberley Wild Brooks wetlands/ nature reserve; Amberley conservation village and castle; Amberley Chalk Pits museum; Arundel Castle and historic town

The pubs: White Hart, Pulborough; Sportsman; Bridge Inn, both Amberley. Try also: Black Horse, Amberley; King's Arms, Arundel

This is classic Sussex scenery: rolling downland, wooded in places and open in others, dissected by wide river valleys. Attractive settlements complement the picture. The walk is a linear transect from the edge of the sandstone Weald at Pulborough across the wetlands of the Wild Brooks Nature Reserve and, for those doing the whole walk, a cutting through the chalk downs to the handsome market town of Arundel. Frequent train services mean that those leaving a vehicle at the start can easily return, and Amberley station offers an escape point at halfway for those who are more tempted by the very good pubs. Be warned that some sections are very low-lying and prone to flooding in wet conditions, so appropriate footwear is advised. The whole walk is the longest in the book at over 13 miles, although in general the terrain is pretty level and undemanding, and over a full day the miles go by pretty easily.

Arundel Castle shimmering across the River Arun

Exit Pulborough station on the 'down' side and take the path which runs along the fence to the left with views of the church, before reaching a small lane and turning left over the railway. Follow the road around to the left, pausing if you wish to look at Old Place Manor on the right: originally a fifteenth century building it has been almost entirely rebuilt but is listed nonetheless. After some 200 yards look for a footpath leading off on the left, with good views all around, notably those opening out very soon across the marshes of the Wild Brooks to the scarp of the South Downs. There's also a good

view back to the parish church at a point where the path passes an old gun emplacement.

Walk up the cinder path on your right, with a wooden fence to the right, past a small house. In the woodland just past the house bear left into the plantation. Inside here, but not very obvious in summer when the trees are in leaf is the Motte and Bailey of old Pulborough Castle, built like the more recent gun emplacement to take advantage of the view across the sweep of the valley. The path winds downhill along a very sandy track, with a feeling of being in a narrow strip of heathland with rowan and chestnut trees guarding the

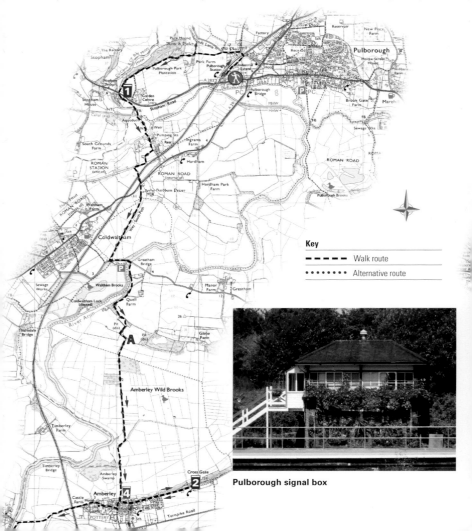

Pulborough signal box

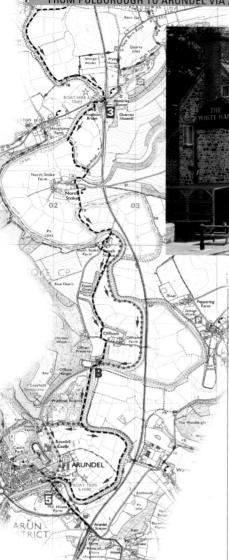

White Hart, Stopham Bridge

the western end, probably a former separate cottage now absorbed into the pub, is of roughly coursed ironstone rubble. It is this section which is most unspoilt internally with a wooden dado and fireplace. The emphasis in the rest of the pub is upon food but there's still plenty of character. Beers are local: expect the likes of Langham's Hip Hop, Arundel Gold and maybe something from WJ King of Horsham. Across the road is an appealing garden which flanks the river, and affords a fine view of the attractive old Stopham Bridge which is now enjoying its retirement.

Leaving the pub, walk up the lane, away from the bridge, and look for a footpath leading off right just before rejoining the busy main road. Cross the meadow, down to the river, and over the footbridge; and then keep well to the left, aiming for the right hand, wooden, of two gates. You may encounter a very marshy section close to the gate. Through the kissing gate with its waymark sign, cross the river again, and turn right just before the level crossing, through the business park. The path doglegs once or twice but it's well signed. Cross the railway line on a bridge, then cross the busy A29 road.

You're now entering a wetland area with willow and other marsh-loving trees. Carry along for some distance with water channels on both sides – quite an enclosed and secluded stretch. At last the noise of the main road recedes and after

drop on the right. Crossing the main road, a new bypass, the **White Hart** 1 is immediately in front of you, reached by a short access path opposite. Arriving here early on a sunny day, it's a very pleasant spot now that the road outside has been bypassed. The building itself is full of interest and deserves its listed status: two thirds of it is ashlar sandstone under a tiled roof while

LEFT: **Hollyhocks adorn many Amberley gardens** RIGHT: **Not a section to tackle after too much ale!**

¾ of a mile you emerge onto another road and turn left. Ignore the first footpath on the right, but continue on the road crossing the river on another attractive old bridge with several stone arches, Greatham Bridge. Just beyond, pick up the signed path running off to the right along the riverside. Across the river to the right can be seen the thickly wooded stretch of the South Downs near Bignor Hill. We're now on the level wetland of the Wild Brooks and most of the next two miles as we wend our way towards Amberley is plain sailing as far as the navigation is concerned.

When entering through a metal gate into the main part of the Brooks (A, ⊛ 031153) note that the path then turns 90 degrees right and is signed on a post to head towards a group of trees ahead of you. There are some wet sections but in general the path is well marked and presents few problems. There's a sense of openness and big skies, and thoughts can turn to the village of Amberley ahead and the next beer!

Nearing the village we leave the floodplain, merge with a rough track and climb gently to emerge on a road in the village via a walled track and turn left. Close by is the **Black Horse** 🔳, but time permitting, a detour half a mile down the lane ahead (don't turn right at the Black Horse) is recommended. The Sportsman has been the local CAMRA Pub of the Year for the last two years, and you are unlikely to regret the journey. On the way, if it's summer, you can enjoy the beautiful displays of hollyhocks growing along the verges, said to have grown from wild seeds scattered by an elderly resident and now jealously guarded by the villagers against the council's tidy-minded roadsweepers. The cottages in this attractive village are built in the main of Bargate sandstone, with brick, half timbering, flint and a little clunch, a type of chalk. At the **Sportsman** 🔳 you'll find a warm welcome, three drinking areas and a rear eatery. The brick-floored public bar is where to head in order to inspect the three rotating ales, which have a local emphasis. Food is served from noon until 2 (2.30 weekends) and from 7 until 9 of an evening.

Return to the Black Horse, which you may want to try: expect a choice of ales including Greene King IPA and Harveys Sussex Best Bitter in a pleasant interior setting. Now this time walk in the

Greatham Bridge

other direction from the emergent track we used earlier, along Hog Lane which then meets Church Street. Turn right and walk down past more idyllic cottages festooned with hollyhocks. At the edge of the village, next to the Norman church of St Michael, the Grade I-listed Amberley Castle towers over you. Looking out over the gap where the river Arun cuts through the chalk escarpment, it dates back to the 12th century and was built as a rural fortress for the Bishops of Chichester. Return to the wide river floodplain and cross the railway carefully at the gate. Straight down to the river embankment, and then turn left to follow the Arun downstream to the bridge.

Emerge on the road just a few yards from the **Bridge Inn** ☒, across the busy road which needs care crossing. It's an attractive white-washed building with sash windows, set back from the main road. The bar area has a stone-

flagged floor, whilst there's an extensive and upmarket dining area. There are three handpumps dispensing mainly local ales (the mandatory Harveys plus the likes of WJ King of Horsham).

If you are finishing your walk here, allow five minutes to get to the station from the pub. Just beyond the station, Amberley's famous working museum is dedicated to the industrial heritage of the South East. It occupies a 36-acre site in an old chalk pit. The museum is home to a number of important architectural structures, some carefully dismantled from elsewhere and rebuilt; there's also a narrow-gauge railway on site.

If you are continuing to Arundel, you have about 100 yards walk along the busy and frankly rather nasty road (with no separate footway) halfway across the bridge where a footpath takes you left to safety. The rewards are immediate: the path crosses the river and follows the embankment into

THE WILD BROOKS

Until the 1960s, the tidal River Arun used to flood the meadowlands of the Wild Brooks regularly. In wintertime many years ago it was possible to take a boat across the valley, passing above fields that were pasture in summer. Since then, the river banks have been raised and the marshland has been criss-crossed by drainage ditches allowing grazing of animals. However, it remains a very special habitat and an area of some 800 acres, including the adjacent Pulborough Brooks has been designated a Site of

Special Scientific Interest, an important habitat both for birds and for wetland plants. The wettest parts of the marsh are dominated by soft rush, sedges and tussock grass, whilst the ditches which dissect the grazing marsh support a wide range of flowering plants. The bird species for which the Amberley Wild Brooks are noted include snipe, teal, wigeon and geese. The area is known as the Fens of Sussex. Even today there are few paths and it's inadvisable to stray from them as the Brooks can still be very wet.

LEFT: **Black Horse, Amberley** RIGHT: **The attractive Bridge Inn**

glorious countryside, and after about five minutes, just after crossing a stile, look for a sign directing the path away from the river, over a second stile, and into a shaded path protected with overhanging hawthorn, with glimpses of the white cliffs of Amberley above, before bringing you out onto a quiet lane close to the hamlet of North Stoke. Walk uphill to the T junction where the footpath continues, signed, a few yards to the left. Up the rise and over rewards you with fine views of the Arun Valley as you head back downhill to the floodplain. Over a dinky suspension bridge which carries the path over an overgrown side channel of the river, and into another pleasing wooded stretch on a raised causeway. Several minutes later, re-emerge on the riverside close to a white footbridge which you cross. If you want stay close to the river, take the stile immediately left over the bridge and keep walking, rejoining the main route at the *Black Rabbit Inn* (below). A pleasant alternative is to ascend the hill into the small hamlet of South Stoke. On your left is the parish church; ignoring the left turn immediately after that, look for bridleway sign another fifty yards further on, also on the left, and take this, which leads through an open riverside meadow at the edge of the floodplain towards Offham. The last section up to the hamlet, through a field gate, is a much narrower and overgrown affair passing a cottage and climbing sharply for a short distance. Turn left at the top and take the first right, a small lane leading through a dark and atmospheric

chalk gorge down to the riverside by the nicely-sited but over-modernised *Black Rabbit Inn* (B, ⦿ 025085). Here, if you selected the riverside option and switched onto auto-pilot for the last section, you will rejoin the main route.

Continue on the riverside path, either all the way into Arundel (admiring the bulk of the castle on a bluff above the floodplain of the river) or as an alternative, about a quarter of a mile along take the right-hand path at a junction leading via a narrow path to the road. Follow the pleasant road left past the precincts of Arundel Castle and into town. The station is about 5 minutes brisk walk out on the road over the river, but the town is well worth exploring, and there are plenty of pubs and restaurants to choose from. As an ale drinker, your best bet may well be the **King's Arms** 5 on Tarrant Street which is more traditional and unpretentious than some of the other outlets in town and you'll get a decent range of ales including beer from the local Arundel Brewery.

PUB INFORMATION

1 White Hart
Stopham Bridge, Pulborough,
RH20 1DS
01798 873321
www.whitehartstophambridge.co.uk
Opening Hours: 11.30-10 (6 Sun)

2 Sportsman
Rackham Road, Cross Gates,
Amberley, BN18 9NR
01798 831787
Opening Hours: 11 (12 Sun)-11

3 Bridge Inn
Houghton Bridge, Amberley,
BN18 9LR
01798 831619
www.bridgeinnamberley.com
Opening Hours: 11-11 (10.30 Sun)

TRY ALSO:

4 Black Horse
High Street, Amberley, BN18 9NL
01798 831700
Opening Hours: 12-midnight

5 King's Arms
36 Tarrant Street, Arundel,
BN18 9DN
01903 882312
Opening Hours: 11-3, 5.30-11;
11-11 Fri & Sat; 12-10.30 Sun

Iping & Stedham Commons

WALK INFORMATION

Start/Finish: Trotton, by St George's church

Access: Trains from London to Petersfield, then Countryliner service 91/2 (Mon-Sat) or Stagecoach service 91 (Sundays)

Distance: Full circuit 6.4 miles (10.3km)

OS map: OS Explorer OL133

Key attractions: Rare lowland heath habitat; ancient church of St George, with medieval wall paintings; Midhurst historic market town (2 miles); Cowdray House and walled garden (4 miles)

The pubs: Elsted Inn, Elsted Marsh; Keepers Arms, Trotton

Iping and Stedham Commons represent a now-rare area of lowland heath habitat in the region; this Site of Special Scientific Interest makes for an enjoyable and easy stroll. It is jointly managed by the Sussex Wildlife Trust and the Sussex Downs Conservation Board. The West Sussex Rother is a minor star in this walk but keeps itself well-hidden, for the most part, even though part of the walk follows its banks. Both pubs on this walk feature in the annual Ballard's Beer Walk, organised by the local brewery, which takes place on the first Sunday of each December. Be warned that the route will lead you through some boggy areas in all but the very driest weather. This is particularly true of Elsted Marsh. Wear appropriate footwear or regret it! After wet weather you may be advised to use the road as an alternative (see map).

Stedham Common looking towards the South Downs

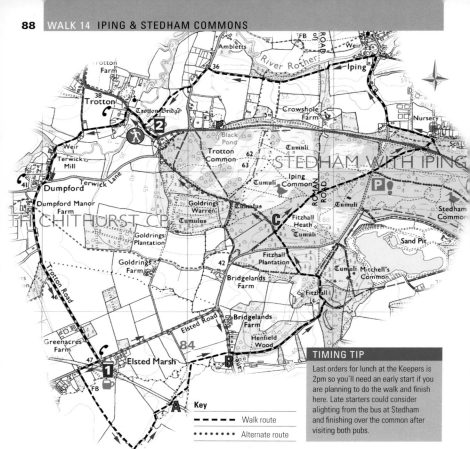

A good bus service connects Petersfield with Midhurst, via the A272, in which case alight at Trotton church, close to the narrow bridge over the Rother and some 200 yards west of the Keepers Arms. The signed path leaves the road on the south side (left turn, coming from the pub) close to the bridge; but the lovely old parish church of St George opposite is well worth a visit if it's open. Inside are some superb medieval wall paintings which depict the Last Judgment and the Seven Acts of Mercy and the Seven Vices. Among several other treasures are fine brasses of the Camoys. Lord Camoy commanded much of the English Army at Agincourt and had a distinguished career as a soldier and diplomat. The Brass of Lady Margaret is thought to be the oldest full-length brass of a woman in England, and dates to 1310.

Back on piste, follow the path through a kissing gate past a couple of old cottages and, joining a rough track, pass some old mill workers' cottages and then across a field and down to the weir over the river and the restored, but clearly once important, old Terwick Mill itself. The little lane leads up to the usually quiet metalled road where we turn right and, shortly, left on another road signed 'Elsted and Harting'. There's little for it now but to follow the road for over half a mile to the far end, but it's a better prospect than it looks on the map: it's quiet, lined for most of the way with fine trees, and has a wide verge to make the going fairly pleasant and easy.

With barely a mile and a half under your belt you duly arrive at the first stop of the day, the **Elsted Inn** 1 . This large double-fronted house was built to serve the once-adjacent station on the now defunct railway and, more recently, was home to Ballard's brewery, which has now moved up the road. One of their beers frequently features on the

LEFT: **A cosy fire inside the Elsted Inn** RIGHT: **Birch scrub invading the heathland at Iping Common**

four handpumps, which also dispense Otter Bitter, Fuller's London Pride and another occasional guest. Like a lot of local pubs it has to major on food to keep going, but its floorboarded front area with a variety of seating, from stools to comfy sofas around the homely fireplace, is a convivial area for drinkers. There's a garden area to the rear as well.

The next section of the walk is pleasantly rural, but is not called Elsted Marsh for nothing. The alternative is to follow the road east from the pub, and then first right to rejoin the route at point B (see map). Otherwise turn left out of the inn and over the ex-rail bridge to take a signed path shortly afterwards on the left, striking out across a wide field on an indistinct path close to a single telegraph post. A gate leads into another field, keeping to the right of the telegraph line. Reaching a metal gate in the hedge, possibly with a precariously perched fingerboard, don't go through the gate but turn sharp left along the field edge, keeping the fence and a tiny stream on your immediate right. Follow around to another gate where a sign, once again propped up against a fence, points into the next field. Cross this wet field to cross the line of the old railway (A, 838204), and keep on the same bearing through the next field, possibly even wetter than the last until, when you see a waymark over on your right marking a path merging from that side (see map), swing left a wee bit towards some trees. If you're on the right bearing you'll reach a gate by another fingerboard, where you take a bearing 90 degrees right climbing gently towards the trees ahead, joining the road via a six bar metal gate at B (839207).

Things change scenically and underfoot straightaway once across the road, where you

enter the sandy soils of the Lower Greensand which forms the higher areas today occupied by Iping & Stedham Commons. In this area you're walking through a thick cover of mature trees. Reach a small pond where the path bears left past a rather large cottage, climbing uphill now within a sunken track with sandstone walls on each side, topped by the rhododendrons of the Fitzhall Estate above you. Veer left at the fingerboard at the top and reach a tarmac road ten yards later. Go straight over here, by the gates to Fitzhall, onto the bridleway climbing up through more rhododendrons. In 150 yards bear right at a split in the paths, reaching and crossing a road. Here you leave the plantation, crossing into a more open area of heathland.

At a crossroads of paths (C, 846216) it's decision time: the shorter route back to Trotton leads straight ahead (see box), but for the main circuit turn right. Walk across the heath, which is not dissimilar in character to some parts of the New Forest. Heathland is not a 'natural' type of vegetation however – it has to be maintained by grazing, otherwise trees will invade and it will

---

SHORT CUT BACK TO KEEPERS ARMS

At point 'C' head directly across at the crossroads of paths. At a blue waymark keep ahead on a narrower, sandy track which now climbs uphill. At the top of this sandy climb meet a waymark and, bearing slightly left, reach another fingerboard in about thirty yards. Keep straight on with a line of birch trees on your immediate right, which starts descending, more steeply later, past another blue waymark (keep straight ahead) bringing you out on the quiet lane just 150 yards or so short of the pub.

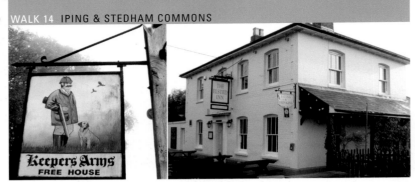

LEFT: **The Keepers Arms** RIGHT: **The homely and welcoming Elsted Inn**

end up as woodland. Grazing has been reintroduced onto Stedham Common using Shetland cattle, a rare breed ideally suited to the rough pasture of heathlands.

Reach the car park and cross the road here through the gate opposite. Take the left-hand bridleway through the silver birch trees of Stedham Common towards the drone of the A272. Climb up to the roadside verge and cross when safe – there is a wide verge and sight lines are good. A short distance to the right take the left turn, School Lane, signed to Stedham. After 150 yards, just before the Hamilton Arms, which you might try if it's open, take the bridleway (blue waymark) on the left: a wide track at the edge of the common with houses on your right. Pass the wide track down to the nursery and, shortly afterwards, join the lane and turn right, downhill, towards Iping village and the Rother Valley. There's no pavement but the road doesn't normally carry too much traffic. At the foot of the hill look out for a signpost on the right, but pointing left, not down the private drive to the converted mill but immediately left of this, on the rising tarmac drive past a white weatherboarded gable end, bearing then immediately right onto an obvious path. There are good views to the restored mill over to your right.

Follow the field boundary into a pleasant area of woodland and into another field. The river is just down the steep drop on the right but there are few views of it until you reach the top of the rise, where you'll

be surprised at just how far below you the river is. Reach a lane by a row of pretty cottages and turn left up the hill. Take the signed path on the right beyond the farm, following the path over the first stile but, once over the second stile, keep hard by the fence (don't drop down to the river footbridge) and follow it almost to the road where you head down into a marshy area to make a somewhat undignified exit onto the road over a stile. There's no pavement here, and it's safer to cross directly to the other side wheres there's an apology for a verge. Retrace your earlier steps/bus journey up the hill to the **Keepers Arms** 2 which, with any luck, will be open. Looking more like a large house than a pub from the driveway and the car park, the Keepers is an upmarket country inn with a very large floorboarded room divided into two or three distinct areas. There's a definite emphasis on dining, as you'd probably expect in this location, and the food, although on the expensive side, is good with the quality having had numerous favourable reviews. It's perhaps a pity that the bar doesn't feel very 'pubby' and lacks the character of some more intimate rural pubs where dining and drinking are more segregated, but the drinker is not forgotten as there may be up to four ales on offer, with Dark Star Hophead a regular and local brewery Ballard's frequently among the guests.

If you're relying on the bus, the stop is back by the church, down the hill and close to the river bridge.

PUB INFORMATION

1 Elsted Inn
Elsted Road, Elsted Marsh,
GU29 0JT
01730 813662
www.theelstedinn.co.uk
Opening Hours: 5-10 Mon;
12-2.30, 5-10.30 Tue-Thu; 12-3,
5-midnight Fri; 11-11 Sat; 11-10
Sun

2 Keepers Arms
Love Hill, Terwick Lane, Trotton,
GU31 5ER
01730 813724
www.keepersarms.co.uk
Opening Hours: 12-3, 6-11; 12-3,
7-10.30 Sun

Banstead & Walton Heaths, & the North Downs Way

WALK INFORMATION

Start/Finish: Tadworth station

Access: Trains from London Victoria via East Croydon

Distance: 9.5 miles (15.4km)

OS map: OS Explorer OL146

Key attractions: North Downs Way; Reigate Fort; Gatton Park gardens and lake

The pubs: Well House Inn, Mugswell; Sportsman, Mogador; Bell (Rat), Walton-on-the-Hill

The only walk in this book which strays inside the M25 nonetheless you'll enjoy a wide variety of scenery – from heathland and parkland, to one of the best sections of the North Downs crest, with fine views. Even the two golf courses crossed on this walk are well above average in terms of scenic appeal. All three of the recommended pubs enjoy an interesting setting, whilst the unspoilt Bell is a real traditional gem not to missed, and listed in CAMRA's Regional Inventory of heritage pubs. There is an option to shorten the walk at Reigate Hill, but you'll miss much of the best of it if you do. The navigation is pretty straightforward and the terrain generally undemanding.

From Tadworth station there's a short section of suburbia: walk left down the road, following the line of the railway, to the junction with Tadworth Street. Turn left here (signed Banstead) and follow the road for some 350 yards before taking the signed path to the right, which doubles as a residential cul-de-sac to start with. Cross the railway and turn left on reaching the

Well House Inn, Mugswell

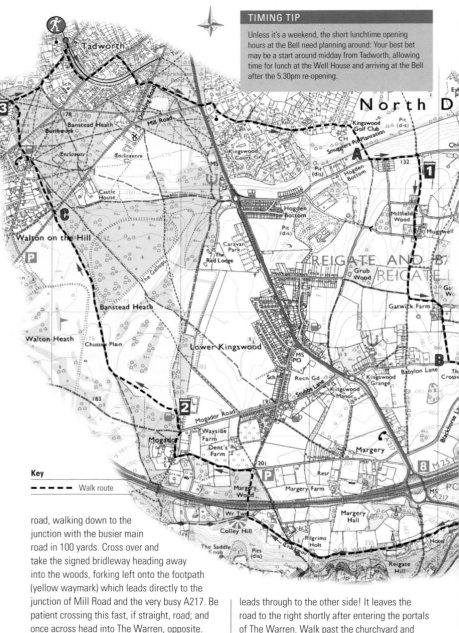

Key

– – – – – Walk route

road, walking down to the junction with the busier main road in 100 yards. Cross over and take the signed bridleway heading away into the woods, forking left onto the footpath (yellow waymark) which leads directly to the junction of Mill Road and the very busy A217. Be patient crossing this fast, if straight, road; and once across head into The Warren, opposite. Kingswood Warren is well-named, a maze of huge detached houses which reinforces all the Surrey stereotypes… fortunately a signed path

leads through to the other side! It leaves the road to the right shortly after entering the portals of The Warren. Walk past the churchyard and continue ahead, ignoring side paths, to merge with a private road after 800 yards. Walk down to the end of this where, by the entrance to the

LEFT: **Lovely garden at the Well House Inn** RIGHT: **The route passes the village pond at Walton**

'Kingswood Golf and Country Club', a footpath sign leads us along the fence and then over a stile and off to the right close to the clubhouse, then down to the tree belt at the lower side of the fairways (A, ⊙, 254554). You should be able to find the waymark posts. The public path heads steeply down through the trees to the lane at the foot, where we turn left (no footpath); it's a safer option, although not a right of way, to stay on the golf course, keeping as close to the tree belt as possible, to another right of way in 400 yards, just beyond the 15th tee, and downhill here, as this option leads right to the pub. You're unlikely to upset the golfers if you keep off the fairways.

Either way you are richly rewarded for the couple of miles of suburban and semi-rural walking for the **Well House Inn** 🔲 feels far more remote than it really is, in a lovely setting in one of the dry valleys which once formed the headwaters of the River Wandle. Mugswell to the south may be named after the well in the pub's garden, but the pub is now in Chipstead parish. The building is made of local flint and brick, seen to best advantage from the pretty garden at the rear; and despite some alterations over the years the place retains a good deal of character. The bar area is enclosed by thick walls, with

further rooms each side, and a carefully-added conservatory used for dining which doesn't adversely affect the character of the historic part of the building. The well-kept beers include three regulars and a couple of guests, often LocAles from nearby micros. Lunches are served until 2.30 but the bar's open all day.

Handily the path heads directly uphill without the need for any further road walking: up a seductive sunken track right by the eastern end of the pub. Good views open out across the valley almost immediately, and the path levels out and crosses two quiet lanes through the hamlet, moving into open country. Join a bridleway and then swing left with the bridleway in a few

Inglis Memorial, Colley Hill

yards, along a wide gravel track between substantial hedges. At the Gatwick Farm hamlet keep right, passing through gates right alongside the new flint and brick buildings, resuming a southerly bearing once again

> This well is credited as being the original St. Margaret's well or Mag's well (hence the name of the area Mugswell) as is mentioned in the Doomsday Book.
> It is probable that St. Margaret's well was the original settlement of Celtic or Anglo Saxon herdsmen.

through farmland with good signage throughout to join quiet Babylon Lane at B (261536). Walk to the left and, at the junction ahead, cross onto unmade Crossways Lane. The M25 drone is distinctly audible now, and indeed is very close. The bridleway drops down and swings under the motorway, continuing downhill now in woodland to meet another road. Straight across here, where stands the handsome Tower Lodge, one of the entrance lodges to the Gatton estate. It's built of the distinctive Gatton Stone, a light sandstone from the Greensand series nearby. Just beyond the lodge bear right onto the North Downs Way (NDW) path by the metal bollard. The next two miles follows the NDW path, offering high quality scenery, with the motorway being less intrusive than its proximity on the map might suggest. Keep on the main wide path through the trees

for some 300 yards, then fork left to enjoy the best views across Gatton Lake below.

Shortly beyond the NDW path swings right at another fork (metal bollard waymark) to reach the car park and café at the Wray Lane viewpoint. It's worth a breather here to enjoy the fine vista south over Reigate and beyond. The NDW path crosses the A217 on a footbridge behind the café, and then heads for the summit ridge of Reigate Hill past the old Reigate Fort. This is one of thirteen so-called 'mobilisation centres' which the military had built around the turn of the twentieth century at a time when they feared a French invasion. It was used during World War I for ammunition storage. It has since (from 1932) passed into the stewardship of the National Trust, and was fully restored in 2000. Having said that, there's not a great deal to see at ground level from the path.

In the unlikely event of anyone 'retiring hurt' here, Reigate station is a mile downhill to the left, via firstly the signed bridleway some 350 yards beyond the footbridge; and then the A217.

Reigate Hill

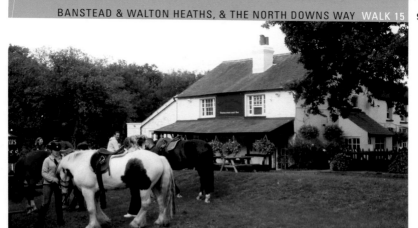

The Sportsman lies adjacent to Banstead Heath

Enter the open crest of the hill by the Inglis Memorial; here the views west along the escarpment are particularly fine. Walk along the crest for another few minutes, looking for an old water tower almost hidden in the trees to the right, with the motorway quite close here now, then just beyond here, a gate with waymark sign (North Downs Ridge Circular Walk) is our route. Cross the M25 straightaway, and then directly into pretty Margery Wood, walking through and emerging by a small car park. Now the views are northwards, down the gentle slope of the escarpment across agricultural land. Look for the good wide path leading left (west) out of the car park at the woodland edge.

You should have worked up another thirst by now but help is at hand: cross a private road after a few minutes and, just 100 yards beyond, bear right onto another wooded lane leading quickly to the pub sign of the **Sportsman 2**. The pub itself is a few yards up the lane to the left. Few who know this popular pub would deny that its setting, in a woodland clearing at the southern edge of beautiful Banstead Heath, is equalled by few other pubs. Externally this ex-Courage pub is still attractive; but as to the inside, there has been much lively discussion on internet forums as to whether it has been taken too far towards being a restaurant or not: personally I would have preferred a more simple and preferably separate public bar for drinkers, for even the main bar room is dominated by rows of dining tables leaving just a small area for casual and stand-up imbibers. Having said that the food is good and it's available throughout the day, useful for hungry and thirsty walkers! And at least it still has a decent beer range, including Otter Bitter, Doom Bar and Young's with a guest. Predictably the place can

GATTON

The park, house and estate of Gatton, now a quiet backwater, was well-known at one time for being one of the infamous 'Rotten Boroughs' which were still electing two members of parliament up until the 1832 Reform Act. This despite its tiny size, and the fact that enormous industrial towns like Birmingham and Manchester had no representation. It was described by the radical William Cobbett around 1820 as 'a very rascally spot of earth'. The gardens and lake were laid out by Lancelot 'Capability' Brown (1716-1783). The last private owners of the Gatton Estate, from 1888, were the Colman Family of Colman's Mustard fame. Sir Jeremiah Colman had the Japanese garden laid out around 1909, along with the rock and water garden a little later. The house, Gatton Hall, was gutted by fire in 1934 and, although rebuilt, it lacks the splendour of its former self. Today Gatton Hall is part of the Royal Alexander & Albert School. The grounds of Gatton Park, about 600 acres, are managed partly by the Gatton Trust and partly by the National Trust – the latter being open to the public all year around.

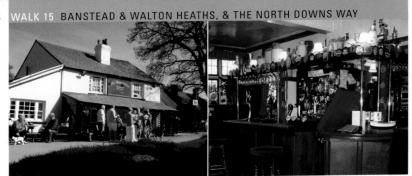

LEFT: **At the Sportsman, Mogador** RIGHT: **The simple public bar at the Bell, Walton-on-the-Hill**

get packed at weekends although there is plenty of outdoor space, either in the rather formal garden or, far nicer, the tables on the grassy woodland margin opposite the pub.

Moving on, walk onto the heath, forking left almost immediately (head for the wooden waymark) and then make across the open parkland, keeping the trees close by on your left. Keep towards the golf course beyond, looking, after a few hundred yards, for a good earthen path which runs up the narrow belt of scrub and trees between the golf course on the left and the open parkland of Banstead Heath to the right. Follow this bearing, keeping the golf course immediately on the left all the way, to join the road at C (230548). Cross directly and pick up the footpath (signed to Mere Pond) to the right of the driveway. This takes us through more pleasant woodland to emerge shortly afterwards by the *Blue Ball* pub in Walton-on-the-Hill. Join the village street right by the Mere Pond. Now there's a sign for the Bell, pointing up the rough drive by the pond. Without the sign one would never know it was here. Fork right immediately as instructed and follow this rutted muddy lane down to the well-hidden **Bell 3**.

The first thing to know about this pub is that hardly anyone who uses it at all regularly knows it as the Bell; to locals it's the 'Rat' and has been for decades. Exactly why it acquired this unusual nickname is not clear, although several diverse 'explanations' abound. The Rat is an uncompromisingly traditional local, with a distinctive, inter-war internal style, following a 1930s rebuild of an older pub on the same site. There are two separate rooms each side of the bar servery; they are now connected by an opening. Fireplaces survive in both the lounge and in the plain public bar with its parquet wood floor and original bar counter. There's even a bar billiards table, and almost needless to say there are 'proper' old fashioned urinals in the gents. Don't expect meals, but the beers are well-kept, and feature Fuller's London Pride and Brakspear Bitter, with the occasional guest.

From the Rat, look for a signed path immediately across the car park in front of the pub, leading 90 degrees away from it. Bear round slightly to the left at the buildings in a few minutes and join the suburban road. A few yards to the right, opposite, a signed path leads down an alleyway. Follow this to the end and voila! You are right back by Tadworth station.

PUB INFORMATION

1 **Well House Inn**
Chipstead Lane, Mugswell, CR5 3SQ
01737 830640
www.wellhouseinn.co.uk
Opening Hours: 12-11.30 (10.30 Sun)

2 **Sportsman**
Mogador Road, Mogador, KT20 7ES
01737 246655
www.timewellspent.info
Opening Hours: 12-11 (10.30 Sun)

3 **Bell (Rat)**
Withybed Corner, Walton-on-the-Hill, KT20 7UJ
01737 812132
www.thebell-therat.co.uk
Opening Hours: 12-3 (not Mon), 5.30-11; 12-11 Sat & Sun

Boxhill & the Mole Gap

WALK INFORMATION

Start: Box Hill & Westhumble station

Finish: Leatherhead station

Access: Frequent trains from London via Epsom and from the South Coast via Horsham. Motorists can use the train to return from Leatherhead. Bus 465 runs frequently Dorking – Leatherhead via Mickleham

Distance: 7.5 miles (12.1km)

OS map: OS Explorer OL146

Key attractions: Box Hill; Chalk downland scenery

The pubs: William IV, Mickleham; Running Horse, Leatherhead

A slight twist on a popular walk, along the Mole from Dorking to Leatherhead via Box Hill, probably the South East's best-known beauty spot. This route takes advantage of riverside paths, but be warned that this is a hilly walk, with several quite sustained climbs. Happily, however, the hard work is done before arriving at the first pub. The scenery is classic downland, with generous amounts of open grassland, riverside paths and shady wooded sections. A sunny autumn day is perhaps the ideal time to enjoy the landscape at its best. Take plenty of water and/or a flask as it's four hilly miles to the William IV. One downside to this otherwise top quality walk: traffic noise intrudes for much of it, particularly from the fast A24 which runs up the Mole Gap.

Start at Box Hill & Westhumble station (for motorists there is a small car park at the stepping stones, a few hundred yards away), an impressive building for a wayside station. Join the road and cross the railway to walk up Chapel Lane. The archway opposite at the entrance to Camilla Drive, built in 1923, has a plaque on it commemorating the 18th-century novelist, diarist and playwright Fanny Burney who was a regular visitor here.

Boxhill from the meadows at Burford

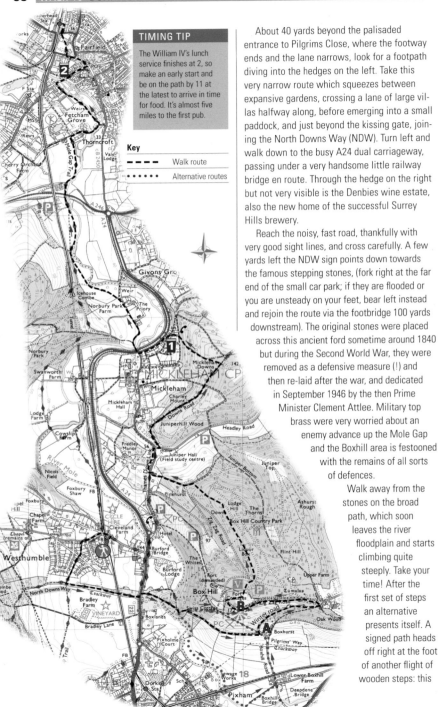

Key

- - - - Walk route

• • • • • Alternative routes

About 40 yards beyond the palisaded entrance to Pilgrims Close, where the footway ends and the lane narrows, look for a footpath diving into the hedges on the left. Take this very narrow route which squeezes between expansive gardens, crossing a lane of large villas halfway along, before emerging into a small paddock, and just beyond the kissing gate, joining the North Downs Way (NDW). Turn left and walk down to the busy A24 dual carriageway, passing under a very handsome little railway bridge en route. Through the hedge on the right but not very visible is the Denbies wine estate, also the new home of the successful Surrey Hills brewery.

Reach the noisy, fast road, thankfully with very good sight lines, and cross carefully. A few yards left the NDW sign points down towards the famous stepping stones, (fork right at the far end of the small car park; if they are flooded or you are unsteady on your feet, bear left instead and rejoin the route via the footbridge 100 yards downstream). The original stones were placed across this ancient ford sometime around 1840 but during the Second World War, they were removed as a defensive measure (!) and then re-laid after the war, and dedicated in September 1946 by the then Prime Minister Clement Attlee. Military top brass were very worried about an enemy advance up the Mole Gap and the Boxhill area is festooned with the remains of all sorts of defences.

Walk away from the stones on the broad path, which soon leaves the river floodplain and starts climbing quite steeply. Take your time! After the first set of steps an alternative presents itself. A signed path heads off right at the foot of another flight of wooden steps: this

LEFT: **Mickleham church** RIGHT: **The route is generally well signed**

path offers a riverside walk described below. The main route takes the next set of steps and, as the path levels off briefly before the main climb up to Box Hill, another waymark (also signed 'Riverside Walk' leads right down into the yews. Take this route (if you're short of time and very fit you might consider the direct route to the summit viewpoint ahead but I don't recommend it: the alternatives are more picturesque and far gentler). The path, fairly level for most of its half mile or so, is far more interesting than it looks on the map, following a tunnel of trees with glimpses out over the river below, the town of Dorking and the countryside beyond. Arrive at a gate (A, ⊙ 182509) where a path heads back sharp left uphill, and through the gate, the old 'winter road' (see box on page 97) curves uphill away from you, fringed with more trademark yew trees.

Once again there are two alternatives. The recommended route leads up the sunken lane to the east, through the trees to the crest of the ridge via a sunken chalky path shaded with box and yew and giving lovely views out across the countryside to the south. Be warned that it's still quite a steep climb even though it tackles the hill obliquely. At the top is the *Smith & Western* eatery, which looks like something which has been flown in from the Wild West. The comments on the Beer In The Evening website sum it up nicely: don't expect me to recommend it even though you've just struggled up the hill and are probably gasping for a drink. Double back sharply

on yourself to pick up the North Downs Way once again, and follow it through the trees and along the contour parallel to the road, until you reach the summit viewpoint (B, ⊙ 179512). A quicker and slightly steeper route to the same point is to take the path doubling back across the face of Box Hill from point A (see map). This joins the North Downs Way close to the top, which is reached by doubling back sharp right onto the wider path. The view from the top is predictably wide-ranging, taking in Leith Hill, the highest point in the South East. The memorial here is

ALTERNATIVE RIVERSIDE ROUTE

Take the first, lower riverside path through the box trees and shrubs with their distinctive small leaves, and head back downhill towards the river. Box timber, which gives the hill its name, was once highly regarded because of its close, fine grain, its rich colour and its density enabling it to be carved precisely. The path simply follows the riverside, an easy and delightful stroll with fine views back up to the top of the hill. Pass a set of twelve weird concrete obelisks, another rather bizarre anti-tank measure at this shallow spot, then under the striking rail viaduct and up to the weir and footbridge. Here the path bears sharp right through a new kissing gate and across fields to join a narrow quiet lane. Admire the fine view of a sweep of the North Downs. Turn left and passing under the railway again head up towards the escarpment. Bear left at the turning circle (waymark) and reach point A by the gate above.

LEFT: **Old bridge over the Mole at Mickleham**   RIGHT: **The yew-clad southern slope of White Hill**

dedicated to Leopold Solomons of nearby Norbury Park, who gave about 100 hectares of land here to the National Trust in 1914 to protect it from development. The Trust's tea rooms and visitor centre, close to the remains of the Old Fort, are a short walk up on the wheelchair-friendly path leading away from the 'summit' triangulation point (which unusually you'll notice is not actually at the summit of the hill). From here, where refreshment is recommended, continue the walk by crossing the car park directly opposite into the green beyond, and making for a double waymark by a bench at its tree-lined fringe. Follow the route of the 'Box Hill hike' onto a good wide path to the left here running directly away from the summit memorial, forking left shortly to keep on the waymarked route of the hike. This wide, shady avenue is an easy ten minute stroll, gently downhill, with a view of the gentle back slope of Box Hill opening out just before reaching a flint tower. Also clearly visible here are the vineyards of Denbies on the far side of the valley, and the church spire at Ranmore on the horizon.

Pausing for breath, head down the fairly steep path straight ahead towards Juniper Hall, the prominent and handsome red brick mansion in the valley below, joining a wider path on the contour halfway down. Bear left here and walk easily down to the old London Road, crossing carefully to continue opposite via the steps which take the path above the road and down towards Juniper Hall, which has for many years

From the summit of Box Hill Denbies vineyard runs up the slopes of the North Downs

now operated as a field study centre. Just beyond the hall turn into Headley Road, and immediately left on the wide bridleway which then climbs up onto Mickleham Downs. It's a fairly painless way of gaining height again, and I promise, the last climb before that first pub which is now almost within grasp. Arrive at the first fork of paths in about half a mile by a direction board; but the confusion of paths on Mickleham Downs make it a bit of a navigational

Sunny garden terrace at the William IV

graveyard, so stick to my directions carefully here if you want that beer!

Keep to the main path ignoring branches to both sides until you reach an indistinct path off to the left opposite a better one on the right through a couple of circular wooden posts. Head down here to merge left into a wider path in about 75 yards. If you miss this turning the same wider track heads back obliquely shortly afterwards at a point where a new wire fence joins the path on your left. Now follow this path down through areas of coppiced and deciduous woodland becoming appreciably steeper towards the bottom, until at the bottom you join a wider well-made earthen path running along the contour. Right opposite a smaller path drops steeply down towards some buildings. Hey presto, the second of these turns out to be the **William IV** ◼1. A tiny pub clinging to the hillside, this regular CAMRA award winner showcases beers from local breweries: Surrey Hills, Triple FFF and Hog's Back, plus an occasional guest. There are two narrow rooms, both with real fires, and although the emphasis inside is towards diners, the place retains a good deal of atmosphere and the décor is tasteful and restrained. In good weather the garden, which affords great views across the Mole Gap towards Norbury Park, is a great spot, although the traffic noise from the A24 road below is unfortunately rather intrusive. Food-wise there is a wide ranging menu of dishes great and small.

Compared with the first section, the stretch from Mickleham to Leatherhead is an easy stroll with no hills to speak of, but if you wish to retire early, the bus stop is just at the bottom of the hill.

To continue, walk down to the foot of the path alongside the pub and, turning left, merge into the pavement alongside the busy A24 for about 200 yards when you reach the junction with the lane running up to Mickleham village. Here, the plan is to cross straight opposite to take what was the old London Road before the fast road by-passed Mickleham. Take great care crossing for even though sight lines are pretty good, traffic is fast. The old lane immediately crosses the Mole on the handsome brick and metal Weir Bridge, before running past Mickleham Priory and then Norbury Park Farm, which these days does a very tasty blue cheese. The landscape around is very rural and only the noise of the main road intrudes. The lane peels off right to cross the river again but here diverge left on

THE 'WINTER ROAD'

The 'winter road' was the former main route from Dorking to London, improbable as it seems! The problem was that the route through the Mole Gap had to cross the Mole at some point to continue up to London beyond Leatherhead. The most suitable crossing point was at Burford (where the modern bridge is, north of Dorking), as today, but at that time there was only a ford and the route could not be made secure against the severe winter flooding which was and remains a feature of the Mole's river flow. The winter alternative was the route up to the summit then via an easy route down the dip slope to Walton-on-the-Hill and Sutton. Even then the route must have been a real trial for heavy loads, but today it makes a pleasant and quiet walk to the top of the plateau.

LEFT: **Running Horse, Leatherhead** RIGHT: **Servery at the William IV, Mickleham**

the good track through a gate and soon the river is close by on the right as you head towards a pleasantly-sited pair of semi-detached cottages which nestle against the hill by the northern portal of the Norbury Park rail tunnel. When this 524 yard tunnel was bored through the hill in 1866, a condition was laid down by the park's then-owner, Thomas Grissell, that there should be no vertical shafts and that the portals should receive architectural treatment. He got his way.

Now follow the good wide path running to the right, signed Leatherhead, and simply keep close to the river for the next mile or so as the route follows the Mole northwards. Head through pleasant countryside crossing under the A246 road, and when reaching the T junction of paths at Thorncroft about half a mile beyond, bear right and, passing the old Thorncroft Manor – now swanky offices, reach the river and here, bear left through a kissing gate on a good path running alongside the river which makes a very fine entrance to Leatherhead. In five minutes you'll arrive at the lovely old town bridge, now carrying a relatively quiet road across the Mole since the town has been bypassed.

Leatherhead is an old Surrey town which has been done no favours, except perhaps economically, by being synonymous to most people merely with a junction on the M25. Recent development has beaten much of the character out of the place, but approaching across the old bridge and coming immediately upon

the **Running Horse** 2 makes the most of what's left. One of the town's oldest buildings, the outside of the pub is a real treasure, which looks its age and beckons one inside. Like the best old pubs there are legends, notably of a forced sojourn by Elizabeth I, caused by yet another Mole flood.

A decade or so back it survived an attempt to 'firkinise' the pub, which would have possibly meant a loss of its historic name and some corporate changes inside; but the barbarians were fought off by a spirited campaign involving locals and CAMRA. Inside there are still two bars plus a couple of separate dining areas. The lounge in particular, with its low ceiling, has plenty of character.

Food is available lunchtimes and evenings, but the place is now a Shepherd Neame house so you can expect a wide range of their ales, both staples and seasonals, plus if you're lucky a guest, perhaps from Surrey Hills.

Upon leaving the Running Horse, make your way up towards the station, which is on the other side of the town centre, but well-signed. You'll pass the *Penny Black*, now a Young's house, en route if you are game for another stop on the way; but if you're headed back towards London, my recommendation would be to take a Victoria stopping train, alight halfway at Carshalton and pop into the award-winning *Hope*, in West Street, two minutes away, (right out of station, left at foot of hill, 150 yards), with one of the best beer ranges in the suburbs.

PUB INFORMATION

1 William IV
Byttom Hill, Mickleham, RH5 6EL
01372 372590
www.king-williamiv.com
Opening Hours: 11-3, 6.30-11; 12-4.30 Sun

2 Running Horse
38 Bridge Street, Leatherhead, KT22 8BZ
01372 372081
www.therunninghorse.biz
Opening Hours: 11-11.30; 12-10.30 Sun

Betchworth

WALK INFORMATION

Start/Finish: Betchworth station

Access: Trains from London & Brighton via Redhill. Arriva bus service 21/22/32 between Guildford and Redhill stops in the village

Distance: (longer circuit) 7.5 miles (12 km)

OS map: OS Explorer OL146

Key attractions: North Downs Way path; Box Hill (2 miles); Polesden Lacey (5 miles)

The pubs: Dolphin; Red Lion, both Betchworth. Try also: Royal Oak, Brockham

Before cutting through the North Downs, the River Mole meanders across the gentle Wealden Clay Vale of Surrey in a surprisingly rural landscape with attractive and affluent settlements nestling among the trees and meadows. There are good views of the steep chalk scarp to the north, and Gatwick is far enough away not to disturb the calm. It's a good place to enjoy the odd pint in the well-pubbed villages. Betchworth itself is now a quiet backwater bypassed by the busy A25. The full walk is undemanding of energy, but as is usual in an agricultural landscape some care is needed with the map and directions to keep to the right path, although you are unlikely to go seriously astray! There is a shorter option which cuts out the pleasant farmland south of Betchworth and makes a beeline straight for the last pub instead.

Start at Betchworth station, which has a reasonably frequent train service. The first section of the walk skirts the foot of the Downs: take the footpath heading up parallel to but above the road as it heads into the trees north of the station, as far as the turning (The Coombe) in 300 yards

where a North Downs Way sign directs you left. Fork left again after 50 yards, past some cottages and through a kissing gate. The attractive path climbs up briefly to level out and lead you along a linear route at the foot of the chalk scarp, with yew trees and (if you're lucky) dappled sunlight.

The Royal Oak overlooks the village green at Brockham

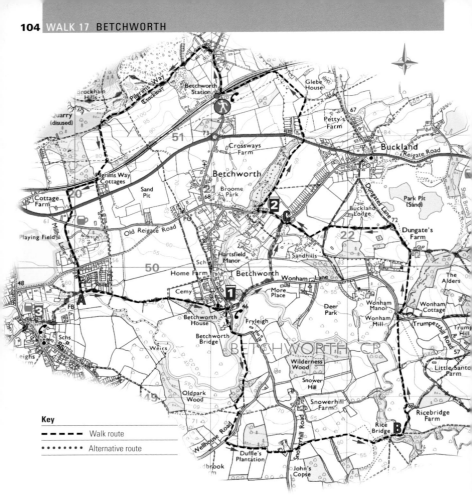

Pass through the old Betchworth quarries with fine views across to the Weald and take the first signed path left, dropping about twenty yards on some earthen steps to resume the same westerly line on a lower path. Disregard the first cross paths in few minutes, but at the second left sign, take this and walk down the field to the post which directs you down to a small bridge under the railway in the far right hand corner of the field. Turn right immediately under the bridge on a rather underused right of way and then look for the telegraph wires running down the field in about 250 yards. These wires mark the line of the right of way accessed via another rickety stile; be warned that the farmer may have planted over the path but be assured that you have the right of way!

At the bottom of the field a stile leads out directly onto the busy A25. Care is needed crossing here as sight lines are poor, but the path continues directly opposite and crosses another smaller road very shortly, into Mill Hill Lane, a bridleway. Wide views are on offer here, across to the chalk scarp slope; the church spire is Ranmore, also visible on the Abinger walk (walk 18). Ahead and slightly to your right is Leith Hill, the highest point in South East England. Cross another road and shortly afterwards the path reaches a T junction with the River Mole ahead (A, 201498).

At this point, there's a short optional detour into Brockham village where suitable refreshments are available, although the first featured pub on the walk is now little over half a mile away. For

 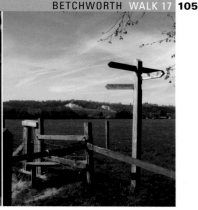

LEFT: **Royal Oak, Brockham** RIGHT: **On the route near Betchworth**

Brockham, take the Greensand Way to the right, past the first of many old wartime pillboxes which are very much a feature of this walk, and cross the Mole by the bridge, the path emerging very shortly just yards from the village green, flanked by its attractive church, handsome houses and two licensed premises. The first has been taken too far upmarket for your scribe to countenance but just beyond, the **Royal Oak 3** still looks like a pub. It's been opened out, but in the smart floorboarded bar you can enjoy a range of beers on three handpumps, with Fuller's London Pride and Sharp's Doom Bar the most likely suspects. There's a restaurant area to the rear, beyond which a garden, but the tables at the front are another attractive option in good weather, offering a pleasant view of the village green, parked vehicles permitting. From here return to the junction of paths on the Greensand Way.

Taking the left hand option on the Greensand Way you have a simple walk with good views left to the quarry, bringing you directly to Betchworth churchyard. The path dissects the churchyard, past the church and some attractive cottages, and emerges via a gateway onto Betchworth's main street with the **Dolphin 1** a few yards away. It's still a characterful old building which has been a Young's house for many years. Inside, a degree of smartening up has seen the formerly basic side bar becoming the Toby Room restaurant, but it hasn't been overdone, and the stone flagged bar area retains a well-worn and homely patina. Through a side arch there's a pleasant lounge with an open

fire. Outside, extensive gardens run round the rear and side of the buildings, whilst a hedged roadside area of tables is always popular.

Leaving the pub, we have two options. The far shorter one takes a short cut to the Red Lion by taking the side road (Wonham Lane) and then the first lane left in about 400 yards, to join the main route at the road junction in a further 400 yards at C (⊙ 215504).

The main, longer route, leads downhill along the wall of Betchworth House opposite the pub to the venerable old river bridge, where the river looks as if it ought to be an anglers' paradise. Take the footpath through the kissing gate on the right immediately after crossing the bridge; you're heading across a field to enter a pretty area of old woodland climbing gently off the flood plain. Just after a second kissing gate bear round to the right, close to the fence, up to a redundant stile by a clump of oaks with a fingerpost beyond. There are two exits left to the lane: at right angles left to a stile, or stay on the field side of the hedge to exit the field in the far left corner.

Just after joining the lane from this far exit, and turning right onto it, look for the footpath sign on the left by a pair of metal gates, take this path leading unerringly in about 500 yards to another lane and across here, keeping ahead but veering slightly right after another 500 yards on a well-defined track downhill towards a line of trees and shrubs, whereupon enter and hold to the path with these trees on your immediate left to reach the meandering Mole once more at Rice Bridge (B, ⊙ 224486).

LEFT: **The comfortable and stylish Dolphin** RIGHT: **The Red Lion, with an attractive garden**

This secluded little spot is an ideal place to draw breath, as it's still over a mile to the Red Lion. Pill-box spotters will be able to tick off the first of several on this next stretch as they cross the river and, just before reaching the stile a few yards further on, a good track leads off under the trees to the left. Take this and look for another, signed, route left after another 150 yards, as the bridleway bears right. Follow the path round the side of the farmhouse keeping to the right of the field.

The path is easy to follow here, keeping close to the river, as we head towards the recently renovated Wonham Mill ahead. When emerging on the road by the mill, bear left on the bend for just a few yards before striking off on another path on the right, just above the mill. Swing left to walk alongside the old millpond then it's plain sailing for the next few hundred yards before you reach the quiet Dungates Lane by a house. There are fine views towards the chalk downs.

Turn left here, and in another 250 yards just beyond another house, left again on another path. Through a couple of new kissing gates, we reach another, well-signed path junction. The direct route, bearing left across the paddock, may entail unhooking an electric fence. If you don't fancy this, take the sharp left option and then sharp right at the junction 100 yards on. Either way you end up on a well-worn track close to the prominent white house. Follow this west to the road, but just before you get there is a surprisingly steep descent. Emerge on the old Reigate

Road, now bypassed and quiet, so bearing left, but ignoring the minor lane left in a few yards at C and keeping to the 'main' road, you'll reach the **Red Lion 2** in just a couple of minutes.

A distinctive pub this, sitting high above the road, getting inside might provide a brief diversion but the three ales in this *Good Beer Guide* regular (Fuller's London Pride and guests, often local) should be in good form. Good use is made of the limited space, with some dining areas around the bar. The outside seating is attractive, the wisteria-covered pergola being a star performer, and cricket was in progress on the rear field on my last visit.

Leaving the Red Lion, the footpath runs up the side of the pub and alongside the cricket field behind it. In the top left corner of the field you'll see the path snaking through the next field (ignore the path diverging right); keep left and at the top of this field emerge via a few yards of shrubbery to the side of the main road.

Cross carefully and over the next stile directly opposite, and keep straight ahead close to the fence. Through the gate at the top of the next field (sign) aim for the left of the big house ahead, and this will bring you to join the right of way running alongside the railway embankment some 50 yards left of the small bridge which comes into view. Through the metal kissing gate, the path then climbs alongside the railway line. Simply follow this along to emerge back at your starting point, Betchworth station.

PUB INFORMATION

1 Dolphin
The Street, Betchworth, RH3 7DW
01737 842288
www.dolphinbetchworth.com
Opening Hours: 11-11; 12-10.30 Sun

2 Red Lion
Old Road, Betchworth, RH3 7DS
01737 843336
www.redlionbetchworth.co.uk
Opening Hours: 11-11 (midnight Fri & Sat); 11-10 Sun

TRY ALSO:

3 Royal Oak
Brockham Green, Brockham, RH3 7JS
01737 843241
Opening Hours: 11-3, 5.30-11; 11-11.30 Fri & Sat; 12-10.30 Sun

Abinger Common & the Hurtwood

WALK INFORMATION

Start/Finish: Gomshall station

Access: Trains from London & Brighton via Redhill, or Arriva bus services 22, 25 and 32 link Gomshall to Guildford, Redhill and local villages

Distance: 9.1 miles (14.6km)

OS map: OS Explorer OL145

Key attractions: Surrey Hills Area of Outstanding Natural Beauty; North Downs Way path (1 mile); Shere folk museum (1 mile); Silent Pool (1 mile)

The pubs: King's Head, Holmbury St Mary; Hurtwood Inn, Peaslake; Compasses Inn, Gomshall. Try also: Gomshall Mill, Gomshall

Despite its high population, Surrey retains some excellent rural scenery, and feels far less urbanised than, say Hertfordshire on the other side of London. The Surrey Hills Area of Outstanding Natural Beauty (AONB) through which this circular walk leads, is one of the most heavily wooded parts of the South East; it's also the highest land in the region. This walk takes in heathland, a habitat with which Surrey is still well-endowed on account of its gravelly and infertile soils, at Abinger Common. It then climbs into the woodland around Holmbury St Mary and Peaslake, relatively remote villages – with an option to visit the viewpoint at Holmbury Hill, one of the highest points in the region – before returning to the start at Gomshall, an old riverside settlement. Some care with navigation is recommended, especially in the woodland, where there are far more paths on the ground than on the map!

Abinger churchyard

Key

– – – Walk route

• • • • • • Optional detour

Autumn on Abinger Heath

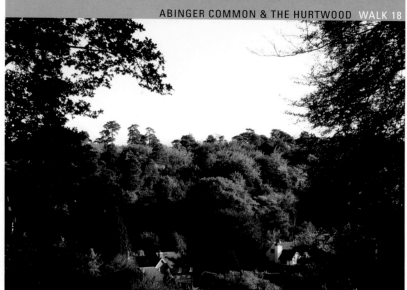

Autumn colours above Holmbury St Mary GP

From Gomshall station, on the Guildford side, take the gate at the far end of the platform and walk down the path to reach the main road. Cross the road carefully and, turning left, walk about 300 yards along the road. Just beyond the bend, by the 30 mph sign, you will see a byway running away from the road. Cross carefully once again and take this track, looking for a footpath leading off to the right in a further 150 yards. Now we're walking east, first pleasantly through some open woodland and scrub and then, beyond a gate, through a field with more extensive views of the scarp of the North Downs. Cross a very minor road and continue into the National Trust's Abinger Common, ignoring paths to the left until, just before a clearing on the right, a path doubles back sharply to your right down to a gate.

Once through the gate there are fine views across to the left towards the wooded slopes of Leith Hill. Passing through another gate the trees close in on all sides and the track down to the busy A25 road is sunken and atmospheric. Great care is needed in crossing since the sightlines are very poor but, once safely across, follow the lane opposite, up to and past Paddington Mill with its pond, up to the farm where the signed bridleway continues uphill to the left of the farmhouse and the barn.

At the top of the rise, by a large oak tree, the bridleway bears first gently left and then sharp right, and at this point leave the bridleway and continue straight ahead on the footpath – a wide track across the field leading down towards a group of farm buildings. Look out for two church spires: the one straight ahead beyond the farm buildings is Abinger which we shall reach shortly; in the distance to the left, atop the North Downs, you should be able to pick out the spire of Ranmore church which is a landmark for miles around. Reach the lane and follow the footpath sign into the farmyard just a short distance down the lane (A, ⊙ 107463) and bear right on the track with the Wootton estate footpath sign; this path leads you directly to the church at Abinger with its attractive churchyard. Directly ahead is the *Abinger Hatch Inn*, not an official stop on our route.

Pick up the path immediately right after passing through the lych gate, along the churchyard wall, to reach and cross a lane, into a meadow and down to a stile leading downhill into a wooded valley. Follow the more sunken path down to the right through the trees, through the valley, and out onto a wider track which winds pleasantly downhill and eventually brings you to the outskirts of Holmbury St Mary, with houses on your right. At a cross path by a gate keep ahead on the good bridleway for another quarter of a mile, ignoring paths to right and left, before merging with a gravel lane at Feldmore Lodge and reaching the road just beyond by a pond with some seats.

Holmbury St Mary is a loose-knit village set deep in the heart of the Surrey Hills, and is none the worse for its slightly old-fashioned ambience. The main village green, where there is another pub, is a little distance down to your right here, but we bear left on the roadside, crossing almost immediately, past the tantalisingly named Hollybush Tavern, not a pub any longer, and taking the little lane diverging right which leads in no time to our first stop, the **King's Head ∏** . Just before the pub, architecture lovers can admire the attractive little Honeysuckle Cottage in local greensand with galletting – a local decorative feature whereby small stones are set into the mortar between the stone courses.

In an area where many pubs have been taken well upmarket to the verge of becoming restaurants, the King's Head retains a good pubby atmosphere despite some recent modernisation. The new owners have said they wish to keep it that way and not turn it into yet another gastro joint. It has long supported local brewers like Pilgrim of Reigate, (but the new owners may change the range) and offers a good range of food up until 2.30 at lunchtimes (all afternoon on Sundays). A star is the extensive and secluded garden. Traditionalists will approve of the retention of the outside gents...

Leaving the pub take the higher road and bear right in a few yards where you merge with a lane coming up from the left. A short distance up the hill look for a track running acutely back to the right, signed to the cricket ground. It doubles back left, climbing up past the ground set in a clearing in the open woodland. A couple of minutes beyond, at a junction of paths and a metal seat, (B, ⊙ 105435) there is an option to climb Holmbury Hill, with its fine views out across the Weald. To do this, simply continue ahead on the main track which, in about ten minutes of steady but not steep ascent, will bring you to the summit. At 857 ft (261m) this is the highest point of any walk in this book. It's one of three prominent hills made of mainly of greensand that project southwards across the Weald in Surrey (the

The summit of Holmbury Hill

The Hurtwood Inn, Peaslake

others being Pitch Hill and Leith Hill). The earth-works around the summit area mark the remains of an Iron Age fort. Its builders obviously had a good eye for a defensive site, for there are views here not just out across the Weald to the South Downs, but also north towards London; on a clear day you'll be able to pick out some of the city's highest buildings. Return by the same route.

Back at the metal seat look for the wide path opposite (on the right as you come from the crick-et ground), heading slightly uphill. This forks after a short distance; take the left-hand, narrower option (bridleway sign), and shortly afterwards cross another path, taking the wider right-hand option at the fork immediately afterwards. Cross another path then head downhill to the valley bottom. Here bear right and simply follow the wide track downhill through the plantation for about half a mile until at the bottom, by a small pond, the route bears sharp left into a much more attractive area of natural woodland. A short distance further on reach a path crossroads by some mature beech trees. Here be careful to take the correct line which continues about 45 degrees right, to the right of the freestanding beech trees and the more obvious path with its 'private land' sign, and towards some open ground with a large house. In a few yards you should pick up a good track running through the trees with the open ground close by on the right. This pleasant bosky path runs downhill and joins a wider path

in about five minutes. We cross, this keeping as close to straight ahead as we can, and in another five minutes or so should find ourselves looking over the rooftops of Peaslake, before dropping steeply down into the centre of this little village which nestles in its wooded valley.

The geography and the eclectic mix of building styles give the place a character of its own which can be appreciated by pausing briefly at the village centre by the vibrant shop. Dominating the village and frankly unmissable is the **Hurtwood Inn 2**: the large 1920s building is primarily an upmarket hotel, taking advantage of its enviable position, but happily the Hurtwood Bar is used to catering for the weary walker too, and offers a good range of well-kept ales in a bright, contemporary setting. Expect Fuller's

The King's Head, Holmwood

LEFT: **A nice array of traditional beer engines at the King's Head** RIGHT: **Gomshall Mill**

London Pride and up to three guests with an emphasis on local microbreweries, and of course an extensive menu. There's outdoor seating too, where you can watch the world go by (or not, as is more usually the case in this pretty, sleepy little place) and admire the scenery.

There's a limited service on bus route 25 back to Gomshall and Guildford if you have had enough by now; otherwise gird your loins for the last couple of miles. Walk down Pond Lane, to the right of the hotel, and at the road junction look for a footpath sign in the angle of the lanes. Go through a stile by a gate, straight downhill across the field, with good views. Follow the path into a small area of woodland to join the road: Jesses Lane. Here bear right onto the quiet lane and follow it past some attractive houses (ignoring paths leading off right and left) to merge with a busier road where you bear left for some 200 yards, crossing when its safe to do so before, on the next bend, peeling off right onto a wide unmade bridleway: Birches Lane. Follow this good bridleway (a small dogleg bend halfway down) to join a public road by the rail bridge. Right under the bridge brings you very quickly down to the A25 at Gomshall. Whether or not you have managed to follow the whole route unscathed by errors, a pint is your reward at this point, and you're in luck: left is the **Compasses Inn 3**, a venerable old building with

timber much in evidence in the roomy, if relatively formal, bar area. Farming knick-knacks adorn the place. In good weather the sunny riverside garden accessed across the tiny Tilling Bourne will appeal, although it's close to the busy main road. Beers are primarily from the very local Surrey Hills brewery, and as a *Good Beer Guide* regular you can expect their ales to be in good form. Meals are on offer (except on Sunday evenings) in a separate dining room. August Bank Holiday weekend sees the 'Gomstock' mini music festival taking place in the garden.

A stone's throw from the compasses is the old **Gomshall Mill 4** which has been converted into an attractive bar and diner, right astride the Tilling Bourne. You might try your luck with the beer menu here with up to four to choose from including rotating guests. The station is about five minutes' walk beyond the Mill along the main road.

PUB INFORMATION

1 King's Head
Pitland Street, Holmbury St Mary,
RH5 6NP
01306 730282
www.kingsheadholmbury.co.uk
Opening Hours: 12 (4 Mon)-11;
12-10.30 Sun

2 Hurtwood Inn
Walking Bottom, Peaslake,
GU5 9RR
01306 730851
www.hurtwoodinnhotel.com
Opening Hours: 12-11 (midnight
Fri); 12-10.30 Sun

3 Compasses Inn
50 Station Road, Gomshall,
GU5 9LA
01483 202506
www.thecompassesinn.co.uk
Opening Hours: 11-11; 12-10.30
Sun

TRY ALSO:

4 Gomshall Mill
Gomshall, GU5 9LB
01483 203060
www.hcpr.co.uk/gomshallmill
Opening Hours: 12-11 (10.30
Sun)

Over the Hog's Back to the Wey

WALK INFORMATION

Start: Wanborough station

Finish: Godalming station

Access: By rail from London Waterloo/Clapham Junction, changing at Guildford. Motorists can return to Wanborough from Godalming by rail (change at Guildford)

Distance: 8.2 miles (13.2km)

OS map: OS Explorer OL145

Key attractions: Watts Gallery and Chapel, Compton; Loseley Park House; Guildford and cathedral (4 miles)

The pubs: Good Intent, Puttenham; Harrow, Compton; Star, Godalming

This linear walk offers a wide variety of scenery through a transect of fine west Surrey landscapes, from the open views north of the Hog's Back, over the famous narrow chalk ridge, and down through the well-wooded sandy heaths around Puttenham and Compton to finish along the banks of the River Wey. Cultural opportunities abound alongside the pub stops, in the form of the manor and barn at Wanborough, and the popular Watts Gallery with its remarkable mortuary chapel close by. If you're sensitive to traffic noise, this is another walk for your personal stereo: the A3/A31 roads are fast and the noise can carry some distance.

Wanborough Church with the Manor House behind

A bosky sunken path near the Watts Gallery

LEFT: **The path down the Hog's Back** CENTRE: **Setting out from Wanborough** RIGHT: **The Good Intent**

Walk from Wanborough station onto the lane which runs south, with the wooded ridge of the Hog's Back on the skyline. At the T junction with Flexford Lane in five minutes bear left, but then almost immediately right onto a signed footpath past a couple of fine old oak trees. Traverse this open landscape, following the pretty clear line of the track across the farmland, heading more or less south the whole time, and emerging on the motor road close to original settlement of Wanborough, as opposed to the modern suburbia by the station. Cross to the footpath opposite and bear left, following the road round the corner. It's highly recommended to detour the few yards into the old hamlet just around the corner (re-cross the road carefully) for here there are centuries of history: the manor house, barn and parish church sit close together within a cluster of other interesting buildings. Cistercian monks from nearby Waverley Abbey owned Wanborough Manor as a grange from 1130 until the Dissolution of the Monasteries in 1536, and it was they who built the impressive 14th-century Great Barn. Just beyond, St Bartholomew Church, Grade I listed, dates back to the 13th century. Behind it the Manor House is 16th century; it was requisitioned during the Second World War and used as a base for training British secret agents.

Continue uphill along the side of the road towards the Hog's Back, a walk more pleasant than it looks on the map thanks to a tree-lined verge separating the road from the footpath. Near the top, as the road bears left, a clear path strikes off right at a manageable gradient to reach the trees alongside the fast A31. Be warned, the path emerges directly onto the carriageway. The road is busy and fast, although sight lines are very good. Be patient and wait for a long gap in the traffic before crossing.

Once safely across both carriageways, find the path in the wider verge opposite which leads to a signed bridleway just twenty yards or so along to the right. The character of the scenery changes immediately as you plunge into one of those lovely sunken paths enclosed and overhung by trees and shrubs. This linear living alleyway offers glimpses out across the wooded and rolling countryside of south-west Surrey as well as very effectively deadening the noise of the A31 which is far less intrusive audibly than on the north side. Enter Puttenham past the village school and turning into the village street, the first pub stop is right here.

The **Good Intent** 🔳 is an old village local that has been extended over the years, but the character has been retained, and there is plenty of exposed timber and brick, creating numerous cosy seating areas. The pub extends a welcome to walkers and cyclists, and seems to fit everyone in happily; excellent food is served without compromising the pubby character, and not at the expense of a serious commitment to beer, with three regulars (Sharp's Doom Bar, Taylor Landlord and Otter Bitter) alongside three more constantly changing guests. If you're arriving on a crisp winter day you'll appreciate the fire in the inviting inglenook. Puttenham has Surrey's last remaining hop garden, on part of the nearby Hampton Estate, and pictures of the garden decorate the walls in one corner of the pub.

LEFT: **A good view over Puttenham** RIGHT: **Riverside meadows on the Wey near Eashing**

Leaving the Good Intent continue up Puttenham's village street, Suffield Lane, towards the war memorial and church, turning right on the footway as the street merges with the main road ahead. A short distance beyond, by the *Harvester* roadhouse, cross the road and head up the North Downs Way (NDW) bridleway (left fork of the paths) opposite. Navigation here is plain sailing, with the golf course on the right. The track starts as a wide unmade road but after half a mile by some pretty cottages and Monks Grove Farm, continue ahead (follow NDW signs) as the path narrows and becomes more shady. The proximity of the A3 road means that noise is increasingly

G F WATTS, THE WATTS GALLERY AND THE MORTUARY CHAPEL.

George Frederic Watts (1817-1904) was, in his own lifetime, widely considered the greatest painter of the Victorian period, but he was also an accomplished sculptor. The Watts Gallery, an early example of an Arts & Crafts building and opened to the public in 1904, is the only purpose-built art gallery to show a single professional artist's collection. It also doubled as a hostel for apprentice potters working under the tutelage of his wife Mary Seton Watts. The Grade II* listed gallery, having fallen into some decay, was re-opened in 2011 after a widely-praised £11 million refurbishment. The nearby cemetery chapel (free admission) is a quite extraordinary, art nouveau, Grade I-listed building, designed by Mary and built by her and the local craftspeople she trained. The celtic-inspired moulded brickwork is very rich, whilst the interior needs to be seen to be appreciated. Modern architectural guru Lucinda Lambton says: 'It is no exaggeration to say that the Watts Cemetery Chapel is one of the most beautiful, one of the most extraordinary, original, marvellous and magical buildings in the whole of the British Isles!'. Admission prices to the gallery are heavily discounted on Tuesdays to comply with the artist's will.

Watts Chapel

Detail from the Watts Chapel

LEFT: **The Harrow, Compton** RIGHT: **The Wey near Godalming**

intrusive however; and you may be relieved to reach the tarred lane where turning right leads one under both the modern dual carriageway and the older A3 just beyond. The lane here follows the line of the Pilgrim's Way, the sometimes ill-defined line of an ancient trackway running broadly along the route of the North Downs from Winchester to Canterbury, this is why the second, older bridge has a pair of crosses on the top.

We're entering the grounds of the Watts estate (see below) and when Surrey County Council wanted to build a bypass through the estate in 1930, George Watts's widow Mary would not consent unless it was designed by Lutyens (1869-1944), the celebrated architect. The much more modern bridge carrying the contemporary road, the bypass of the bypass, makes no such concessions!

Beyond the bridges, the lane reaches the Compton road at a T junction. The North Downs bridleway leads left, then right, right past the well-known Watts Gallery which, if you have factored in the time, is well worth a visit (see box). The cemetery chapel is free to enter and is about 300 yards down the road to the right.

Continue along the North Downs Way which runs up alongside the gallery, on a soft sandy track climbing gently uphill at first, becoming more interesting as it enters a sunken stretch after passing a metal barn. Another 250 yards further on reach a cross path at a shady spot where we turn right downhill through the trees into the Loseley Estate nature reserve. Yes, this is the same Loseley which is responsible for the yoghourt… Join Polsted Lane, (A, ⊙, 966475) and walk down this usually quiet road (keeping ahead at the junction halfway down) to join the B3000 road

in Compton village. Walk along for another 300 yards or so to reach the **Harrow 2** opposite. We found this road more difficult to cross than the A31 but it was a Sunday?! Assuming you survive, you'll find a smart food-oriented pub which has recently had a change of management, and a promising hike in beer quality. The three ales are sourced from all parts, but Sharp's Doom Bar makes a regular appearance by all accounts. Service is attentive and food is available lunchtimes and evenings, whilst the pub itself opens throughout the day. There are three fairly distinct areas, including a lower room with comfortable seats and sofas to enjoy your pint.

Unless you're making a short cultural detour to view Compton's noteworthy 11th-century parish church, a few hundred yards further down the street, the footpath leaves right by the pub car park at its western edge (although the first few yards looks like a private drive-cum-car park itself). It improves straightway, however, and once over a stile leads you uphill on a well-worn route towards a second stile where there are two waymarked options – take the right hand one alongside the fence towards, and then along, the edge of the woodland area, and follow this uphill with great distant views towards the east and north to the top of the field, and a kissing gate. Pass through here and head uphill to the right into the woodland and a 500 yard section running across a couple of swanky roads and past the back gardens of some seriously large houses, reinforcing all the Surrey stereotypes (well, Charterhouse is less than a mile away…). The path steepens and merges into another path which runs downhill in a wooded valley; ignore side paths however tempting, but

The Star, Godalming

hold to the valley bottom until you reach the foot of the slope by a very large and handsome house at the wide valley floor (B, ⊙, 952449).

Now, bear left (public footpath sign) and follow what is the edge of the River Wey's densely wooded floodplain, although the river is only occasionally visible on this stretch. The path keeps left of Milton Wood (the house in a few yards) but aside from that is very straightforward indeed, bringing one out to the end of a suburban road in half a mile, at which point the right of way continues downhill to the right: keep straight ahead to reach the river. This is a very attractive spot and the overflow sluice a few yards upstream would make a good place to open that afternoon flask of tea and the packet of hobnobs or whatever. The actual route follows the river downstream however: simply keep as close to the riverbank as possible when confronted with a choice of paths. It's a very nice stretch of the route, and the river feels far more rural than the reality. Cross the entrance to 'Westbrook Mills' these days a soulless looking office complex with a security gate more suited to a detention centre, to reach the road just beyond by a very attractive three arch bridge. In fact the original Westbrook Mills

was one of several which once made Godalming an important industrial town, and notably it was a dynamo at Westbrook Mills which supplied the power for the world's first public electricity supply system, established here in 1881. Turn right, under the railway bridge, and walk up to the handsome parish church of St Peter and St Paul with its impressive spire. At the T junction, noting that the railway station is only 100 yards to the right, bear left and walk past the church along Church St where just around the bend lies Godalming's best real ale destination, the excellent **Star** **3**.

With a robustly traditional interior, with lots of beams, it retains a very nice front snug and further drinking areas along the bar to the side, with a covered outside area leading to a rear patio. It takes its ales very seriously, with a constantly changing, wide selection on offer. The website keeps you abreast of upcoming beers and the frequent festivals and events so you could plan ahead for one of these if you wish. Additionally the Star, which is a *Good Beer Guide* regular, offers a choice of real ciders and Belgian bottled beers, although food is confined to lunchtimes.

It's a good pub to hole up in knowing that the station is only five minutes away…

PUB INFORMATION

1 **Good Intent**
60-62 The Street, Puttenham,
GU3 1AR
01483 810387
www.thegoodintentpub.co.uk
Opening Hours: 12-2.30, 6-11;
12-3, 7-10.30 Sun

2 **Harrow**
The Street, Compton, GU3 1EG
01483 810594
www.theharrowcompton.com
Opening Hours: 11-11; 12-
10.30 Sun

3 **Star**
17 Church Street, Godalming,
GU7 1EL
01483 417717
www.thestargodalming.co.uk
Opening Hours: 11-midnight;
12-11 Sun & Mon

Along the Thames: Boulter's Lock to Cookham Dean

WALK INFORMATION

Start: Maidenhead, Boulter's Lock (or Cookham station)

Finish: Cookham station

Access: Trains from London Paddington to Maidenhead then hourly bus (Courtney service 78) to Boulter's Lock, or for shorter option change at Maidenhead for train to Cookham.

Distance: 7.5 miles (12km) from Boulters Lock; 5.7 miles (14km) circuit from Cookham station

Key attractions: Thames Path; Cookham village and Stanley Spencer Art Gallery; Cliveden

The pubs: Bounty, Cookham; Jolly Farmer, Cookham Dean; Old Swan Uppers, Cookham

It would be a significant omission for this book not to contain at least one walk along the Thames; and, in the view of many, it doesn't get any better than this. It's a lovely walk all the way with great views of the river and the steep tree-clad terraces either side of the floodplain. Culture vultures are also catered for in the Stanley Spencer Gallery. It's a pleasant surprise that in an area oozing affluence there are still some unpretentious pubs serving a good pint without being completely transformed into restaurants. That said, you'll be able to eat well at any of the places on this walk. Although you can shorten the walk by starting at Cookham station, you'll miss the best stretch of the Thames by doing so. The *really* soft option is to alight from the train at Bourne End and cross the river which takes you almost straight into the Bounty…

The delightful Cliveden Reach

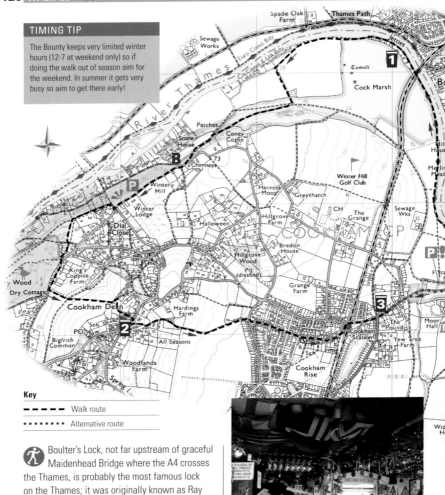

TIMING TIP

The Bounty keeps very limited winter hours (12-7 at weekend only) so if doing the walk out of season aim for the weekend. In summer it gets very busy so aim to get there early!

Key

– – – – Walk route

•••••• Alternative route

Boulter's Lock, not far upstream of graceful Maidenhead Bridge where the A4 crosses the Thames, is probably the most famous lock on the Thames; it was originally known as Ray Mill Lock after the family who owned the nearby mills. The mills were demolished a century ago but the lock was a noted resort, with carnivals and pageants a frequent occurrence.

Shortly after leaving the lock and walking upstream the Thames path diverges from the road and enters the Cliveden Reach, one of the prettiest stretches of the whole river. The opposite bank carries a wide variety of trees so expect plenty of colour; and there are several islands or eyots in the river itself. On the Maidenhead side some stately-looking houses line the banks. Cliveden itself is not very obvious from the river path but briefly comes into view at one point.

Plenty to look at inside the Bounty, Cookham

It's an easy and very pleasant mile and a half along the river from the lock before the path turns abruptly inland, and makes its way across the meadows under a shady avenue of trees to join a quiet lane and thence the main road just close to Cookham village (A, ⊙ 897852). Cross the road and bear right, crossing School Lane, and down

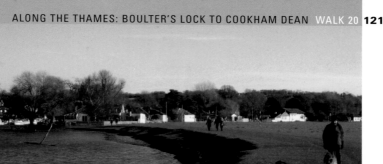

Thames Path at Cock Marsh, Cookham

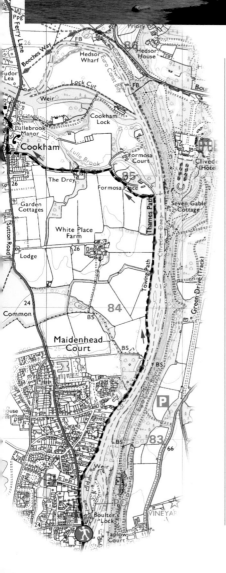

to the Stanley Spencer Gallery on the next corner. Dedicated to the life and work of the celebrated artist and Cookham resident Sir Stanley Spencer R.A. (1891-1959), the gallery was opened three years after his death and is run entirely by volunteers, a fine example of the Big Society at work, no doubt...

If you're taking the shorter route from Cookham station (see box), join here. Cross the busy junction and follow the main road round to the right, bearing next left into Church Gate, then follow the Thames Path through the churchyard of Holy Trinity church. The churchyard is the setting for Spencer's famous painting *The Resurrection*.

Rejoin the Thames beyond the churchyard. You find yourself alongside another lovely stretch of the river with a riverside meadow beyond the boat club, and views ahead to the prominent terrace of Winter Hill rising steeply from the river's floodplain. It's difficult to believe that Maidenhead is just a few miles away.

Pass through a kissing gate into the National Trust's Cock Marsh Meadow where the Thames Path hugs the open banks of the river closely, with the intermittent shade of willows, whilst on the opposite bank the humble dwellings of the poor artisans of Bourne End back onto the water's edge. Passing under the rail bridge, a line of riverside bungalows line the south bank of the river too. There's only access on foot or by water here, which makes it all the more surprising to come across the **Bounty** 🍺 a short way along. This must be one of the quirkiest pubs in the region, not only by virtue of its beer being delivered by river, but the building itself and

Near Boulters lock, looking upstream towards Cliveden

the highly unusual winter opening hours add to the sense that this is no ordinary boozer. The boat-shaped bar servery is surrounded by a spacious room with several tables, and there's a dining area out the back with views over the river meadows; on the walls and ceiling, all manner of ephemera catch the eye. Beers are from Rebellion, the local micro from Marlow across the river: expect a choice of three. Its location right on the riverside is a real draw and the numerous outside tables can fill up quickly if the weather's right so get here early if you want some space. Dogs abound: everyone in the area seems to own several and bring them to the pub.

Continue along the Thames Path, through more riverside meadows, with the river cliff

of Winter Hill ahead, rising steeply from the floodplain. Before very long the path again leaves the riverside and bears left of some riverside villas before turning inland towards Winter Hill across a field. Take the obvious path to the right once through the kissing gate, climbing gently but steadily up the hill. Predictably the views are quite wide, across the river and towards Marlow and the Chilterns. Reach the summit of this easy climb via another kissing gate and continue along the track, following the Chiltern Way sign in a couple of hundred yards; this keeps just below the crest of the ridge to join two small lanes, Stonehouse Lane and Gibraltar Lane at B (⊙ 874864). Here, turn left up to the junction to join the lane running right, along the top of the crest,

---

WALKING FROM COOKHAM STATION

It's actually quite a pleasant walk down from the station: the lane runs down over a mini roundabout into a narrow stretch past the Old Swan Uppers, which I recommend you save for later. Beyond this, you walk alongside the riverside meadows of Cookham Moor, over an old bridge, now a footway, and into the High Street with its numerous old buildings and several other pubs, to the gallery at the corner, where you turn left to join the main route.

Old Swan Uppers, Cookham

and continue west along this quiet road which continues to climb giving good views across the river.

Just beyond a viewpoint and at the junction with Startins Lane, where the road narrows considerably, a footpath leaving to the left at the entrance to 'Rivendell' on your right, takes you on a bosky but level path contouring along the crest of the hill with a steep wooded drop below you, and occasional views through the trees. Bear

Holy Trinity Church, Cookham

left in some 300 yards at the path junction, and walk through a pretty coppiced area of woodland (bear left, then right in 10 yards when you meet a fence) to rejoin the road opposite another area of woodland, Quarry Wood. If you have time on your hands this woodland would make an interesting diversion, and with some map reading you could rejoin the route close to

Cookham Dean Common. Otherwise head down Grubwood Lane almost opposite for some 200 yards, looking for a path on the left accessed via a kissing gate adjacent to a driveway into a large turkey farm. Drop down past the turkeys into the dry valley below and straight up the other side (ignoring the cross paths), reaching a stile where once again you enter the trees.

CLIVEDEN REACH

Immediately upstream of Boulter's Lock the beautiful stretch of the Thames is known as Cliveden Reach after the great house on the top of the terrace on the opposite bank. The present Cliveden was built in 1851 after the previous house had been destroyed by fire. The architect was the prolific Sir Charles Barry, better known for rebuilding the Houses of Parliament. The grounds

were landscaped by Lancelot "Capability" Brown. Royalty and Cabinet worthies were entertained at parties and political gatherings in Cliveden, which in the early 20th century was home to Waldorf and Nancy Astor. In the 1960s Cliveden became associated with the Profumo Affair: it was here that Profumo and Christine Keeler, reputed mistress of an alleged Russian spy, met for the first time.

LEFT: **The Jolly Farmer, Cookham Dean** RIGHT: **Inside the Old Swan Uppers, Cookham**

Immediately afterwards a fork in the paths presents itself. Take the right hand option, for although not marked on the map this path leads very conveniently through a small wooded area directly into the rear garden of our next stop, the **Jolly Farmer 2**. The core of this lovely old 18th century house, brick and flint with not a plastic window in sight, is the cosy public bar with its tiled floor and open fire. There are eating rooms off to both sides. For some 25 years this pub has been community owned, and you can expect efficient service and good beer: Brakspear Bitter and Courage Best are regulars, but expect Rebellion to feature strongly among the three guests. I can vouch personally for the quality of the food. If the interior is too busy, there is the large garden at the rear, which you've already met, and pleasant tables at the front overlooking the little green and Cookham Dean's attractive flint church, St John the Baptist.

It's an easy walk back to Cookham: cross the road to the church and, walking past the lych gate, pick up the signed public footpath leading pleasantly downhill with good views ahead to the river valley. Ironically you'll get probably your best view of the day of Cliveden Reach from here, at almost the furthest distance from it. The path leads down through a fringe of hedges and trees to reach the

road in about half a mile. Here take the road almost opposite, High Road, which leads in another half a mile or so directly to Cookham station. From here, having checked the train times for later, it's an easy few minutes further on down the road over the level crossing to the last pub of the day, the **Old Swan Uppers 3**. As the interesting pub sign suggests, the curious name derives from an ancient ritual of catching young cygnets for counting and tagging, and a picture in the bar dating to 1890 shows a group of men armed with their long poles ready to do the business. The stone-flagged main bar sports one of the largest stoves you're likely to see and which, on a chilly winter's day, you'll be keen to enjoy. There should be at least five beers to choose from, including Fuller's London Pride, Brakspear Bitter and guests. If you're settling in for the rest of the day you can eat here, and there's a separate rear dining area.

PUB INFORMATION

1 Bounty
Riverside, Cookham, SL8 5RG
01628 520056
Opening Hours: 12-11 (winter 12-dusk Sat & Sun only)

2 Jolly Farmer
Church Road, Cookham Dean, SL6 9PD
01628 482905
www.jollyfarmercookhamdean.co.uk
Opening Hours: 11.30-11 (11.45 Fri); 12-10.30 Sun

3 Old Swan Uppers
The Pound, Cookham, SL6 9QE
01628 521324
www.theoldswanuppers.co.uk
Opening Hours: 11-midnight (11 Sun)

North of the Thames Group

Inside the Blue Boar, Maldon

West Wycombe, Naphill & Downley Commons

WALK INFORMATION

Start/Finish: West Wycombe High Street

Access: Trains from London Marylebone to High Wycombe, then bus 2a, 40 to West Wycombe from bus station. Bus 300 runs frequently, and until late, between High Wycombe and Aylesbury via the Wheel

Distance: 6 miles (9.6km)

OS map: OS Explorer OL172

Key attractions: Classic Chilterns woodland and downland; West Wycombe village; West Wycombe Park (National Trust); Hellfire caves; St Lawrence church and Dashwood Mausoleum, West Wycombe Hill

The pubs: Wheel, Naphill; Le De Spencers Arms, Downley Common; Swan, West Wycombe. Try also: Red Lion, Bradenham

Although I'd argue that the walking south of the Thames generally has a lot more to offer, this lovely round is as good as any of its length, in wonderful Chiltern chalkland. In addition to the woodland, commons and downs which make this short walk a pleasure from start to finish, there are plenty of cultural attractions, from the stately West Wycombe Park to the numerous associations with the rakish Francis Dashwood, 15th Baron le Despencer and founder of the Hellfire Club. There are plenty of pubs, at regular intervals; and using the bus links enables one to shorten or lengthen the route. The steepest hill is right at the start, the paths are well-marked and well-trodden, and navigation generally easy. If you're making a day of it and relying on the train back from High Wycombe, I'd consider starting and finishing at the Wheel, Naphill, rather than West Wycombe, as the 300 service runs very late, unlike buses back from West Wycombe. Alternatively, book a cab to collect you from the Swan.

On West Wycombe Hill

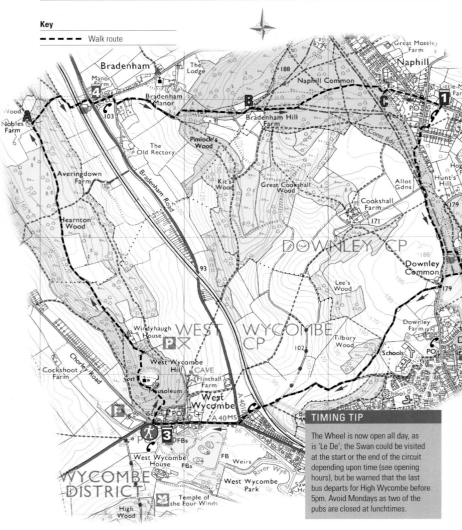

Key

---- Walk route

West Wycombe's pretty main street is virtually a line of listed buildings from one end to the other, spoilt only by the heavy traffic along the A40 road which cuts it down the middle. Look for the Swan towards the western end (the bus stops outside): this old pub has an entry in CAMRA's National Inventory of unspoilt interiors and is a must-visit for lovers of thirties pubs. We'll 'officially' save it for the end of the circuit, but if you wish to drop in before you get going, see the entry towards the end of this route description.

There's more than one way to scale the prominent West Wycombe Hill which rises steeply behind the village street and which is home to St Lawrence's church and Sir Francis Dashwood's mausoleum: if you love old cottages walk back eastwards past the *George & Dragon* and head up Church Lane (through the archway beyond and opposite) past the picture-postcard terrace and then up onto the hill to the church. Alternatively, the quickest way is to head west from the Swan to the junction with Chorley Road

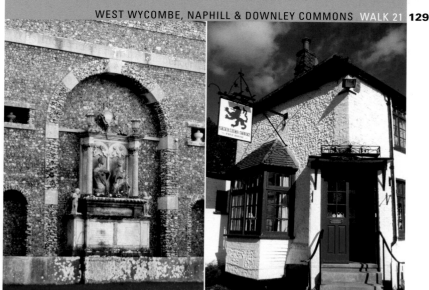

LEFT: **Detail from the Mausoleum, West Wycombe Hill** RIGHT: **Red Lion, Bradenham**

and then straight up the hill to the mausoleum, the remarkable flint building visible above you on the hillside. If you take this latter route you should be able to look across and get a glimpse of West Wycombe Park, the Palladian mansion set in the eponymous parkland by a lake across the valley to the south. Either way it's a steep climb, to be taken slowly.

Once at the mausoleum pause to admire both the remarkable Portland stone and flint monument, and the views across the Chilterns and back towards High Wycombe. Said to take its style from Constantine's Arch in Rome, the mausoleum houses the remains of members of the Dashwood family, including the notorious Sir Francis, who had it built. Almost equally remarkable is St Lawrence Church whose tower is crowned by a very curious golden sphere.

Having drawn breath at the church make for the gate at the far end of the small churchyard out into an informal car park/turning space. The ridge levels out ahead, and the wide, easy-to-follow track makes its way towards the woodland to the left of the entrance drive to Windyhaugh House ahead. Under your feet is one more surprise: in 1740 Sir Francis Dashwood began a project to mine chalk from under the hill, supposedly to build the main road

from West Wycombe to High Wycombe. But being Sir Francis this was no ordinary mine. Using local labour, glad of employment following successive harvest failures, he had excavated over half a mile of caves, caverns and curios, all accessed through a grand entrance which looks like a gothic church. The Hellfire Club was another of Sir Francis' schemes: it consisted of various political and social 'big cheeses' who formed a chapter and met here. The caves are now privately owned and open to the public.

Enough culture for the while: you've now over a mile's easy stroll through the trees on the track, keeping straight ahead, towards Nobles Farm (A, ⊙, 819968). When you reach the farm take the footpath branching off to the right and follow this quite steadily downhill, emerging from the trees with good views across the valley and Bradenham village to the wooded Naphill Common which we will cross later. At the foot of the hill your path joins the main road almost opposite the **Red Lion** 🄰 which, once we've crossed safely, is an optional stop if you are ready for an early drink. Walkers can expect a friendly welcome in this attractive pub which has a front bar and also rear room which now serves as a restaurant. Between the two is an unusual little drinking lobby with a nice tiled

LEFT: **Autumn colours on Naphill Common** RIGHT: **Le De Spencers Arms, Downley Common**

floor. Two beers are available, with Brakspear Bitter likely to be one of them.

Walk up the lane away from the main road and reach the road junction by Bradenham's long village green in a few yards. The church sits at the top end of the green, but we wish to aim for the top right (south-east) corner as we look at it. The bridleway in fact follows the unfenced lane rising up the far side of the green. The path then winds round the wall of Bradenham Manor on a well-signed route to enter the trees of Naphill Common.

Naphill Common is an extensive area of mixed oak and beech woodland with remnants of a formerly more extensive heathland. The beech in particular was planted in the nineteenth century for the furniture industry which was once strong here. Nowadays these woodlands are regarded as one of the most natural in the Chilterns. It has numerous venerable old trees which have helped to ensure its status as a Site of Special Scientific Interest (SSSI). It certainly offers some lovely walking and, although there are numerous paths, the route described here is pretty easy to follow. Walk up the bridleway (blue waymarks) to reach an interpretation board in about 450 yards (B, 835969). At this point there is a clear fork in the bridleway, and we take the right hand fork. Continue for about five minutes, at which point, close to an area of marshy ground, a footpath (yellow waymark) bears off to the left. The wetter areas in the woodlands are the result of clay-with-flints deposits which are often found towards the tops of chalk hills. The flints, of course, were very much in evidence in the buildings of Bradenham which you have just passed. Follow this clear path through the woodland,

hopefully with dappled sunshine playing on the leaves, and ignore paths to both sides until, after a further few minutes, you emerge from the woodland onto an unfenced lane with a few houses, the edge of the village of Naphill. There should be another interpretive board nearby. (C, 844971) Take the residential road opposite this (it's Chapel Lane but there's no obvious sign) and follow this round to the right to join the main road very shortly. Here continue in the same broad direction (north east) across the junction and just beyond what looks like a pub sign but turns out to be the village hall, you'll see the sign for the **Wheel 1** opposite.

Dashwood Mausoleum, West Wycombe Hill

Looking southwest from Downley Common

From near-closure five years ago the current licensees have not just turned the pub around but steered it to the winning post in the 2011 local CAMRA branch Pub of the Year award. It's a popular community local with friendly service and a variety of seating areas, as well as plenty of garden space. The smaller front bar leads around to a rear room, off which large dining extensions have been added. It's a Greene King tenancy so expect their IPA and Abbot, but two or three interesting guests as well. Food is available lunchtimes and evenings.

The Wheel is right on the route of the frequent 'beer bus', route 300 which stops right outside; it runs every twenty minutes or so. If you have the time, it's an easy journey from the stop across the road to Lacey Green a couple of miles away where both the *Black Horse* and the *Whip* offer some tempting beers, and both make it into the 2012 *Good Beer Guide*. The Whip is open all day too…

Otherwise (or having returned by bus) cross the road outside the Wheel and head right across the field opposite towards the far right-hand corner where an alley leads onto Downley Road. Here turn left and walk down to the edge of the common once again. Reference to the map shows that the next stretch of the walk follows a narrow strip of wooded common land towards Downley; heading a few yards into the trees on the path enables you to pick up a wider path,

follow this to the left past a small pond (it may be dry). You'll probably then merge into a still wider bridle path – don't worry too much: as long as you're heading south east in the trees you're on the right track! You'll cross a farm track and continue in the same direction. Look for a row of terraced houses brightly painted on the right in a few minutes and, shortly afterwards, you'll see some houses to the left through the trees. Head across to these and join this rough lane, once again running down the side of the trees with houses on one side. Happily one of the houses further along has a special appeal as it is also **Le De Spencers Arms 2**. As noted above, Francis Dashwood was the 15th Baron le Despencer. His legacy lives on in this attractive flint building looking onto the woodland across the lane. The small interior has separate drinking areas, with a stone-flagged floor at one end and an open fire. Home-prepared food complements the well-kept beers from the Fuller's stable including a couple from the ex-Gales portfolio.

Upon leaving *Le De*, as they like to call it, continue along the rough lane to join the tarmac a little further down; and here bear right along the lane at the edge of Downley Common. There are wide views across the open woodlands to the south east, with houses dotted in the landscape. Not readily visible but nearby in this direction is the country seat of Disraeli's Hughenden Manor,

The well-preserved thirties interior of the Swan, West Wycombe

now in the care of the National Trust. Disraeli himself was born nearby in Bradenham.

Follow the lane as it turns sharply left along the edge of the common and look for, in quick succession about 100 yards down the lane, a footpath and then a bridleway both leading off to the right. It's the bridleway we wish to take. It's a wide, tree-lined avenue which leads off the plateau and back down towards the valley at West Wycombe, easy walking with wonderful views beyond the avenue of trees and shrubs out across the Chiltern downland. This excellent path leads right down to the road junction of the A40 and A4010, from where it's just few hundred yards back to your starting point outside the **Swan** 3 which it's now time to visit, assuming you have got your timings correct. This 18th-century pub, owned by the National Trust (like most of the village) was refitted and extended in 1932 and is the only Buckinghamshire pub to make it into CAMRA's National Inventory of Historic Pub Interiors. That means that in my book it's a must-see. The bar off the road frontage is the saloon, which is in the original building. The parquet

floor and brick fireplace are classic thirties. The plain public bar is in a similar style and is accessed at the side of the pub. In between is the ultra-traditional gents with the original Shanks urinals and washbasin. Ladies are well-catered for too on the heritage front however with the 'penny-in-the-slot' door still surviving! Beers (Brakspear Bitter plus two from Marlow micro Rebellion) are served from casks stillaged behind the servery; there are no dispensers on the bar counter. Traditional lunches are served on Monday to Friday lunchtimes in the dining room at the rear: the Swan doesn't do 'bar meals' or a wide menu! A real gem to finish the day.

PUB INFORMATION

1 **Wheel**
100 Main Road, Naphill,
HP14 4QA
01494 562210
www.thewheelnaphill.com
Opening Hours: 12.30-2.30
(not Mon), 4.30-11; 12-midnight
Fri & Sat; 12-10.30 Sun

2 **Le De Spencers Arms**
Downley Common, HP13 5YQ
01494 535317
www.ledespencersarms.co.uk
Opening Hours: 12-11 (midnight
Fri & Sat); 12-10.30 Sun

3 **Swan**
High Street, West Wycombe,
HP14 3AE
01494 527031
Opening Hours: 11.30-2,
5.30-11; 11.30-2.15, 6-11 Sat;
12-2.30, 7-10.30 Sun

TRY ALSO:

4 **Red Lion**
Bradenham, HP14 4HF
01494 562212
www.redlionbradenham.com
Openining Hours: 11.30-2.30
(not Mon), 5-10 (9 Mon);
11.30-4 Sun

Magical Metroland: the Chess Valley & Chorleywood Common

WALK INFORMATION

Start: Chalfont & Latimer station

Finish: Chorleywood station

Access: Trains from London Marylebone or via Underground Metropolitan Line

Distance: (to the Land Of Liberty) 7.25 miles (11.6km)

OS map: OS Explorer OL172

Key attractions: Classic Chiltern chalk stream; Chenies Manor House and garden; Chiltern Open Air Museum, Chalfont St Giles (4 miles)

The pubs: Red Lion, Chenies; Rose & Crown, Chorleywood; Land of Liberty, Peace & Plenty, Heronsgate. Try also: Cock Inn, Sarratt Church End

In 1889 the Metropolitan railway was extended from Rickmansworth to Chesham via Chorleywood. And thus 'Metro-land', as the company marketed it in about 1915, pushed into the Buckinghamshire countryside. Chenies and Chorleywood were dubbed the 'Gateway to the Chilterns' and the wealthy moved in. Fortunately the line, and the ribbon of urbanisation kept at a respectable distance from the lovely River Chess, one of the finest chalk streams in the South East. This linear walk follows the river through a landscape that remains surprisingly rural, before climbing into Chorleywood which retains its well-wooded common. The walk finishes at one of the best beer pubs in the region. If you're arriving by car with a designated driver, consider parking with permission at the Land of Liberty and taking the train to Chalfont & Latimer from Chorleywood.

The Land of Liberty, Peace & Plenty

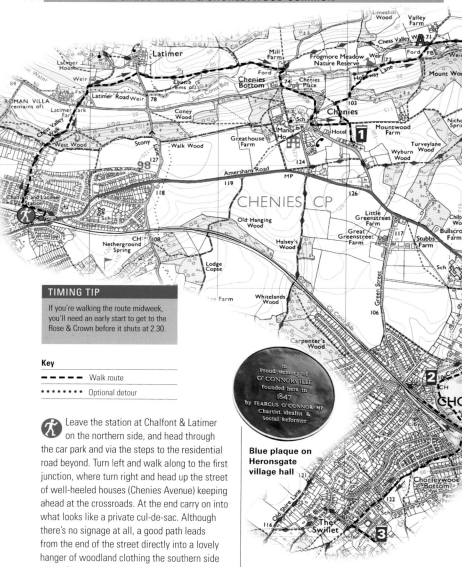

TIMING TIP

If you're walking the route midweek, you'll need an early start to get to the Rose & Crown before it shuts at 2.30.

Key

— — — — Walk route

•••••••• Optional detour

Leave the station at Chalfont & Latimer on the northern side, and head through the car park and via the steps to the residential road beyond. Turn left and walk along to the first junction, where turn right and head up the street of well-heeled houses (Chenies Avenue) keeping ahead at the crossroads. At the end carry on into what looks like a private cul-de-sac. Although there's no signage at all, a good path leads from the end of the street directly into a lovely hanger of woodland clothing the southern side of the Chess valley. Almost immediately cross a bridleway contouring the slope, pass through the posts, and head downhill through the woods on an excellent path, passing what appears to be an old quarry on the way, until you join another lateral path at the foot. Look for a gate below leading out of the trees down to the valley floor. Once through here, a well-worn path makes straight for the road. The large red brick mansion

Blue plaque on Heronsgate village hall

ahead of you is Latimer House, built in 1863. Cross the quite busy B road and walk down to the River Chess. This charming chalk stream is a rich habitat as well as a wonderful landscape feature, but the idyllic scene is under threat from the usual problems of water abstraction, habitat loss and invasive species as well as threats to water quality from pollution.

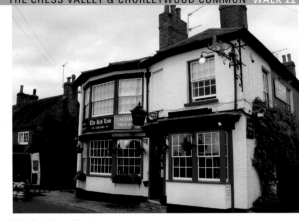

The Red Lion, Chenies

Immediately over the bridge, take the footpath on the right to walk alongside the river. Cross the road at Latimer and continue on the well-walked path which, on this next section, holds to a terrace just above the river floodplain, with fine views of the woodlands on all sides, which in autumn are a mass of varied colours. At the next road leave the river path to divert to our first stop. Pass the former Dodds Mill which has seen duty as a flour, paper and fulling mill during its 700-year history. Reach the valley road again and, checking the traffic, turn left (no pavement) for a few yards before crossing carefully to the path rising above the road on the other side, opposite Chenies Place. This path climbs pleasantly above the road through the trees and rejoins it a few hundred yards later just short of Chenies village. Head up the last hundred yards to the pretty green with its well-kept village sign. By May Cottage opposite, a signed footpath leads off to the east on a tarmac lane, and an easy level walk for a few minutes brings you to a footpath crossing the lane; take the right hand arm across a field towards a jumble of attractive looking cottages and, passing between a couple of them, emerge on the street right by the **Red Lion 1**. Once past the rather unfriendly warning about muddy boots (why do some pubs in the countryside insist on carpeting the whole place?) you're met with a smart interior which does however still retain three fairly separate areas around the servery. The main draw here is the good range of consistently well-kept beers which have earned the pub almost continuous inclusion in the *Good Beer Guide* over the years, evidenced by an array of awards on the wall. Expect four ales from Vale, Wadworths, and a guest, alongside the house beer brewed by Rebellion. There's a good menu too if you're intending to eat here.

The Chess at Latimer

LEFT: **Chorleywood Common** RIGHT: **The Rose & Crown, Chorleywood**

From the Red Lion retrace your steps to the tarmac lane and cross straight over, walking back down towards the valley. It's a rural scene with very few buildings in the mixture of woodland and fields. Join a second, narrower, traffic-free lane (Holloway Lane on the map) and turn right to walk down it with excellent views over the valley. Just around the left hand bend a footpath (via the prominent stile) cuts the corner across the field down to the valley floor, rejoining what is now little more than a tarred footpath.

A pleasant walk for another few hundred yards (ignore the first footpath sign, on the corner) leads you to a picturesque little wooden bridge across the river (A,  026990). Turn right onto the wide track, passing the last remaining watercress beds on the Chess here. At the terrace of four white cottages follow the Chess Valley walk waymark to the right, along the valley floor, past a couple of pretty cottages and along a road signed 'no through road'. Occasional glimpses are caught of the river flowing in the meadows beyond the hedge. Were it not for the sound of the odd plane this scene could easily transport one back the best part of a century, and it would make an ideal spot for a pub...

Beyond a row of handsome flint cottages the roadway peters out into a path. A short way ahead a kissing gate marks a path crossroads, and an information board explains the origins of the "lynchets": ancient terraces visible on the field to your left here at Sarratt Bottom. They are thought to date from the 9th century and probably grew wheat and barley, possibly even holding vineyards when the climate was warmer. On the right as we continue along the valley, are some particularly attractive water meadows. These are being grazed to maintain plant diversity and in turn sustain ideal conditions for wetland loving birds such as Redshank, Snipe, and occasionally Water Rail. This is probably one of the most attractive stretches of the whole walk, although the drone of the M25 now makes itself audible as we head towards another kissing gate to leave the water meadows, by a house. At this point a path heads up the hill to the left: this is the point at which to head up to the **Cock Inn** 4 at Sarratt Church End, if you wish. The pub is a few hundred yards up the hill, just beyond the prominent white house, and adjacent the flint church of the Holy Cross. Expect up to four beers from the Hall & Woodhouse stable. Otherwise, or on return, continue along the valley path, crossing New Road at the next gate, and through another meadow before the path turns to cross the river by a short avenue of tall lime trees. This is another idyllic spot (apart from the traffic noise) and there's a seat close to the unfenced riverside just downstream of the bridge if you wish to enjoy it to the full for few moments.

Continue downstream through a stretch of riverside parkland until merging with a driveway to an isolated house, just beyond which is a waymark and information board with a path heading off to the right, uphill into the trees, towards Chorleywood House Estate. The grounds of the estate were bought by the Chorleywood Urban District Council in 1940 and remain as public open space today. The wooded ascent makes a pleasant contrast with the lengthy stretch of riverside walking that has preceded it. The last section of the climb leads up to an avenue of horse chestnut trees, then reaching a small car park and a tarmac lane at a junction of paths (B,  034970) bear left to walk up past the lawns of Chorleywood House across to your right, and join the main A404 road by the old lodge.Cross over onto Chorleywood Common, with Christ Church and its odd spire across to the left. The route takes the obvious line through an avenue of trees, slightly to the right of the pavilion. Chorleywood Common with its lovely mature trees is another highlight of this walk particularly once the noise of the busy road recedes. As buildings come into view ahead in a few minutes make for the terrace of cottages, with a road coming in on your right. The building at the right hand end of this terrace is the next refreshment stop, the **Rose & Crown 2**. This small free house, like the cottages next door in this older part of Chorleywood, predates the railway. Note the unusual wrought iron pub sign before you go in. The front bar is now the drinking area, the rear a smart restaurant. Expect four beers, with regulars Fuller's London Pride and Young's Bitter joined by two changing guests (check the website for current offerings); the pub is accredited in CAMRA's LocAle scheme, making good use of local breweries like Tring, Buntingford and Vale.

Leaving the pub, if you are really pushed for time the railway station is accessed in a couple of minutes by bearing right and right again downhill via a path; otherwise cross over to the Common again and walk across to the information board

by the car park. Pick up a footpath-cum-horse track which takes a pleasant line through the trees above the road, which soon drops out of view on the right behind the gorse bushes. To your left the common is now occupied by a golf course but there remain plenty of fine trees along the fairways to enhance the landscape, whilst to the right across the valley lies the suburban development which Betjeman called 'essential Metro-land'. In three hundred yards or so cross the railway on a road bridge with metal sides, and head up the road straight ahead, keeping the *Old Shepherd* pub on your right and heading down the hill on Chorleywood Bottom. Take the first left into Turneys Orchard and almost immediately pick up a path on the right (signed 'Stag Lane and Copmans Wick') which leads uphill between the houses in a leafy alley. Continue directly ahead over a road, ignore the left hand path beyond, and instead keep ahead with the woodland on your immediate left and the housing estate on the right. Emerge on a road junction and head up Stag Lane past Chorleywood Primary School to the pub, the *Stag*, at the junction ahead. Now here turn left and walk down the road towards another pub sign which soon appears ahead, but take care, since this lane, although narrow, does lead straight off the M25 a mile or so ahead and at times can be fairly busy: there's no footway. The reward is that the last pub

Chenies village green

LEFT: **Crossing the Chess near Chenies** RIGHT: **The Land of Liberty, Peace & Plenty**

of the walk, the **Land of Liberty, Peace & Plenty** ▣ , is the sort of place you'll not regret visiting. This unpretentious alehouse, winner of numerous CAMRA awards which you can view inside, deserves all the accolades it has received for its well-kept beers. The wide range of rapidly changing ales (which can be viewed on the website) includes a house beer, Liberty Ale, brewed by Tring. It's a proper community pub where conversation dominates, and which sticks to what it does best, so don't expect Sky TV or fruit machines! The 'Lib' doesn't do meals, but pies, pasties and baguettes are available along with nibbles.

There's an extensive garden and a covered pavilion to the side if the pub gets too crowded, which, as it's small, it can do at popular times.

The history of the name and the immediate area is very interesting. You may have spotted that the pub sign has, unusually, a different picture on each side. One depicts the signing of the Magna Carta in 1215, an early forerunner of modern constitutional law limiting the powers of the monarch. The other side shows a scene from the Chartists' mid-nineteenth century campaign for electoral reform. The local connection with this radical reform movement was that in 1846 Fergus O'Conner, a Member of Parliament and Chartist Leader, bought nearby Heronsgate Farm and renamed it "O'Connorville: Land of Peace and Plenty". His aim was to resettle families from the industrial north on parcels of land which they could farm to support themselves; but also enfranchise working people by

allowing them to buy freehold land (for at this time those men who had no freehold land could not vote). O'Conner would not allow alcohol to be sold in his land of peace and plenty so a beerhouse was built on adjoining land and was called "The Land of Liberty". Sadly but predictably these settlers, with no knowledge of agriculture didn't do at all well; but fortunately for us the pub has survived and flourished!

If you're settled for the evening and/or darkness has descended it may be worth either booking a cab for the journey back to Chorleywood or Rickmansworth stations, (at quieter times licensee Gill has been known to drop visitors at the station, it's that kind of place). To get back on foot, the easiest option is simply to retrace your route right back to the railway bridge at the foot of the Common (don't miss the footpath a few yards on the right once you've headed left beyond the school); and then taking care (no footway for a short distance) follow the road alongside the rail cutting for the few hundred yards to Chorleywood station.

PUB INFORMATION

1 Red Lion
Latimer Road, Chenies, WD3 6ED
01923 282722
www.redlionchenies.co.uk
Opening Hours: 11-2.30, 5.30-11; 12-3, 6.30-10.30 Sun

2 Rose & Crown
Common Road, Chorleywood, WD3 5LW
01923 283841
www.roseandcrownchorleywood.co.uk
Opening Hours: 11.30-2.30, 5.30-11 (midnight Fri); 11.30-11 Sat; 12-10 Sun

3 Land of Liberty, Peace & Plenty
Long Lane, Heronsgate, WD3 5BS
01923 282226
www.landoflibertypub.com
Opening Hours: 12-11 (midnight Fri & Sat)

TRY ALSO:

4 Cock Inn
Church Lane, Sarratt
Church End, WD3 6HH
01923 282908
www.cockinn.net
Opening Hours: 12-11; 12-9 Sun

A circuit of Chesham's dry valleys

WALK INFORMATION

Start/Finish: Chesham station (Metropolitan line)

Access: Tube from London via Metropolitan line

Distance: 11 miles (17.8km); (6.8 miles to the Black Horse)

OS map: OS Explorer OL172

Key attractions: Chess Valley; Chesham museum; Chiltern open air museum, Chalfont St Giles (5 miles); Ashridge Estate (7 miles); Hughenden (7 miles)

The pubs: Crown, Ley Hill; Black Cat, Lye Green; Black Horse, Chesham Vale; Queen's Head, Chesham. Try also: Swan, Ley Hill

Chesham is the furthest you can go these days on the London Underground network, although you won't see many tunnels on the journey from central London. Chesham was once a significant industrial town, with water mills, tanneries, and breweries pre-eminent. It lies at the confluence of four dry valleys and the sources of the well-known River Chess are all close by. This circular walk heads up into the Chilterns, which surround the town, and traverses some of the dry valleys which converge on Chesham. Expect typical chalk scenery of rolling downs and plenty of woodland, with fine views. The pubs are well-spaced and offer plenty of choice and, provided you arrange transport, you can cut the walk a lot shorter by finishing at the Black Horse and getting a taxi back to Chesham, where the Queen's Head is not to be missed. Be warned that some parts of the walk are liable to be muddy, so it's important to be sensibly shod.

The Queen's Head

Key

- - - - Walk route

Turn sharp left out of Chesham station and pick up a footpath running back alongside the rail tracks. Follow the Chess Valley walk sign in a couple of hundred yards, dropping down to the main road below you. Cross the road and turn left, following the young River Chess (which may well be dry at this point) through Waterside, a pleasant linear water meadow alongside the road. Pass some old sluice chambers suggesting a former mill stood hereabouts, before rejoining the road just short of a roundabout. Cross carefully to the left, and walk down Moor Road. Pass underneath the railway and keep to the path on the riverside on the left hand side of the walk. When the path reaches a footbridge, don't cross but turn down to the right to rejoin the road and bear left (Chess Valley Way sign). At the end of this road, by a T junction, cross straight over onto a (signed) path, crossing a tiny stream and entering an area of valley floor parkland. Keep to the left hand edge of the grass with the river to your left. Ahead of you are the wooded sides of the Chess Valley.

At the far end of the grass, an earthen path runs out at the left hand corner down to some

Autumn in the woodlands at Tylers Hill, near Chesham

stepping stones across the stream; continue on the opposite side in a pleasant wooded section with more evidence of old mills. In a couple of hundred yards, by a large weir, leave the Chess Valley Way and head up left to the road, crossing directly over into Hill Farm Road which strikes up the slope in front of you. Continue uphill on the obvious bridleway (signed 'Pump Lane and Botley'), passing some attractive old farm buildings and ignoring right and left-hand paths before entering a hedge-fringed green lane with a very rural feel. The shady sunken lane then drops down into a dry valley to cross another similar lane at A (975013) before (very slightly to your left) rising again uphill onto agricultural land but with a wide grassy margin. The best views of the day so far open out behind you, notably down towards the Chess Valley; and in autumn the colours here are tremendous.

At the top of the spur the houses of Tyler's Hill come into view – reach and pass through the first of two kissing gates, and walk down to the second (Chiltern Heritage Trail (CHT) waymark) and opposite, up what looks like a private drive, past half-timbered Chantry Cottage with the little churchyard on your right. Over a stile into a large field, head for the kissing gate in the far right hand corner. Passing through, bear right into a

delightful area of beechwood. This next section is potentially confusing so take care: almost immediately you'll come upon a large dip, possibly an old quarry. Bear left here and in about thirty yards there's another waymark. At this waymark, bear right, passing another deep pit, and through the trees to and over a wooden stile. It's now plain sailing across a paddock and, entering a narrow path flanked by fences, emerging onto the side lane at Leyhill Common by the old Methodist chapel. Swing right here and across to the main road at the junction where, as reward for negotiating the woodland, there is a choice of two pubs adjacent each other, fronting the common. Both are worth a stop. I preferred the **Crown** 1 with a traditional-style bar wrapped around the wood-panelled servery. There's an open fire, dartboard and floorboards, but also modern touches like a decadent sofa at one end. More important perhaps, there's enthusiasm for interesting beers, attested to by the impressive display of pump clips on the wall by the fireside. Most of the guests, barring supporting regulars Hobgoblin and Doom Bar, come from nearby micros like Red Squirrel and Tring. Gentlemen can recycle their beers in some fine traditional urinals… If you want an early food stop you can eat in the bar or the restaurant, and the menu is on the pub website.

Next door, the **Swan** 5 is a heavily modernised interior encased in a handsome old building. There are several separate drinking areas, and a dining area at the rear. As for beers, expect St Austell Tribute, Taylor Landlord, Brakspear Bitter and a local guest. There are tables outside on the edge of the common which are loosely shared between the two pubs.

From the pair of pubs walk away, slightly to your left, crossing all three of the roads here, looking for a bridleway sign on the verge of the far road. Take this bridleway through a pair of posts and into the trees, following closely the edge of the golf course for a while on a stretch that may well be rather sticky underfoot. In about 500 yards swing round to the left, keeping within the trees, onto the CHT again. You're now dropping down into the floor of another dry valley although, as just noted, it may not be as dry underfoot as you might hope. Follow this bearing for about half a mile in pleasant woodland before merging into another path. Keep ahead on the same line, towards traffic noise ahead. You're walking on the grassed-over former road now, before reaching the busy road at B (⊙ 996032), ignoring the bridleway leading off to the right just before you get there. The road is surprisingly busy and very fast, so take care crossing, and making for the CHT sign opposite and some fifty yards to your right. Again expect some mud, as there is horse traffic here. We've reached the plateau of the Chilterns here, at about 500' so, where the vegetation permits, the views are extensive.

Keep straight ahead, through an industrial yard after a few minutes, and back into open country, before reaching Grove Lane in just over a quarter of a mile further. The path continues almost opposite, still heading west; keep to the field boundaries until it turns away at right angles, here head across one last small field to the trees ahead and emerge onto another lane via a gate (C, ⊙ 981038). Cross over onto the footpath margin and bear left for about 100 yards, then right through a gate where there's a choice of paths. Take the left fork, visible as a track across the grassy field, this leads to the green at Lye Green. Make for the right hand side of the green to join the motor road and, walking round the corner for another 150 yards or so, you'll see the sign for the **Black Cat 2** , not that you'd be left wondering about the name of the place for long without the sign, since black cats of all shapes, sizes and styles pop up pretty well everywhere inside, keeping a close eye on your every move. Notwithstanding this, the traditional interior feels very cosy and homely with an open fire at each end of the (now single) room. The pub, which was runner-up in the local CAMRA 2010 Pub of the Year competition, has built a very good reputation for both its beer and its food: the informative web site gives you the current run down on both, but expect three beers, Young's Bitter, Taylor Landlord and a rotating guest. Food is served until 2 at lunchtimes, and again in the evening.

Leaving the Black Cat, continue down the rather narrow road for another 250 yards or so, then take a turn on the right hand side signed 'Pressmore'. The first few yards look like the entrance to a secret nuclear bunker, but perse-

Rolling landscape typical of the Chiltern foothills

LEFT: **The Swan, Ley Hill** RIGHT: **Attractive frontage of the Black Horse**

vere: sidestep the gate on the left, following the fence of the installations in a pleasant tree-lined alley which opens out into farmland beyond. Join and carefully cross a very busy main road to the path continuation opposite (note that the path then bears left in another 25 yards at Pressmore Farm). Just beyond the farm buildings you come across possibly the best view of the day so far: a wonderful vista up the wide Chesham Vale, one of the four dry valleys referred to earlier.

When you reach the valley bottom and join the road turn right. Be warned that the road, although not too busy, is quite narrow and has no footway; fortunately we only have about a four or five minute walk (make a mental note of the path leading off left by a tall hedge after some 200 yards: this is the path we'll take later). For now, make for the pub sign which is visible after you've passed the hedge: and the **Black Horse** 3 has a very good pub sign too, showing off a fine old building set back from the road. Inside the place still has plenty of evidence of a long innings as a pub, with low beams, some nooks and crannies, and a wonderful inglenook fireplace. The rear of the pub is a dining room. Beers are usually Tring Side Pocket for a Toad, plus a couple of guests, with a traditional cider.

It's four beer-free miles back to Chesham, so decide here if you want to walk on, or call it a day and ring that cab. If you choose the latter, don't miss the Queen's Head (see the description below) – get the taxi to take you straight there. To continue the walk, return down the road and take the signed path on the right by the tall hedge.

Walk uphill until you get to a path branch and a couple of stiles. Take the left hand option, which bears left straight down to the floor of a side valley. Turn right here and head along until there's a branch in about 250 yards: the byway carries on, a footpath diverges slightly left and heads uphill; it's quite steep for a while before entering the woods, merging with another side path and levelling off. At the T junction by the back of a terrace of houses bear left and walk down to join the road. Cross over and take the right of way immediately opposite towards Mount Nugent Farm. Keep on the same bearing, negotiating the gates and paddocks, with the handsome farm buildings over to your left. Once over the stile, take the left-hand option when reaching the good track a few yards into the trees. Follow this through the predominantly beech woodland.

Disregard the first path crossroads after a couple of minutes, by a gate on your left, but then peel off to the right in another 100 yards, following a couple of white waymarks painted on trees. This good path makes its way steadily downhill, crossing a bridleway and dropping steeply into yet another dry valley where you meet the Ashridge Road (D, 947033). Once again there is no footway. Turn left and, walking carefully along the lane for some 250 yards, take the signed path on the right. Be careful not to miss it: it's just before the first house on the left and just after an agricultural barn on the left. This is the last steepish climb of the day: keep to the right of the field, making for the line of trees on the right further up, and picking up a track in the grass running up to the top right hand corner of the field at the end of a row of detached houses. Here exit via a stile and a confined alley (with excellent views right across the valley) to join the road at the top. Cross over and bear left, following Chartridge Lane, the larger of the two roads forking here. This one does have

LEFT: **The comfortable inglenook at the Black Horse** RIGHT: **The Queen's Head**

a pavement, but we're in the suburbs of Chesham now. After the road starts curving round to the left look for the prominently signed path (tarmac at first) on the right, veering to the left after fifty yards on a good path with views across Pednor Bottom, the next valley in this anticlockwise journey around Chesham. It's just over a mile back into town and it would be hard to go wrong now, so you can switch onto autopilot and enjoy the scenery. As you approach Chesham you'll enter Lowndes Park, given to the town in the 1950s, and see a pond fringed by a road lower down. Just before you reach the pond pass the parish church of St Mary's on the right and turn through the gate immediately after, between two brick pillars, which leads down an appealing alley and merges into Church Street in the heart of old Chesham. Despite a lot of twentieth century suburban sprawl to the north, the old town is still a very attractive spot in its own right, with numerous venerable old buildings. Now simply walk along the street, passing several handsome cottages to reach the **Queen's Head** 4.

The smart brick frontage is inviting but doesn't prepare you for the interior beyond the lovely etched glass windows in the lobby doors leading to the 'Public Bar' and 'Bar Parlour'. The latter, now the pleasant saloon with separate sections, is an amalgamation of several older rooms which lead towards the rear of the pub, but the public bar to the right is, in my book, a

candidate for my list of 'desert island pub rooms'. It's got that informal, relaxing, comfortable ambience that comes from decades of use. Aged tables and benches are arranged around a wonderful fireplace, set off by tasteful windows and curtains. The TV and other intrusions are in a smaller room leading off at the rear leaving conversation in charge here. Don't miss it.

Oh, the beer: The Queen's is a Fuller's house, and you'll find four of their beers, as well as (slightly incongruously maybe) Thai food which comes recommended.

To get back to the station head right, back up Church Street, to the bottom; use the crossing and head up East Street, parallel to and just beyond the pedestrianised High Street. Station Road is then first right; allow twelve minutes from the Queen's Head.

PUB INFORMATION

1 Crown
Ley Hill Common, HP5 1UY
01494 783910
www.thecrownleyhill.co.uk
Opening Hours: 12-midnight

2 Black Cat
Lycrome Road, Lye Green,
HP5 3LF
01494 773966
www.blackcatchesham.co.uk
Opening Hours: 11-2.30, 5-11;
11-11 Sat; 12-10.30 Sun

3 Black Horse
Chesham Vale, Chesham,
HP5 3NS
01494 784656
www.black-horse-inn.co.uk
Opening Hours: 11-3, 5.30-11
(11-11 Sat summer); 12-4, 7-11
(11-11 summer) Sun

4 Queen's Head
120 Church Street, Chesham,
HP5 1JD
01494 778690
Opening Hours: 12-11 (midnight
Thu & Fri); 11-midnight Sat;
11-10.30 Sun

TRY ALSO:

5 Swan
Ley Hill Common, Ley Hill,
HP5 1UT
01494 783075
www.swanleyhill.com
Opening Hours: 12-2, 5.30-11;
12-10.30 Sun

Hertfordshire's Ash Valley & Much Hadham

WALK INFORMATION

Start/Finish: Widford, adjacent to Green Man (optional extension to Wareside)

Access: Trains from London Liverpool St or Tottenham Hale to Bishop's Stortford/St Margarets/Ware then (in all cases) bus 315 to Widford

Distance: main circuit 7.3 miles (11.8 km)

OS map: OS Explorer OL194

Key attractions: Much Hadham village and Forge Museum; Rye Meads Nature Reserve, Stanstead Abbots (4 miles); Bromley Hall garden, Standon (2 miles); Top Events GB, Ware (2 miles)

The pubs: Prince of Wales, Green Tye; Bull, Much Hadham; Green Man, Widford. Try also: Chequers, Wareside

This is one of the most rural parts of Hertfordshire. It's an agricultural landscape, but the attractive Ash Valley has some pretty waterside meadows and woodlands where, in spring, you can enjoy wonderful displays of bluebells. Fairport Convention fans will be familiar with the tiny river Ash, immortalised in their 1971 instrumental 'Bridge over the River Ash'. The album on which it featured, *Angel Delight*, was named after the Angel pub, now gone, in Little Hadham. The pubs that remain offer a contrast in styles, from simple rural beerhouse to smart village pub. Much of Hadham village is full of listed half-timbered buildings, and if you're here at the weekend you could pop into the Old Forge Museum, a few doors down the lane from the Bull. In summer stronger walkers can easily continue down the valley to Wareside where the Chequers offers well-kept beers, and beyond this into Ware itself. Navigation should present few problems, and the terrain is hardly strenuous.

Half timbered houses at Much Hadham

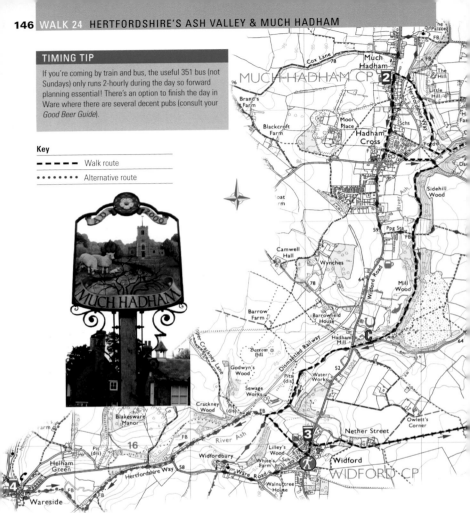

TIMING TIP

If you're coming by train and bus, the useful 351 bus (not Sundays) only runs 2-hourly during the day so forward planning essential! There's an option to finish the day in Ware where there are several decent pubs (consult your *Good Beer Guide*).

Key

- - - - Walk route
.... Alternative route

If you're arriving on the bus alight at the stop in the centre of Widford village by the Green Man, which you have an option to visit later. Like its neighbours it's a pretty village, with a quarter of its buildings listed by the Department of the Environment as having architectural or historic merit. Head north up the street (taking the parallel slip road rather than the main road which heads downhill with no footway) until, opposite the pretty thatched cottage, take the path on the right signed 'Nether Street'. Quickly leave the houses behind and walk downhill to join a byway at a row of pretty cottages. Here simply turn right and it's about a

mile of level, easy walking along what becomes an unmade track, with wide views and big skies. Ignore footpaths and bridleways to both left and right. It's a very quiet area here and, apart from birdsong, you shouldn't hear much noise.

Reach the end of this straight and bear left, joining tarmac again at Turtle Farm and its little duckpond. Beyond Minges Farm (note the unusual sculpture opposite) join another lane and turn right, passing the entrance to St Elizabeth's Centre, into Perry Green. Here, by the green and post box in this tiny hamlet, a signed bridleway continues in the same direction ahead. It promises to be a delectable shady

Half timbered houses at Much Hadham

track with a canopy of trees but, along the latter part of it, the hedges have been grubbed up and you're out in the open again; but the compensation is the all-round view. Follow the track as it swings first left and then right, keeping a pond and a green agricultural shed on your right. The route then heads round to the right again for a few yards to a path junction (A, 445177) – the waymark at the time of survey was lying on its side here – where you bear sharp left to follow the hedge rather than going straight ahead into an enticing tree-lined byway. Keep straight on (Hertfordshire Way) at the next path junction, into another pleasant wooded area but then, almost immediately, leave on the left on a wide, shady little byway, passing an appealing old thatched house, to reach the hamlet of Green Tye in a couple of minutes.

You'll be drawn on by the pub sign for our first stop, the **Prince of Wales** **1**. This little pub, pleasantly sited on a quiet lane, remains a plain unfrilly rural local where the emphasis is firmly upon good beer and traditional values. Fittings are simple, with a quarry tiled floor, dartboard and a couple of open fires, although there's a carpet in the 'lounge' part of the L-shaped bar. Now independent of the Green Tye brewery to

the rear of the pub, the place nonetheless keeps their Union Jack ale as a regular, as well as Wadworth's Henry's IPA and a couple of guests, including Green Tye specials. No-nonsense food is offered at lunchtimes until 2. There are a couple of beer festivals each year, held over May Day weekend and in early September, at which you can enjoy the spacious garden.

On departure, head to the left (west) along the lane for some 300 yards, taking the bridleway on the right signed 'Danebridge Road'. Where this

Nether Lane trackway, near Perry Green

LEFT: **The Prince of Wales, Green Tye** RIGHT: **Sidehill Wood**

bridleway opens into a field in some 250 yards (B, ⊙, 440185) some care is needed to pick the correct route: bear slightly left at first (disregard the footpath leading right) but then bear round to the right, following the edge of the field, keeping the large building in the middle distance ahead of you and slightly to your left. In another hundred yards or so, at a waymark post, you'll spot a series of two more posts striking ninety degrees left across the field. Follow this line, passing underneath the telegraph wires. At the last post the path turns right at ninety degrees again to lead you into the wooded valley ahead. This is a beautiful stretch in the right conditions, with bluebells in spring and rich colours in autumn. Cross a stile and, before reaching the pantiled house ahead, swing right to cross the tiny stream, often dry, and join the quiet lane. Turn left and follow it round to the right, over the ford at the junction. Some 150 yards ahead turn right again onto the signed Hertfordshire Way. Go through a paddock and pass through a kissing gate, keeping on the well-worn path which stays on the flood plain (don't climb up the brae ahead) and joins the minor lane just a few yards from Much Hadham's main street. If you wish to visit the parish church it's a short way up

**Wayside 'busker'
at Perry Green**

the lane to the right; otherwise turn left to walk up the few yards to the village street, and emerge just a few yards south of the **Bull** ②.

In a street of wonderful half-timbered buildings the Bull's heavily altered exterior is hardly striking, although it's plain to see that it's an old building. Inside it's far more impressive, with the modernisation having taken account of the character of the place: there are plenty of old beams, and suitably uneven walls. Each side of the open fire there are some attractive seating areas, with further nooks and crannies elsewhere; whilst if you fancy being more formal there's a dining area at the right-hand end. Matchboard has been retained in some parts of the pub including the attractively plain bar counter. Expect a minimum of two, usually more, beers from the Punch Taverns guest list: this included Black Sheep Bitter and Brakspear Bitter on my visit. The Bull is a good place to eat if you haven't brought a picnic: there's a wide menu.

A few yards south, continuing along the main street having turned right on leaving the Bull, is the Forge Museum housed in an interesting collection of buildings; but opening hours are restricted to Fridays to Sundays.

It's about half a mile further along the main street, past some handsome almshouses, to the southern end of the long village, Hadham Cross. If you're in the mood for another pint before leaving the village you could try the *Old Crown*, where there should be up to four ales including Greene King IPA and guests, but frankly the Bull has a good deal more character. By the congregational church, with the pub sign of the Old Crown in view beyond, take the footpath down the alley to reach Malting Lane, facing the riverside meadows, in 200 yards. Emerging on Malting Lane there's another signed path through the railings a few yards to your right: head through here and across the meadows to reach another narrow lane on a bend. Starting to climb the road for thirty yards before taking another track: a bridleway (Hertfordshire Way) signed 'Bourne Lane'. This leads very pleasantly through Sidehill Wood, a valley-side hanger which, in spring, is carpeted with the lilac of thousands of bluebells. This open mixed wood is a lovely place at any time of year though, with views between the trees across the valley back to the village — one of the highlights of the walk.

Keep straight head at the junction of paths, with more of the same before emerging onto the waterside meadows and merging with Bourne Lane itself at C (425169).

Walk right, down to the main B1004 road again, and cross straight over on the Hertfordshire Way into a more open landscape, with the spire of Widford church ahead of you. It's now a simple stroll along the track, past the water works, sharing their concrete trackway for a stretch to a junction of paths; here carry straight ahead on the riverside path for another 250 yards to the next path junction and ascend the riverside bluff on your left, which rises into Widford, crossing a residential street just before emerging in the village back at the **Green Man** 3. At one time there were five public houses in Widford. Now this is the only one and even this was threatened with closure a few years ago, but successfully retained following a campaign by the local community. The double-fronted building has been knocked around inside and won't get you very excited architecturally but it feels like a village local and offers a couple of decent ales

The Ash Valley at Much Hadham

LEFT: **Pub sign at the Prince of Wales, Green Tye** RIGHT: **Green Man, Widford**

including Adnams, and often one from Green Tye. There were some internal alterations taking place when I visited and the kitchen was closed; so to be safe, phone ahead for food times if you are hoping to eat here: the popular fish and chip night will be retained, I'm sure.

Depending upon your timings and your energy/enthusiasm levels, you might be happy to finish here and return to the bus stop or your car. When the evenings are long, the two mile walk to the Chequers, further down the valley at Wareside is a pleasant one; the pub re-opens at 6. Briefly, the directions are: retrace your steps to the riverside path in the valley. Head straight down to and cross the little footbridge over the Ash close to the path junction, and then simply follow the clear path to join the road in a little under half a mile. On the way, you can't fail to be impressed by the Grade II*-listed 13th century Church of St John the Baptist as you pass under it; it's an eye-catching building which sits on a bluff with a commanding view over the valley. Walk in the same direction along the road for a couple of minutes (take care as there's no footpath here, surprisingly seeing as it's still the Hertfordshire Way) until the path departs the road again at the corner ahead, on the other side of the road. Now the bridleway keeps close to the old railway trackbed for another 750 yards; look out for

the signed footpath leading off ninety degrees to the right and, taking this, cross the river for the last time towards the cottages ahead at the fringe of the hamlet of Wareside. When you reach the road, the **Chequers 4** is a short walk further down, on the bend. It's a traditional roadside building with three distinct bar areas and a restaurant, the latter with a good reputation for home-cooked food including vegetarian options. Expect a couple of changing guests, often with a local emphasis, alongside Adnams Bitter and Taylor Landlord on the beer front.

From here, it's a further two miles' walk into Ware, which hardened walkers might attempt armed with their own map; for lesser mortals who are without their own transport, I suggest phoning for a cab to take you into Ware (there's no public transport to speak of in Wareside) where, ale-wise, the best bet is probably the *Crooked Billet* on Musley Hill (and it is a hill), north of the centre.

PUB INFORMATION

1 Prince of Wales
Green Tye, SG10 6JP
01279 842517
www.thepow.co.uk
Opening Hours: 12-3 (3.15 Wed),
5.30-11 (1am Fri & Sat); 11.15-
10.30 Sun

2 Bull
High Street, Much Hadham,
SG10 6BU
01279 842668
Opening Hours: 12-3, 6-11
(7-10.30 Sun)

3 Green Man
High Street, Widford, SG12 8SR
01279 843119
Opening Hours: 12-11

TRY ALSO:

4 Chequers
Ware Road, Wareside, SG12 7QY
01920 467010
Opening Hours: 12-3 (3.15
Wed), 6-11; 12-4, 6-10.30 Sun

Wildhill

WALK INFORMATION

Start/Finish: Little Berkhamsted, St Andrew's church

Access: Trains from London Moorgate/Finsbury Park to Bayford, then walk or taxi

Distance: Circuit from and to Little Berkhamsted 6.4 miles (10.3km)

OS map: OS Explorer OL182

Key attractions: Mill Green Museum & Mill (3 miles); Hatfield House (5 miles); Welwyn Garden City (5 miles)

The pubs: Candlestick, Essendon; Woodman, Wildhill. Try also: Baker Arms, Bayford

Where Hertfordshire hasn't been covered in urban sprawl, the countryside is usually very attractive. This walk traces a circuit in a pocket of pleasantly undulating and relatively rural landscape between two railway lines. Expect a mix of open views and shady woodland paths. The star of the show is the award winning Woodman pub, which has won the local CAMRA Pub of the Year award no less than seven times. Coming by rail will add two miles (in each direction) to the walk from Little Berkhamsted, so booking a cab ahead may be a good option. Another possibility is to make it a linear walk and book a cab from the Woodman. The walk is not strenuous and the navigation is pretty straightforward.

Start at the church of St Andrew in Little Berkhamsted (nowhere near its larger twin in the north west of the county). If you're walking up from Bayford station, see the box below.

From the church walk down the lane, away from the war memorial, past the village shop. Opposite the *Five Horseshoes* pub a signed footpath to 'Danes and Epping Green' leads across the edge of the cricket pitch. Go through the gate and turn right onto the track which joins a lane in just thirty yards. Here, bear left a short distance (there's no footpath) before leaving the lane in 100 yards at a lodge, Terra Cottage, where the right of way, here part of the Hertfordshire Way, follows the driveway up through an open landscape with wide views. The distinctive red brick building across on

The Woodman nestles in the small hamlet of Wildhill

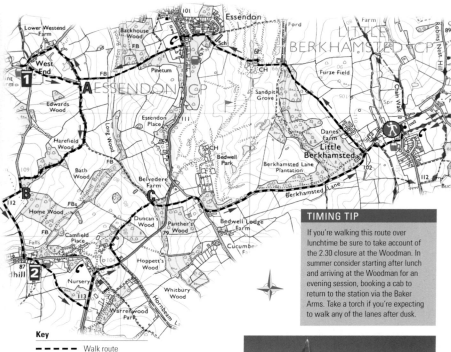

Key

- – – – Walk route
- • • • • • • Optional link route

TIMING TIP

If you're walking this route over lunchtime be sure to take account of the 2.30 closure at the Woodman. In summer consider starting after lunch and arriving at the Woodman for an evening session, booking a cab to return to the station via the Baker Arms. Take a torch if you're expecting to walk any of the lanes after dusk.

the left is Bedwell Park. This listed Victorian 'Gothic Revival' mansion, formerly a golf clubhouse, is set in twelve acres of landscaped gardens, the rump of an ancient 300 acre park. Much of the park is now occupied by two golf courses used by the club, and which you'll encounter shortly.

The path drops down into woodland and bears left; at a path junction in the valley bottom continue straight ahead, climbing up through the fairways of one of the golf courses. Reaching the club buildings obey the blue waymarks which lead you around the right-hand side of them, passing a couple of ponds and climbing uphill. Join a wider track towards the top of the rise, emerging on a lane by a modern house (bridleway sign). Here bear left, passing the Essendon village hall and join a busier B road. Turn left, walking down to the *Rose & Crown* pub but, before you reach it, take the signed path to the right along the edge of another cricket square. Views are wide here: an extensive view to the north-west opens out as you leave the sports field and start heading downhill through

Little Berkhamsted church

some lovely woodland, on what is one of the nicest stretches of this walk; in autumn sunshine the colours are particularly appealing.

At the foot of the hill cross the stream and head uphill to join a wide unsurfaced byway at A (⊙ 267083). Reference to the map here shows that the waymarks just a few yards to your left mark the later continuation of the track to Wildhill but,

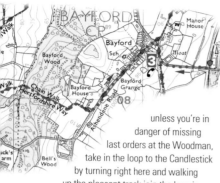

Venerable old trees near Little Berkhamsted

unless you're in danger of missing last orders at the Woodman, take in the loop to the Candlestick by turning right here and walking up the pleasant track join the lane in Essendon West End in about five minutes. Turn left here along the lane, soon reaching, in splendid isolation at the road junction, the **Candlestick 1**. Clearly a modern and extended version of an older building, it still has a bit of internal character and retains a separate public bar, although sometimes this is occupied by a large dining table; but they have to make a living and as you might expect in this rural spot, the pub, which is now leased by the folks at the Woodman majors on food, for which it's building a good reputation. Nonetheless the beer is in good form too: expect a choice of three, with Greene King IPA often joined by another from the GK stable, and a (frequently local) guest. The benches on the green are well used in summer.

Why the 'Candlestick'? Formerly known as the Chequers, its colloquial name derived from the days before electricity when the older pub was lit by a single candle and plunged into darkness whenever the landlord took the candle to the cellar to fetch the beer! The nickname stuck and was adopted as the pub's new "official" name in 1966.

Leaving the pub you can simply walk left down the lane and rejoin the route at B below, but a more pleasant option is to turn sharp right and take the signed path running along the garden and northern side of the pub downhill pleasantly to reach point A once again on the byway. This time turn right and follow the tree-lined route south, crossing a valley and, in a few minutes, at a junction of routes keep ahead on the byway (red waymark) which veers gently to the right, entering Harefield Wood and offering a very pleasant saunter to work up a renewed thirst. In no time you'll rejoin the lane which leads directly down from the

Candlestick (B, 263074). Follow this to the left and simply walk downhill, enjoying the views southwards; although there's no pavement this shouldn't prove a problem since it's a very quiet lane. At the road junction you're in the little hamlet of Wildhill: turn to your left and at the foot of the slope sits the **Woodman 2**. This is, for the ale drinker, a place of superlatives, being a very regular winner of the local CAMRA branch Pub of the Year award. The fact that on my visit, a mid-week lunchtime in autumn, it was packed despite

---

WALKING FROM BAYFORD STATION TO LITTLE BERKHAMSTED

Exiting from the station onto the lane, turn back over the rail bridge and walk up the lane to Bayford village at the top of the rise, taking care since there's no footway. Swing left around the Baker Arms but save the pub for later. The main street of the village running south of the pub has a couple of pretty old cottages but overall it's rather suburban. It's about a ten minutes walk up the road; just beyond the 30 mph signs and Bayford House you'll see a signed path leading off right. Walk up here on an easy-to-follow route along the field edges and into a pleasant area of woodland, crossing a small stream and then re-ascending and emerging from the trees with a view of a curious looking folly up ahead. This is Stratton's Tower, a 150' tall observation tower which was built in 1789 for Admiral John Stratton who lived nearby; according to folklore he had it built to see ships in the Thames, but a more likely explanation is simply to assist his stargazing. It's now a residential property and listed at Grade II*. The path soon reaches a quiet lane at the edge of the village and crosses it, continuing some fifteen yards to the right, leading you through a field and, in just a couple of minutes, to the church of St Andrew.

The Woodman is proud winner of the local CAMRA 2011 Pub of the Year award

being somewhat geographically challenged speaks volumes for the popularity of the place. The main room, which stretches across the width of the pub has several seating areas but it's primarily for socialising over the excellent range of real ales on offer, so expect the hum of convivial conversation rather than the clatter of knives and forks: food plays a strong supporting role at lunchtimes, but no more than that. This is primarily an old-fashioned rural local where the drink comes first. As for the beer, expect a choice of six ales with Green King's IPA and Abbot Ale joined by four changing guests. In summer the spacious garden is a popular retreat, as is the small forecourt.

As suggested earlier, it's an attractive proposition to have booked ahead for a cab to fetch you from the Woodman, since the return walk involves a fair bit of (albeit lightly trafficked) road walking. Ideally you should ask the cab to drop you at the Baker Arms (see below) since from here it's little more than five minutes back to Bayford station.

If you do decide to walk back to Little Berkhamsted or beyond, the path leaves alongside the far end of the pub into the car park, and left through a kissing gate before you reach the bottle banks. Follow the path diagonally uphill through another kissing gate and around a woodland area to join the Kentish Lane, which is rather fast, but there's a verge on the opposite side which you should use to walk up to the left towards the road junction and the entrance gates to Camfield Place, the country estate of the late Barbara Cartland. It's probably safer now to cross the road (very carefully near this bend!) and, bearing right, walk along the verge on the left hand side of Kentish Lane for a further 200 yards before taking a track on the left opposite Hornbeam Lane, signposted 'Hertfordshire

Way'. It bears right after about 100 yards and runs through Duncan's Wood, and out into a field. Reach a cross path at C (272072) where the Hertfordshire Way heads left, and ahead is a small track down to a bridge over Essendon Brook, a pretty spot; but we want the right hand option, where the path climbs slightly before dropping down to another footbridge across the river. Cross this and climb some wooden steps cut into the bank and then a further set of steps leading to the road again. Cross with care and continue on the footpath on the opposite side, signposted 'Berkhamsted Lane'. Walk through here until the path reaches quaintly named Cucumber Lane by a bungalow, and bear left along the roadside margin path until it disgorges you opposite Berkhamsted Lane. Cross and proceed along Berkhamsted Lane: unfortunately, this last part of the walk involves the best part of a mile of road walking. Nonetheless it's usually quiet, and the views are pleasant. Once you encounter the 30 mph and welcome signs at outskirts of Little Berkhamsted, simply retrace your steps into Little Berkhamsted (right in about 100 yards on the path, then left through the gate and across the field to the *Five Horseshoes*). If you're going the whole hog and walking back to Bayford station, simply reverse the route outlined in the box, map in hand. This will enable you to drop in en route at the **Baker Arms 3** in Bayford. This is a smart McMullen's pub in handsome brickwork, which retains an unfussy public bar with floorboards, benches and wooden dado around the wall. In summer you may prefer the spacious garden. There are three beers from McMullen's range available. If you want to eat here before your train, the separate restaurant is open for business well into the evening each day except Sunday: check the website for times.

PUB INFORMATION

1 Candlestick
West End Lane, Essendon,
AL9 6BA
01707 261322
www.thecandlestickpub.co.uk
Opening Hours: 12-11 (8 Sun); closed Mon

2 Woodman
45 Wildhill Road, Wildhill,
AL9 6EA
01707 642618
Opening Hours: 11.30-2.30, 5.30-11; 12-2.30, 7-10.30 Sun

TRY ALSO:

3 Baker Arms
Ashendene Road, Bayford,
SG13 8PX
01992 511235
www.bakerarmsbayford.co.uk
Opening Hours: 12 (3 Mon)-11; 12-6 Sun

St Albans town trail

WALK INFORMATION

Start/Finish: St Albans City station

Access: Trains from London St Pancras/Farringdon/London Bridge/Blackfriars

Distance: 3.7 miles (6km)

OS map: OS Explorer OL136

Key attractions: Historic Roman town with cathedral, museums and Roman theatre; Gorhambury House (2 miles)

The pubs: Mermaid; Blacksmiths Arms; Boot; Six Bells; White Lion; White Hart Tap. Try also: Lower Red Lion; Portland Inn; Ye Olde Fighting Cocks; Goat; Garibaldi; Farmers Boy, all St Albans

An obvious choice for a guide like this, St Albans combines cultural attractions with arguably the best range of drinking options in the South East outside central London. What's more, it's less than half an hour by train from the capital. Unless you already know the place well, allow plenty of time for cultural diversions: the cathedral is a must-see, and for those interested in Roman history, the Verulamium museum, and the nearby remains of the Roman theatre and city walls, is essential visiting. Choosing the best pubs for the discerning drinker is not easy: the standard is high and the real ale scene is changing quickly. What follows, unusually, is half a dozen pubs on the 'main' circuit with quite a few 'try also' suggestions for those who want to go the whole hog.

🚶 Arriving at St Albans City station, head up onto Victoria Street (there's an exit on Platform 4 which takes you directly out to the road junction by the *Horn*). If it's before midday,

your best plan is to head straight up into the town centre for some early cultural touring or to catch early breakfast at the Blacksmiths, taking in the Mermaid later on (consult your map). Otherwise

The venerable Ye Olde Fighting Cocks

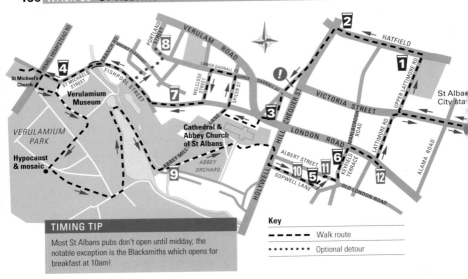

Key

━ ━ ━ ━ ━ Walk route

•••••••• Optional detour

walk up to the next junction, with Lattimore Road, and turn right, walking up past the walled grounds of Loreto School to meet Hatfield Road. Turn left here and the first pub stop is visible almost immediately. The **Mermaid 1** is a single bar traditional pub with a 'local' feel to it being just outside the town centre, and is well worth a visit on account of its wide range of well-kept beers: expect around seven real ales and at least one draught cider. Tring and Oakham are well represented, but there should be an interesting guest or two for the beer ticker here as well. Tastefully furnished and with a sensible wooden floor, there's a range of comfortable seating around the L-shaped bar.

Head left up Hatfield Road into town, past the handsome Marlborough Buildings, the town's principal almshouses and, opposite, the Museum of St Albans, worth a visit and host to interesting special exhibitions as well as the permanent galleries. At the top of the hill by the junction is the **Blacksmiths Arms 2**. This large mock-Tudor pub has been transformed from previous incarnations and currently offers the widest choice of real ales in St Albans. A range of seating areas at different levels is arranged around the L-shaped bar servery and the décor is tasteful. There's also a large patio/garden to the rear of the pub which hosts occasional beer festivals but, frankly, with this choice of beer the place is pretty much a permanent beer festival as it is: there are ten handpumps dispensing all sorts of tempting and well-kept ales, including local brews from the likes of Red Squirrel and Buntingford. The Blacksmiths opens early for breakfast and food service continues throughout the day.

Head across the road and turn left by the *Cock* into St Peter's Street, the main shopping axis of St Albans. Walk down towards the market place at the southern end of the street and fork right past the

St Albans' medieval clock tower overlooks the Boot

St Albans Cathedral

entrance to the tourist office located in the Georgian town hall. There's your first glimpse of the cathedral rearing up over the rooftops of the old buildings clustered around the town hall and the surrounding streets. You'll soon reach the medieval clock tower, close to the site of the now-gone Eleanor Cross, one of a dozen which King Edward I had erected in memory of his wife Eleanor of Castile, marking the nightly resting-places of her body en route to burial in London. The clock tower, which acted as a semaphore station during the Napoleonic war, was restored by Sir Gilbert Scott in 1864.

Right opposite the clock tower is pub number three: the **Boot** 3 . As you'd expect from a pub in this location it is a bustling building with a rambling interior and lots of history. Despite modernisation it's still easy to get a sense of the age of the building here, with its low ceilings and exposed beams.

Once again you're spoilt for choice as regards the beer range, with five regulars including Tring's tasty Side Pocket for a Toad and up to three guests. It can get busy at times but as you can see into the bar easily you can make a decision about entry very quickly on that score; there are plenty of other options if you don't fancy the crowds...

Leaving the Boot, cross the road to the left at the lights and duck straight down the covered alley towards the cathedral. Turn right through the graveyard along a path which brings you right to

the front of the cathedral. This is an obvious point at which to visit if you so wish (although we pass close by later on, too).

Displaying work from a wide variety of periods like almost all English cathedrals, it's as an example of Norman architecture that the Cathedral and Abbey Church of St Alban is best known. Paul Johnson in his *British Cathedrals* regards it as the best introduction to the Norman version of Romanesque, showing the style 'at its most elemental'. The late Sir Alec Clifton Taylor, our greatest scholar of buildings, called it a building of 'austere majesty', but, never one to excuse poor work, was scathing about the Victorian restoration including the insertion of a 'deplorable window' in the north transept! Judge for yourselves, and check the official guide and the website for more information.

Whether you pop into the cathedral or not, the walking route exits onto Romeland by the entrance to St Albans School. Turn right onto Romeland and cross into Spicer Street, and left into Lower Dagnall Street to pass the *Farriers Arms*, with its plaque outside showing it was the venue for the first branch meeting of the first constituted local branch of the Campaign For Real Ale, South Hertfordshire, in 1972. It's still in business today serving ales from the local McMullens brewery.

Turn left at the next corner by the *Verulam Arms*, and then right to join Fishpool Street. This is one of the most attractive streets in town, with some nice old houses lining the street as we head downhill towards the river floodplain. There are a couple of opportunities for optional extra pub stops before we get to the river and our next 'main' visit: around the curve in the street is the **Lower Red Lion** 7 , an attractive old inn dating back to the seventeenth century. Expect a wide range of ales including three regulars (Oakham JHB, Sharp's Doom Bar and Brains Rev James) and up to three guests. Beyond the Lower Red, look for a narrow path on the right about 50 yards before reaching the St Michaels Manor Hotel, with its hanging sign. Take the steps, and walk right to the top, reaching a road where you turn left and first right to find the **Portland Arms** 8 . This is a Fuller's house with a good range of their beers including Chiswick Bitter. There's a homely little room off to the right with an open fire and an old matchboard ceiling. Food here comes recommended.

LEFT: **Lower Red Lion** RIGHT: **Distinctive architecture on Fishpool Street**

Back on Fishpool Street pass the *Black Lion* and *Blue Anchor* on opposite sides of the street and, ahead, the Kingsbury Watermill, which has been largely subsumed in a popular eatery, the Waffle House. The mill still operates, however. Ahead, yet another pub, the *Rose & Crown*, with several ales on cask, and a vine on the frontage of the building. Just a step beyond is the next official watering hole, the **Six Bells 4**. Another characterful old building with genuinely old timbers set into the painted brickwork, it is the only pub in town within the boundary of the old Roman city walls; not unconnected with this, the pub featured on the *Pub Dig* series on TV's History Channel. The main bar room has a parquet wood and quarry tile floor and, at one end, an enormous open fire. It's a regular in the *Good Beer Guide*, so expect the ales to be on good form. There are three staple beers including Oakham JHB, and a couple of guests – check the website for the current offerings. As with many pubs in town you can eat well here if you're ready to.

Leaving the Six Bells, head towards the next corner by St Michael's church, where accompanied by a heritage signpost the main walk route leads off to the left and round into Verulamium Park. However, a short detour to the impressive walled remains of the Roman theatre is strongly recommended. Reach the main road and cross carefully – the road is fast and busy (there's a controlled crossing to the left). The remains are in a compound just beyond the kiosk on the path to Gorhambury opposite. There's a small admission charge to view the ruins, which by Roman remains standards are really rather impressive. Leave the theatre by the way you came and cross back over the main road. Bearing right, head through some wooden gates into St Michael's churchyard.

St Michael's lies among the foundations of the old basilica (law-court) of Roman Verulamium, where Alban was condemned to die. The church was built to receive pilgrims and prepare them for their visit to his shrine within the cathedral. It contains a monument to the church's most famous parishioner, Francis Bacon (1561–1626). Exiting the churchyard at the far side, bear right to reach the entrance of Verulamium Museum, depicting everyday life in Roman Britain. Among other worthwhile exhibits it contains a number of recreated Roman rooms and some Roman mosaics and wall plasters.

Beyond the museum keep left and enter Verulamium Park, bought by the City of St Albans in 1929. On your right is *Inn on the Park* – not an inn in our sense, but a café – albeit one offering a limited selection of bottled beers including local Tring and Saffron brews. Take the gravel path from the far side of the café, past a playground and up to a low, modernist concrete building which houses an 1,800-year old Roman hypocaust and mosaic floor uncovered during excavations in the 1930s.

Taking in the fine views across the expansive park, walk straight across the front of the building and head through a gap in a row of trees. Continue diagonally downhill across some sports fields, with the cathedral sitting imposingly to your left, to meet the end of a hedge line at the far corner. A blue signpost indicates the ruins of part of the Roman town wall and an old gatehouse to your right. Turn left at the signpost, down towards the lake, forking left after a few yards where the path divides. There is a wealth of aquatic bird life on and around the lake and in the warmer months the RSPB staff an information point with telescopes. Head left around the lakeside then across the stone bridge and back along the far side where the path runs between the lake and the river Ver.

At the end of the lake, cross the bridge to your left to reach **Ye Olde Fighting Cocks** 9. It's an attractive and unusually-shaped building with plenty of antiquity and well worth a visit on those grounds. Pubs like this one, claiming to be the oldest in the country, are of course numerous, and Geoff Brandwood and Andrew Davison in their authoritative work *Licensed to Sell* devote a chapter to some of the more outlandish hyperbole on this subject. In this case, claims of 'dating back to the 8th century' can be safely dismissed as ridiculous; the first recorded licensee dates to 1822, although there may have been a monastic brewhouse here before that time. Be all that as it may, many noteworthy features survive, such as low ceilings, various nooks and crannies and a bread oven next to one of the fireplaces. In the 21st century however, this place caters mainly to the tourist trade. Beer tourists like us are reasonably well catered for too with Greene King Abbot Ale, Harveys Sussex Best and Taylor Landlord joined by two or three guests.

Leaving the pub, head uphill through the cathedral grounds to the southern side of the cathedral, before taking a cobbled lane to the right (at the eastern end) down to busy Holywell Hill. Turn right and cross the road towards the art deco *Café Rouge*. This glasshouse and the adjacent Comfort Hotel are notable as the former headquarters of seed merchant, local mayor and Ryder Cup founder, Samuel Ryder (1858–1936). The city's Verulam Golf Club is home to the tournament.

Take the second road on your left which is Sopwell Lane, leading into the district of the same name. This lane was, improbably, part of an old coaching route from London. For the pub goer this area is the best in the city for back-street pubs, which have survived in some numbers here. What's more, most of them are good. First up, and worth a try, is the **Goat** 10, an old coaching inn of genuine antiquity which still has its carriage archway at the right-hand end of the building. Inside, St Austell Tribute is available along with a couple from the Wells/Young's empire. Literally a stone's throw further down is the **White Lion** 5, another cosy old pub which is hard to pass by. It retains two separate main rooms in the homely interior, which still have a real feel of age and long use. It's a pub which takes its beer seriously as evidenced by a separate entry for beer on its website, the best place to check the latest brews. Expect eight ales (and a cider) including Tring's Side Pocket and St Austell Tribute, with a discount for CAMRA members (which you'll also find at the Goat and at the next pub).

If you leave the pub via the secluded garden to the rear, you will exit right opposite the next pub on this punishing itinerary, the **Garibaldi** 11. This traditional brick-built Fuller's house offers up to seven ales from the brewery's range in what is now a single room wrapped around the central servery. There are no less than three real fires to keep you warm in winter.

The White Harp Tap – a great backstreet boozer

Head left on leaving the pub (right from the White Lion's garden) down Albert Street to the end, and the next pub is just up the hill on the left. This is the **White Hart Tap** 6 in an elegant double-fronted house sitting up on the next corner. The bright, tastefully-modernised interior with floorboards and dado-clad walls around the servery, and a wood-burning stove at one end, is more likely to appeal to a younger clientele than the old traditionalists like me who probably prefer to find a dark corner to sit in, but the beer range is once again very good. There are half a dozen to

choose from, including Taylor Landlord and Sharp's Doom Bar. There's a large garden at the top end which with a bit of planting could be a very pleasant oasis; it's a bit stark at the moment...

Right, almost there… you can safely give the *Beehive* a miss as you climb up beyond the Tap to join the main London Road; but as you turn down the road past the traffic lights, if you still have any energy and capacity remaining, consider a brief stop in the **Farmers Boy** 12 just along on the right. In a handsome former cottage, this is the only brew pub in town, brewing two regulars: Clipper IPA and the darker Farmers Joy. Reviews of the beers are mixed, and there are other beers on show too, but after what you've been through it'd be rude not to try the local stuff. It's quite a small pub, so pray for a seat.

To return to the station, return a few yards to the traffic lights and head up Lattimore Road opposite. Then turn right at the next lights, on Victoria Street, retracing your route to the station.

PUB INFORMATION

1 Mermaid
98 Hatfield Road, St Albans,
AL1 3RL
01727 837758
Opening Hours: 12-11 (midnight Fri & Sat); 12-10.30 Sun

2 Blacksmiths Arms
56 St Peters Street, St Albans,
AL1 3HG
01727 868845
Opening Hours: 10 (11 Mon)-11; 10-12.30am Fri & Sat; 12-10.30 Sun

3 Boot
4 Market Place, St Albans,
AL3 5DG
01727 857533
Opening Hours: 12-midnight (1am Fri & Sat); 12-11.30 Sun

4 Six Bells
16-18 St Michaels Street, St Albans, AL3 4SH
01727 856945
www.the-six-bells.com
Opening Hours: 12-11 (11.30 Fri & Sat); 12-10.30 Sun

5 White Lion
91 Sopwell Lane, St Albans,
AL1 1RN
01727 850540
www.thewhitelionph.co.uk
Opening Hours: 12-11

6 White Hart Tap
4 Keyfield Terrace, St Albans,
AL1 1QJ
01727 860974
www.whitehearttap.co.uk
Opening Hours: 12-11

TRY ALSO:

7 Lower Red Lion
36 Fishpool Street, St Albans,
AL3 4RX
01727 855 669
www.lowerredlion.co.uk
Opening Hours: 12-11 (10.30 Sun)

8 Portland Arms
63 Portland Street, St Albans,
AL3 4RA
01727 370575
www.theportlandarmspub.co.uk
Opening Hours: 11-3, 5.30-11; 11-11 Fri & Sat; 12-10.30 Sun

9 Ye Olde Fighting Cocks
16 Abbey Mill Lane, St Albans,
AL3 4HE
01727 869152
www.yeoldefightingcocks.co.uk
Opening Hours: 11-11.30 (midnight Fri & Sat); 12-11.30 Sun

10 Goat
37 Sopwell Lane, St Albans,
A1 1RN
01727 833934
www.goatinn.co.uk
Opening Hours: 12-11 (11.30 Wed, midnight Fri & Sat)

11 Garibaldi
61 Albert Street, St Albans,
AL1 1RT
01727 894745
Opening Hours: 11-11.30 (midnight Fri & Sat); 12-11.30 Sun

12 Farmers Boy
134 London Road, St Albans,
AL1 1PQ
01727 860535
www.farmersboy.net
Opening Hours: 12-11 Mon & Tue; 12-midnight Wed & Thur; 12-2am Fri & Sat; 12-11

Via the Essex Way to Pleshey

WALK INFORMATION

Start/Finish: Great Waltham war memorial

Access: Frequent trains from London to Chelmsford then bus 42/42a to Great Waltham

Distance: 6.2 miles (10km)

OS map: OS Explorer OL183

Key attractions: Pleshey Castle motte and bailey; Pleshey village; Essex Way long distance path

The pubs: Leather Bottle; White Horse, both Pleshey; Walnut Tree, Broads Green

Rural Essex has plenty to offer even though it is in general far less hilly and less wooded than locations a comparable distance south of London. This particular walk traverses some pleasant if unspectacular agricultural landscapes to the north of Chelmsford, the highlight being the attractive village of Pleshey with its pretty cottages and Norman defensive earthworks, topped by the motte and bailey of its old castle. The first half of the route follows the very well-signed Essex Way. All three pubs on this easy rural saunter have internal features of interest and two feature in CAMRA's Regional Inventory of Historic Pub Interiors. As with most agricultural landscapes, mud is a potential issue so come prepared.

Start at Great Waltham with its substantial church, opposite the *Beehive*. If you wish to buy some snacks, a well-stocked village shop lies a few yards up the side lane beyond the pub. The walk, however, starts down the main road keeping the Beehive on your left; note the pargetting (decorative plasterwork) on some of the houses on the way down the hill. At the foot of the hill, by another bus stop, look for the Essex Way heading off to your left.

Colourful cottages on Pleshey's main street

TIMING TIP

The Leather Bottle opens at 12, so work backwards from that in planning your day.

Follow the path through open meadows towards the white house ahead, crossing the small lane and skirting a small reservoir behind the trees. The way is well signed. Pass a large oak tree at a double bend in the path (few of the trees hereabouts have much antiquity), and keep left of another reservoir, continuing down to the left to join (via a new metal gate) an overgrown but attractive and well-wooded stretch of land close to the line of the tiny Walhambury brook. Emerge onto the lower right hand edge of another field, and follow this line. At the end of the field here the track appears to turn uphill, look for a small wooden footbridge in the trees to your right, crossing the brook (more like a ditch here!) to emerge on the left hand side of much larger field (A, ⊙, 678140). Bear left along the footpath, and then navigation for the final 10-15 minutes into Pleshey is quite straightforward. On reaching the road at the eastern end of the village, walk down the street past some picture-postcard cottages and you'll arrive quickly at the **Leather Bottle** 1 .

Externally it is an inviting brick building fronting directly onto the village street, but with a largish garden to one side. A former Ridley's of Chelmsford house with a fair bit of old breweriana inside, the real star here is the unspoilt public bar: it was once two rooms itself, and has had a wee bit of a makeover in the recent past but still retains lots of character imparted by homely simplicity. Painted wooden panelling lines

LEFT: **Leather Bottle, Pleshey**   RIGHT: **A woodland path along the Essex Way**

Key

— — — — Walk route

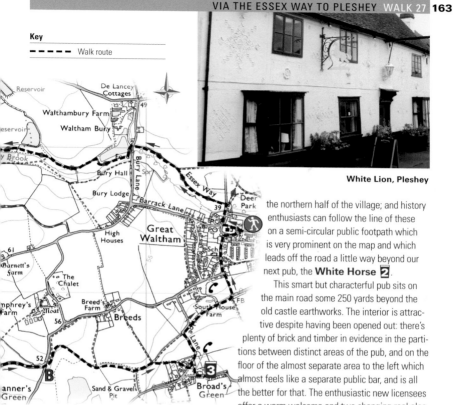

White Lion, Pleshey

the walls and ceilings, and there are some good bench seats. An opening has been made by the bar counter into the once-separate lounge, which has been recently refurbished to appeal to diners. There is food until 3 at lunchtimes (4 at weekends). Beers are Greene King IPA, Woodforde's Wherry, and up to two rotating guests.

Just down the road a few yards from the Leather Bottle is a garden and pond, part of the moat of the old castle which once sat on the prominent flat-topped grassy mound, or motte, in front of you here. Pleshey originated as a Saxon settlement, but the village is now much better known for this Norman motte and bailey castle, built by Geoffrey de Mandeville on land gifted to the family by William the Conqueror. Today nothing remains of the castle apart from the 14th-century brick bridge, believed to be the oldest in Britain. The ditches are still in evidence though, and we'll come across more shortly. The ground plan of the village also shows very clearly the earthworks which encircled

the northern half of the village; and history enthusiasts can follow the line of these on a semi-circular public footpath which is very prominent on the map and which leads off the road a little way beyond our next pub, the **White Horse ②**.

This smart but characterful pub sits on the main road some 250 yards beyond the old castle earthworks. The interior is attractive despite having been opened out: there's plenty of brick and timber in evidence in the partitions between distinct areas of the pub, and on the floor of the almost separate area to the left which almost feels like a separate public bar, and is all the better for that. The enthusiastic new licensees offer a warm welcome and two changing real ales on the pumps, with Mighty Oak's Maldon Gold a popular choice. Food is available at lunchtimes and evenings but, unlike the Leather Bottle, the place shuts during the afternoon.

Retrace your steps a short distance and turn up into Pump Lane on the right. There's a good spot here to view the moat on the left, before making your way diagonally across the cricket green, keeping the church on your right. Make for what looks like a gate in the far corner of the field. On arrival, spot the waymark pointing straight ahead on the concrete track, which is the right of way. Suddenly a wide view opens out to the east (left).

Keep on this bridleway for several minutes until, just as the path starts to rise uphill from the foot of the gentle valley, look for and take a bridleway bearing 90 degrees left. 200 yards further fork right onto a footpath, still a wide track, with a beech hedge on the right and woodland to the left. Cross a minor road and continue, on a well wooded stretch of the wide bridleway, taking

LEFT: **The public bar of the Leather Bottle** RIGHT: **Walnut Tree**

the odd twist and turn, for quite some time, until you arrive at a junction of tracks and a three-way fingerboard. Go left, crossing another bridleway and passing several cottages in succession until, in about half a mile, reach a lane (B, ⊙, 684125). Cross straight over, and bear sharp left to walk parallel to the road for a while in a nice tree-lined cocoon. Now keep your wits about you and look in about 100 yards for a gap in the trees on the right with a rather indistinct path cutting through the tree screen to join a much better path by a reassuring white painted waymark post, only a few yards distant. Merge into this path bearing right to keep to the side of a very large field. There's a reservoir over to your right.

Keeping more or less the same bearing, the route dog-legs slightly (ignore the alternative right of way heading left) and then forks left to lead across a plank bridge almost immediately. Then just 100 yards ahead, a crossroads of paths presents itself with waymarked white posts. Turn right here, keeping close to the wooden fence as we gently climb the hill, and finally through a short tree-fringed section and an alleyway to emerge, satisfyingly, on the village green at Broads Green with the **Walnut Tree** 3, our next stop, right opposite.

A surprisingly large pub for this small village, this place is a rural gem. The front door leads, unusually, into a tiny snug between the two main bars, which may have been the original 'off sales' counter. The lounge to the right is unexceptional, so instead go left into the public bar which is another welcome time-warp, with painted matchboard panelling, parquet flooring and padded bench seats (my favourite!). A screen separates this room from the snug, and there's a small serving hatch to the bar counter. As at the Leather Bottle, old Ridley's brewery posters adorn the walls. Idiosyncratically however there's also a pictogram from Wainwright's famous Lake District guides showing the panorama from Scafell Pike, England's highest mountain. The well-kept beer range is predominantly from the Greene King stable, with a genuine guest. Finally, approving mention must be made of a good example here of that dying breed, the proper outside gents!

It's a short stroll back to Great Waltham: turn right along the little lane fronting the pub and right again, following the road down to the bottom of the hill, where you take the path running right at the corner, along a bank above the lane and along the edge of the field towards a white waymark post some 350 yards away. It's pleasing to see how throughout this walk farmers have left good wide field margins where rights of way cross their land, so one doesn't have to negotiate ploughed or planted ground. If this is the work of the Essex Rights of Way officer(s), then he/she/they should take a bow. Turn right at the waymark on the path up into the village, keeping straight ahead to arrive at the church. The Beehive, bus stop and village shop are all close by.

PUB INFORMATION

1 **Leather Bottle**
The Street, Pleshey, CM3 1HG
01245 237291
Opening Hours: 12-11 (midnight Sat & Sun)

2 **White Horse**
The Street, Pleshey, CM3 1HA
01245 237281
www.whitehorsepleshey.co.uk
Opening Hours: 12-3, 6-11; 12-11 Sat & Sun

3 **Walnut Tree**
Broads Green, CM3 1DT
01245 360222
Opening Hours: 12-11.30 (11 Sun)

Maldon maritime trail

WALK INFORMATION

Start/Finish: All Saints Church, High Street, Maldon

Access: Witham station then bus 90; or Chelmsford station then bus 31/31X

Distance: 5.3 miles (8.5km)

OS map: OS Explorer OL179

Key attractions: Maldon town; Thames sailing barges at The Hythe; Beeleigh Falls; canal and riverside walks; Heybridge Basin

The pubs: Maltsters Arms, Heybridge; Queen's Head; Blue Boar, both Maldon. Try also: Queen Victoria, Heybridge

Maldon is second in antiquity only to Colchester within Essex, and the place still has plenty of interest to offer the visitor. It's also home to two successful micro-breweries, giving you another reason to visit! This interesting circuit takes in not only the old town of Maldon itself but the Chelmer & Blackwater Navigation up to the pretty Beeleigh Falls, as well as the maritime archaeology of the waterfront at The Hythe and Hey-bridge. The walk can easily be extended down to the Blackwater estuary at Heybridge Basin from where there is a limited bus service back to Maldon and Chelmsford. The recommended pubs are well dispersed, and both the walking and the navigation are very straightforward.

Start in the High Street by the war memorial in front of All Saints' Church. Pass the Blue Boar, to which we will return later, along Silver Street, which leads into Beeleigh Road. Walk down along this lane past some old cottages, with views between them across the Blackwater Valley. When the road peters out follow the footpath which is its continuation, which leads,

The jettied Blue Boar has genuine antiquity and character

Key

– – – – – Walk route

in a couple of minutes, steeply down to the busy bypass road. It looks the sort of spot where a footbridge should have been built but the money ran out! Cross the road carefully (there are good sight lines), beyond which the footpath resumes its way pleasantly, passing the site of old Beeleigh Abbey and joining a very quiet lane. Turning right here, the lane leads down towards the complex waterway network at Beeleigh Falls by the Chelmer & Blackwater Navigation.

Just before reaching the waterways, on the right, stands a fine house and some extensive ruins. This is the site of Beeleigh Mill, once owned

by the abbey nearby until the Dissolution in 1536. Sadly the mill was destroyed in a huge fire in 1875 and never rebuilt. Some remains of the water mill building survive along with the adjacent steam mill with the original beam engine and gear, and Elephant boiler. There are plans to capitalise on the heritage and educational potential of the site once a colony of rare bats have been relocated!

The waterway layout around the falls beyond the old mill, approached through a shady and atmospheric path, is quite complex, but the route across is straightforward: cross the first bridge over the Chelmer falls, pausing perhaps to enjoy the scene and, if you have one, open your flask; then follow the path to the right through the woods and marshy vegetation to join the navigation

LEFT: **Alongside the Chelmer & Blackwater Navigation** RIGHT: **The Blue Boar**

towpath by a lock. Turn right and walk down over the weir to Beeleigh Bridge by the confluence with the Blackwater. The Chelmer & Blackwater Navigation is 14 miles long, and was opened in 1797 to enable goods to reach Chelmsford by water from Heybridge Basin. Almost needless to say it was bitterly opposed by Maldon who envisaged a loss of revenue from transhipment. The canal is used primarily for leisure today of course: the scene by Beeleigh Bridge is a remarkably peaceful and rural one.

Almost immediately over the weir bridge, and without crossing the canal, leave the tarred path which now runs alongside the navigation to pick up a path darting into the trees on your right and leading to the 4th tee of the golf course. Now simply follow the permitted path alongside the tidal river at the edge of the golf course. This makes a more interesting walk back into town than the canal cut. Ahead are good views of Maldon itself, sitting above the river on a prominent bluff and, once under the bypass, a view of some of Maldon's maritime buildings, marred somewhat by the large new supermarket. Just as you reach the car park of the latter, leave the riverside on a tarred path running left to cross the Navigation in 100 yards, and turn right on the path alongside. This ducks under the bypass a second time, and leads down alongside some new houses. Here look for the towpath in the vegetated margin on the right – it may run parallel only a few yards away but feels like a different place altogether, and although close to the centre of town it's one of the best stretches of the walk. The waterside vegetation is diverse and habitat value high.

Leave the canal at the road bridge and join Holloway Road, crossing the canal and walking down to the junction with the main road, and continue in the same direction, passing St Andrews church. Cross the road when safe to do so and look for the turning for Hall Road a few yards beyond the *Heybridge Inn*. A short step along here, set in the street of terraced houses, stands the **Maltsters Arms** **1** . The three external doorways of this traditional Gray's house suggest a traditionally

Plain and simple – Maltsters Arms, Heybridge

divided former layout, but once inside you'll find an opened out space with a couple of separate areas. The décor will transport older readers back to the seventies, but of more importance is the reliable ale quality of this *Good Beer Guide* regular. Beers are served by gravity – and are a mix of Greene King and two guests. The rear patio overlooks the Heybridge Creek, the old course of the tidal river prior to the construction of the navigation.

It's possible to walk down to Heybridge Basin, and link up with the pubs on walk 29, by walking further down Hall Road and turning onto the signed path which runs round the Heybridge Hall Lake; but to continue the Maldon route return to the main road and this time turn right, walking the 150 yards or so to the Wave Bridge and the imposing Bentall's Warehouse on the canalside.

Descend to the canal and head inland (west) to rejoin your earlier route at the next bridge, and then retrace your steps to the supermarket car park, re-crossing the canal bridge and walking back across to the River Chelmer.

Now, turn left and follow the river down the short distance to the Fullbridge, the ancient crossing point of the river, with the steep road to the town centre up to the right. Cross the bridge and bear sharp left into Fullbridge Quay (footpath sign) passing the twee little toll house and bearing left into Chandlers Quay through a new estate of quite attractive riverside houses. The footpath disgorges onto another road, running above the river, with a small park on your left. The less said about some of the domestic architectural confections on the right, the better! At the end of this road, bear left down to The Hythe, the old port of Maldon.

Once, The Hythe was separate from but owned by Maldon; hythes and quays being rented to individuals. By the early nineteenth century most of

LEFT: **Public Bar at the Queen's Head**   RIGHT: **Inside the Blue Boar**

Maldon's wealth derived from the quayside here. Today most of that source of wealth has gone but still trading is the Maldon salt works, one of only a tiny handful of English salt makers. The restored Thames sailing barges which are moored up on the quayside are also a familiar sight here. During the 19th century sailing barges, with their distinctive reddish ochre sails, became the most important cargo vessels on the Blackwater and east coast rivers, carrying hay, straw and grain up to London to feed the urban horse population, and returning with manure. Today there are only a couple of dozen fully operating craft remaining, mostly based here at Maldon and available for charter. Meanwhile, on terra firma, the **Queen's Head** 2 is unmissable, enjoying a prime spot right on the quay: the Riverside Bar has great views out across the estuary whilst the public bar, land-side, has a more pubby character, smart but in traditional brick and timber cladding with maritime pictures on the walls. A good range of several ales is available, staples being from Adnams and local brewer Farmer's. You can eat here all day, notably in the Port Hole restaurant adjacent to the Riverside Bar.

Leaving the pub bear right by the *Jolly Sailor* up past the handsome St Mary's church to join Maldon's long High Street by the *Ship & Anchor*. Bear right and walk right along to the far end. On the way you'll pass old St Peter's church, now home to the Maeldune Centre, Maldon's heritage museum, and the Thomas Plume Library. A little way beyond is All Saints' Church, and just across Silver Street here is the **Blue Boar** 3 which you passed by longingly earlier.

The imposing Georgian frontage of the Blue Boar gives this fine old coaching inn a dignified unity but walk through the coaching archway and a jumble of much older buildings is revealed, notably the timber framed range immediately to the left. The building to the right of the arch is still a hotel today although the London 'fly' coach no longer calls. Our interest is in the cosy bar to the left, entered via the coach yard alley. The place oozes character with antlers and other trophies hanging off the walls and old beams. On top of all this the Blue Boar is home to Farmer's Ales which are brewed in the stable yard; so unsurprisingly a good range of their beers is available here, served on gravity from the rear room. Adnams Bitter is a regular guest. As you'd expect there's plenty to eat on offer here too from a tempting menu.

If you're keen to drink elsewhere before heading home, the best bet is the **Queen Victoria** 4, out on the Spital Road. It's a simple walk from the Blue Boar, of about half a mile. It's also on the 31X bus route back to Chelmsford. Once inside, past the splendid summer hanging baskets, expect beers from both local micros Mighty Oak and Farmer's in this Gray's house, along with Greene King, making it well worth the trip if you have time.

PUB INFORMATION

1 Maltsters Arms
Hall Road, Heybridge, CM9 4NJ
01621 853880
Opening Hours: 12-midnight
(1am Fri & Sat; 10.30 Sun)

2 Queen's Head
The Hythe, Maldon, CM9 5HN
01621 854112
www.thequeensheadmaldon.co.uk
Opening Hours: 11-11 (midnight Fri & Sat; 10.30 Sun)

3 Blue Boar
Silver Street, Maldon, CM9 4QE
01621 855888
www.blueboarmaldon.co.uk
Opening Hours: 11-11

TRY ALSO:

4 Queen Victoria
Spital Road, Maldon, CM9 6ED
01621 852923
Opening Hours: 11 (12 Sun)-11

Heybridge Basin & the Blackwater Estuary

The Essex estuaries, including the Blackwater, represent a special and increasingly valued habitat. This walk dovetails with the Maldon walk, leaving Heybridge to strike out along the good shore path, and with the option of returning inland through quiet countryside. The Chequers at Goldhanger is a very worthwhile quarry for this walk, and if you have had enough when you leave the pub there are buses back if you time things correctly. Stephensons' infrequent service 90 from Witham takes you to Heybridge Basin which will shorten the walk. I can confidently sat that this is the lowest pub walk in any of CAMRA's books so far: hardly getting above 20 feet above sea level the whole way round – so if you like beer but don't like climbing hills you've come to the right place.

From St Andrew's church in the centre (such as it is) of Heybridge walk down the main road, away from Maldon, for a couple of minutes to reach the Wave Bridge over the Chelmer & Blackwater Navigation (for information about the canal see walk 28). The impressive warehouse building by the bridge has a connection with Goldhanger, for it was built by William Bentall, a Goldhanger ploughmaker, who transferred his business to Heybridge when the canal arrived.

The Old Ship and the Jolly Sailors compete for your attention

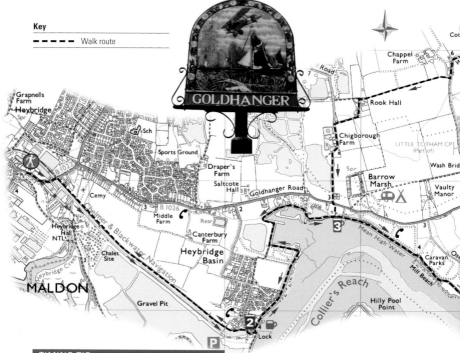

Key
– – – – – Walk route

Join the canal here and head out along the towpath towards the basin. It's a long, straight mile past some old navigation cottages, the cemetery where many salts made their final journey, and the many pleasure boats which line the banks. The mile will pass quickly enough, and you'll arrive at the lock basin with the handsome lock-keepers cottage and the two pubs, the *Ship*, and round the corner, the Jolly Sailor, which I would recommend leaving for later in the day. If you want to stop off already, see the description further down. The shore path continues past the Jolly Sailor, and the navigation instructions for the next three miles or so are pretty simple: follow the coast! The first section twists and turns a bit around some smaller

basins, then heads east. Seawards there may be mud or water, or a bit of both, depending upon the tide. The unremarkable looking land across the channel is Northey Island, now in the hands of the National Trust but, believe it or not, this is the site of one of the few successful invasions of Britain. The Battle of Maldon took place here in 991 AD, making this the oldest recorded battlefield in Britain. The Vikings landed on the island and successfully fought their way against the Anglo-Saxons to the mainland.

After about fifteen minutes' walk the coast path reaches the beer garden of the **Mill Beach 3**. If it's open you may wish to pop in for a break: the place is far from your average real ale emporium, more like a Canvey Island rock n' roll ranch *a la* Dr. Feelgood, but the rambling building is an eclectic and interesting confection. The single beer, Wells IPA was, however, in pretty good form when I sampled the place.

Moving on if the tide is low the salty air will fill your nostrils as you traverse a pretty large and frankly gruesome caravan park; when you finally leave it behind the second of the estuary's islands,

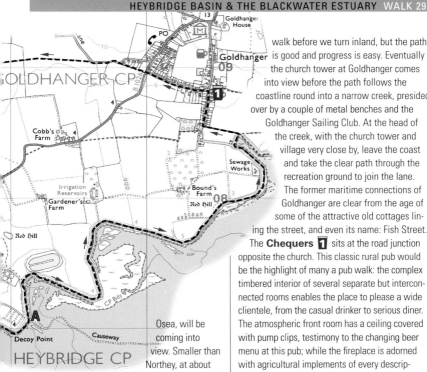

walk before we turn inland, but the path is good and progress is easy. Eventually the church tower at Goldhanger comes into view before the path follows the coastline round into a narrow creek, presided over by a couple of metal benches and the Goldhanger Sailing Club. At the head of the creek, with the church tower and village very close by, leave the coast and take the clear path through the recreation ground to join the lane.

The former maritime connections of Goldhanger are clear from the age of some of the attractive old cottages lining the street, and even its name: Fish Street.

The **Chequers** sits at the road junction opposite the church. This classic rural pub would be the highlight of many a pub walk: the complex timbered interior of several separate but interconnected rooms enables the place to please a wide clientele, from the casual drinker to serious diner. The atmospheric front room has a ceiling covered with pump clips, testimony to the changing beer menu at this pub; while the fireplace is adorned with agricultural implements of every description, set around a stove. Another room has a bar billiards table. Outside, the patio garden catches the sun. The whole place feels comfortable yet tasteful, homely and welcoming: not a place you'll want to leave too soon, especially when you see the beer range. There's a wide choice: expect regulars like Young's and Crouch Vale Brewers Gold alongside several guests, with an emphasis upon local sourcing. If you're here in good time

Osea, will be coming into view. Smaller than Northey, at about 375 acres, it also has more history than one might think, having been a World War I torpedo boat base, a film set, and more recently host to a rehab centre that has had at least one famous visitor. At low tide a causeway runs out to the island from Decoy Point (A, 891070).

Beyond the sea starts to dominate, the estuary opening out more with distant views of the Bradwell Nuclear Power station. It's still a fair

Marshes near Heybridge basin

LEFT: **At Heybridge basin** RIGHT: **Inside the Chequers, Goldhanger**

I recommend choosing from the tempting food menu before considering that 2.40 bus, although the afternoon walk is hardly strenuous with about 10 ft of ascent!

For those hardy souls doing things properly, take the street opposite the pub when leaving and walk down to the far end, crossing the main road by the village sign into a path opposite. This is, in effect, a short cut to a narrow rural lane which we join in no time at all. Join this unfenced lane, with wide views over the agricultural landscape on both sides, for a couple of hundred yards to another footpath sign pointing out over a wide flat prairie. It's probably not a very well-used route but, to his credit, the farmer has left a clear un-ploughed line which is easy to follow and straight. It leads, in about 600 yards, to another lane. This time bear left onto the road and, once again, you'll be lucky to meet any traffic. Pass Chappel Farm on the next bend and, shortly after passing a thatched cottage on the left, look out for a footpath leading off to the right. Take this path towards Rock Hall, the prominent building with a tiled roof visible a few hundred yards away. A newly-created pond on the left just before Rock Hall provides a pit-stop for wildfowl.

At Rock Hall itself the right of way swings round to the left in front of the house, and bends right to join the public road in a minute or so. Turn left, walking past the extensive Chigborough Lakes Nature reserve. This 45 acre reserve has been created from worked-out and flooded gravel pits. Although the lakes are large they are also shallow, offering a wide variety of habitats, including willow carr, marsh and ponds as well as blackthorn and hawthorn scrub. In a few minutes you'll reach the B1026 Goldhanger Road, almost opposite the Mill Beach pub which we passed earlier. Turn left for a few yards, cross the road and make your way back to the shore path. From here, it's simply a question of retracing your steps along the path to the **Jolly Sailor 2**. Open all day from 11, this attractive little pub by the Heybridge Basin still has a traditional layout, with vestiges of the old off-sales counter by the central door, and two rooms leading off: the right-hand a dining room, and the appealing bar room to the left. On the beer menu, expect Adnams Bitter and Broadside; and Mighty Oak's Maldon Gold. Food is available until 8pm, so if you missed out at the Chequers, now is your chance!

For further drinking options, one could either try the *Ship* nearby or, for stronger walkers, take the sea wall path across the canal mouth and around the far side of Heybridge Hall Lake with good views across to Maldon, and join Hall Road to the *Maltsters*. The final alternative is a bus or cab back into Maldon itself. In either of these last two cases refer to the Maldon route (walk 28) for details.

PUB INFORMATION

1 Chequers
The Square, Goldhanger, CM9 8AS
01621 788203
www.thechequersgoldhanger.co.uk
Opening Hours: 11-11; 12-10.30 Sun

2 Jolly Sailor
Basin Road, Heybridge Basin, CM9 4RS
01621 854210
www.thejollysailorheybridge basin.co.uk
Opening Hours: 11-11

TRY ALSO:

3 Mill Beach
Goldhanger Road, Heybridge, CM9 4RA
01621 852650
Opening Hours: 12-midnight Mon; 8am-midnight (1am Fri & Sat, 11 Sun)

Rail-aleing the Braintree branch

WALK INFORMATION

Start: White Notley station

Finish: Cressing station

Access: Trains from London Liverpool Street via Witham

Distance: Main circuit 11.3 miles (18.1km); longer option 14.8 miles (23.8km)

OS map: OS Explorer OL183

Key attractions: Cressing Temple; East Anglian Railway Museum (10 miles)

The pubs: Square & Compasses, Fuller Street; Vine, Black Notley. Try also: St Anne's Castle, Great Leighs

A physically undemanding circuit in pleasant, if unspectacular, landscape with a very rural feel. There are some appealing cottages to look at in the villages. Expect plenty of Essex mud in the fields during wet spells. Navigation, as usual in agricultural land, needs care: signage is good along the Essex Way section, more variable elsewhere. It's quite a long walk with no obvious intervening refreshment opportunities (not even bad pubs!) so don't leave home without a drink and snacks in your rucksack. Car drivers note that the walk starts and ends at different rail stations, but a fairly frequent service will get you back to your car at White Notley station.

Typical old Essex cottage and garden

Alighting from the train at White Notley cross the line and walk down the road to the ford at the foot of the hill. Immediately before the river turn left on the Essex Way, passing some pretty cottages. Follow this along through several fields, once clear of the water company's driveway, before turning right to cross the little River Brain on the concrete footbridge in a few hundred yards. Now, simply walk up the hill through pleasant agricultural landscape, disregarding side paths, to join the road by Forge Cottage, where you turn left. There's no footway, but you're only on this road for about 100 yards before leaving by the bridleway (Essex Way waymark) on the right by Maltings Farm.

The line of the bridleway at first is an old sunken lane, although the first section is rather overgrown and progress may be easier at the field margin instead. Further up though, the lane, named as Pink Lane on the map, is wide, shady and a very attractive way to gain height and keep interest whilst passing through the open landscape to either side. The old route takes a few convulsive twists and turns further ahead, but the way should be clear, until you pass Troys Hall (A, ☉, 776170) where the road surface improves and leads you down to join the public road in a few minutes further.

Turn right, and in 200 yards at the junction, bear left at the hamlet of Fairstead. Scenery here is rural and undulating, with some handsome farm cottages, many now no doubt occupied by commuters and retirees. Look out for the Essex Way post on the left just before the road drops downhill; pass a small, informal cemetery. There are wide views all around. Watch out for the waymarks as once again the right of way turns one way and then the other, crossing a small woodland at one point, and making several ninety degree turns, but with generally good

TIMING TIP

The Vine closes during the afternoon until 6.30, so to complete the circuit without missing a drink needs pre-planning. Consider either a later start at the weekend when the Square & Compass is open all day; or a longer weekday walk with your map, taking in the *Good Beer Guide* listed St Anne's Castle at Great Leighs.

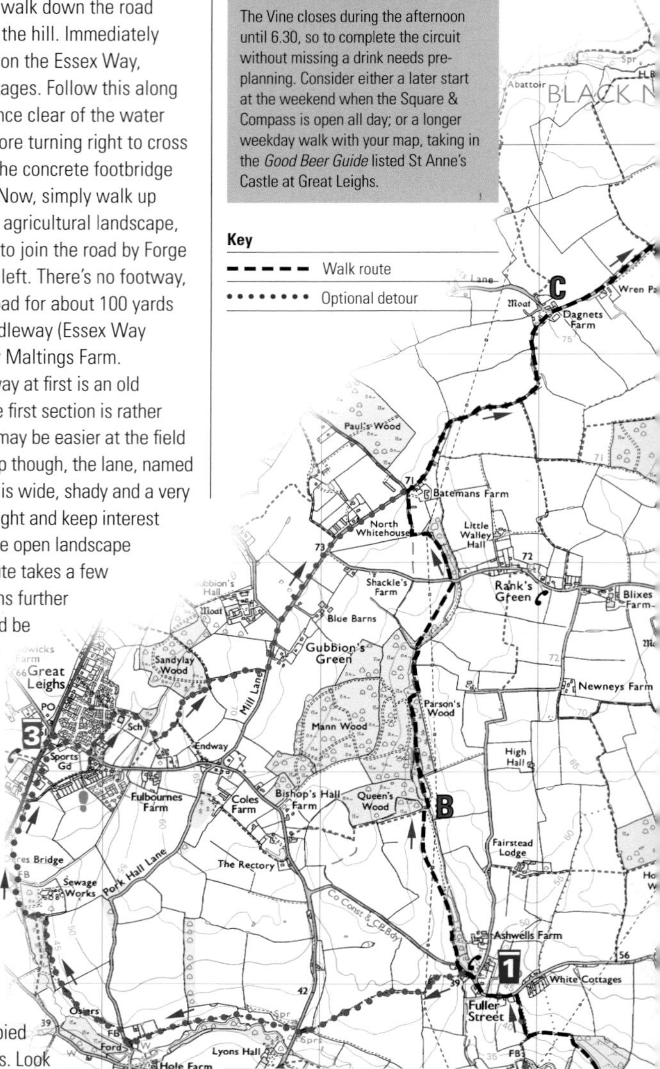

Key

– – – – Walk route

• • • • • • • Optional detour

Terling Mill

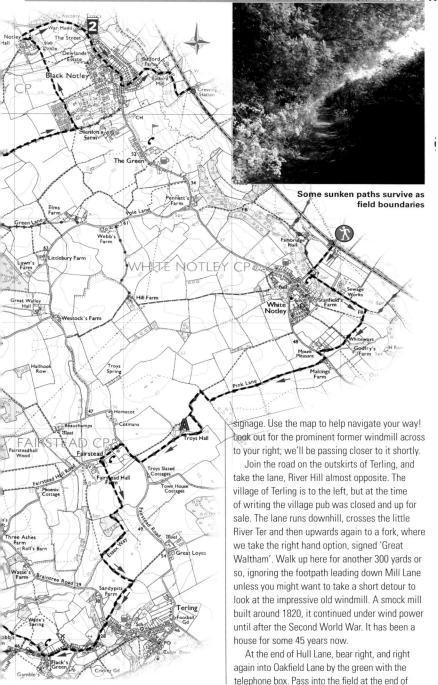

Some sunken paths survive as
field boundaries

signage. Use the map to help navigate your way!
Look out for the prominent former windmill across
to your right; we'll be passing closer to it shortly.

Join the road on the outskirts of Terling, and
take the lane, River Hill almost opposite. The
village of Terling is to the left, but at the time
of writing the village pub was closed and up for
sale. The lane runs downhill, crosses the little
River Ter and then upwards again to a fork, where
we take the right hand option, signed 'Great
Waltham'. Walk up here for another 300 yards or
so, ignoring the footpath leading down Mill Lane
unless you might want to take a short detour to
look at the impressive old windmill. A smock mill
built around 1820, it continued under wind power
until after the Second World War. It has been a
house for some 45 years now.

At the end of Hull Lane, bear right, and right
again into Oakfield Lane by the green with the
telephone box. Pass into the field at the end of

LEFT: **Square & Compass interior** RIGHT: **The remarkable mezzanine drinking area at the Vine**

the lane, keeping to left hand extremity along the waymarked margin. Follow the path over a stile and down to the stream at the bottom of the hill, curving round slightly to the left as you approach the valley foot to follow the line of the stream which you're more likely to hear than see, particularly in summer. Remain on the south side of the stream by the metal gate and stile, continuing into an avenue of tall willows, passing through another small willow plantation and then following the waymark to cross the brook on a metal-sided wooded footbridge. The right of way now strikes across the field to exit at the top right corner by the prominent pylon. If there's a crop growing it may be easier to skirt the field clockwise to reach this point. Moving into the large field where the

pylon stands, turn left along the wide margin underneath the transmission cables, and finally enter the hamlet of Fuller Street by making a right-angled turn at the field boundary and making for the wooden waymark by the white cottage with the pantiled roof ahead.

There's not a great deal in Fuller Street, but given you've been walking for quite a while by now, you're no doubt ready for a drink; so bear left onto the road, again taking care as there are no pavements; and walk down to the road junction where help is at hand in the form of the **Square & Compass** 🔳 . Proudly displaying its local CAMRA best food pub of the year award (at the

The Square & Compass is a rural oasis

time of survey anyway) this rural oasis offers a welcome respite for the weary walker. It's under competent new management having been closed for a couple of years. The three main areas inside vary from smart to very smart, but the nearest thing to a public bar (to the right at the rear) retains character with tasteful renovation of timber features including the ceiling. Old woodworking tools adorn the walls, and there's a wood burning stove in one of the pub's two inglenooks. With food (and wine) very much in evidence, it's good to see that beer hasn't been forgotten either: the house beer is brewed by Nethergate and there are up to three changing guests.

Leaving the pub, return the few yards to the road junction, and turn right. If you're tackling the longer version of this walk and taking in the **St Anne's Castle** **3** at Great Leighs then this is the point at which you'll leave the described trail and continue on the Essex Way which leaves on the left after just a few yards. You'll rejoin the route at Batemans farm (see below) but you'll need your map to navigate. One of many pubs claiming to be the oldest in England, it has a licence going back to the 12th century. Expect a good range of ales, up to three guests alongside regulars Adnams, Woodforde's Wherry and Courage Best.

The 'official' route leaves the road on the right, opposite the Essex Way, and leads straight into the lower margin of a large field with a tiny stream in a ditch by a wooded strip to our right. On the map the next mile or two looks like a breeze, but life is never so simple: at the time of writing the farmer has taken liberties by ploughing very close to the field boundary making progress more difficult than it should be. The direction is clear all the way to the next lane however, broadly northwards, never far from the valley bottom and the electricity transmission cables. At the far end of this large field the path crosses the stream on a small wooden footbridge and enters the woodland shortly afterwards (B, 746168). If you have sunshine, this section is surely one of the highlights of the walk.

Exit the woods briefly via a stile and keep to the left hand field boundary, re-entering soon into the woods and trusting the waymarks to guide you on an indistinct section emerging into the bottom of another field and passing under the power lines again to walk up to a small lane in a few minutes. Almost opposite, slightly left, the path continues, towards another pylon. The stile leading out of this field would be the hardest to spot in the whole book were it not located literally right under the pylon. Even so the entry is very overgrown.

There may be inquisitive horses in the next field, which we cross diagonally to a gate, and then round to the left hand side of the buildings of Batemans Farm and through a small car park to the road. This is the point at which walkers having done the longer option will rejoin the main route.

The parish church of St Peter & St Paul, Black Notley

The Vine is an attractive roadside pub

Look for the public byway sign pointing to the right which appears to lead into the private driveway of the pink house, but keeping left of the house you'll find the byway opening up. It's now a pleasant, easy walk for about 10-15 minutes until you merge (briefly) with a tarred road (C, 🔘 751192) and follow this until it peters out at a house; it's simply a case of following the byway once again for another mile or so. Eventually reach a path crossroads where the left hand option, which we take, points to the parish church, and leads through a new housing estate at the outskirts of Black Notley.

Follow a line through the quite attractive modern development (there are a couple of waymarks along the open strip and mature trees between the houses) and out onto open country again (with distant and not-too-flattering views of Braintree), and traversing a small valley heading towards the church of St Peter & St Paul, with its flint walls and slender wooden spire. Walk through the churchyard, exit to the road beyond the church and follow the churchyard wall around to the right to join the road, which is quite busy but has a footway. Walk down to the junction and head right again (signed 'Witham') and the **Vine** 2 sits on the roadside not very much further.

An attractive building inside and out, dating back to the

16th century, the interior is long and narrow with distinctive diners' and drinkers' ends. In the latter, the star is the surely unique 'minstrels' gallery' style mezzanine where you can watch the proceedings below. It's just large enough for a table and six chairs, a great spot for an evening session! In winter, there are log stoves for comfort, whilst out the back, there's a dinky but pretty little decked patio festooned with flowers for those sunny days. Beers are from Adnams, with one or two guests.

It's an easy fifteen-minute walk back to the railway station at Cressing. Continue along Black Notley's surprisingly dismal main street until you reach Bulford Lane on the left. The road drops steeply, and leaving the houses behind, curves round by the railway line, narrows and passes Bulford Mill, carefully restored and winner of two Environmental Heritage Awards in 1993 and 1995. The station is a few minutes beyond.

PUB INFORMATION

1 Square & Compasses
Fairstead, Fuller Street, CM3 2BB
01245 361477
www.thesquareandcompasses.co.uk
Opening Hours: 11.30-3,
5.30-11.30; 11.30-midnight Sat;
12-11 Sun

2 Vine
Witham Road, Black Notley,
CM77 8LL
01376 324269
Opening Hours: 12-2.30, 6-11;
12-4, 7-11 Sun

TRY ALSO:

3 St Anne's Castle
Main Road, Great Leighs,
CM3 1NE
01245 361253
www.stannnescastle.co.uk
Opening Hours: 12-midnight
(1am Fri & Sat)

Transport links

All of the walks can be accessed using public transport. The majority start and end at train stations, and timetable information can be found at **www.nationalrail.co.uk**, or by calling 08457 48 49 50. Where the walks involve a bus journey at the start or finish, local bus information can be found at Traveline **traveline.info** or by calling 0871 200 22 33.

In addition, links to local bus timetable information are detailed below.

Walk 4
Bus 6/6A Paddock Wood–Matfield
www.travelinesoutheast.org.uk
Bus 297 Tumbridge Wells–Matfield
www.arrivabus.co.uk

Walk 6
Bus 594/5 Oxted–Westerham
www.busmap.co.uk/tt4/595.pdf

Walk 12
Bus 54 Chichester–Matfield (no Sunday service)
www.countryliner-coaches.co.uk

Walk 14
Bus 91/2 Petersfield–Trotton (Mon-Sat)
www.countryliner-coaches.co.uk/timetables.asp
Bus 91 Petersfield–Trotton (Sun)
www.stagecoachbus.com\

Walk 16
Bus 465 Dorking–Leatherhead via Mickleham
www.londonbusroutes.net/times/465.htm

Walk 20
But 78 Maidenhead (Frascati Way)–Boulters Lock
www.courtneybuses.com/services.asp

Walk 21
Bus 300 High Wycombe–Aylesbury via the Wheel; see the CAMRA guide at
www.swansupping.org.uk

Walk 24
Bus 315 Bishop's Stortford/St.Margarets/Ware–Widford www.intalink.org.uk

Walk 25
Taxis from Bayford www.hertford-taxis.co.uk

Walk 27
Bus 42/42a Chelmsford–Great Waltham
www.firstgroup.com

Walk 29
Bus 90 Witham–Heybridge
www.stephensonsofessex.com
Bus 73/75 Chelmsford

Places index

Pubs index

HARVEYS
The Sussex Brewers

HARVEYS BREWERY, known locally as 'Lewes Cathedral', sits on the banks of the River Ouse in the old industrial heart of the County Town. Founded in 1790, the brewery is proud to carry on the age old tradition of local sustainability and hop contracts are placed four years in advance to support the local growers in their native and adjoining counties. Some have supplied them for over sixty years. Distribution of their beers is limited to a self imposed sixty mile radius of Lewes.

Their *Sussex Best Bitter* is renowned, but Harveys is by no means a 'one beer brewery'. They maintained uninterrupted supply of their dark mild and old ale, as well as the lower gravity bitter introduced when rationing was in place during the Second World War. A stronger, dry hopped bitter was added to their portfolio in 1988 - *Armada Ale*. *Old Ale* is brewed seasonally between October to March and is greeted each year with the 'Old Nouveau' celebrations in the brewery yard.

In 1990, their bicentenary year, Harveys decided to launch a 'Seasonal Brew - available for one month only'. This had long been the case with their draught *Christmas Ale* and the following year saw production of *Tom Paine* for 'Independents Month' each July. Soon afterwards the range was expanded - *Kiss* for February; 1859 *Porter* in March; *Knots of May Light Mild* for 'Mild in May'; *Copperwheat Beer* for June; *Southdown Harvest Ale* for September; *Star of Eastbourne* for October; and *Bonfire Boy* for November. These brews enjoy a consistent demand and are tied into the local traditions and folklore of their environs.

Recently Harveys produced a Golden Ale - *Olympia* - to replace their Winter Warmer between April to September. They are also proud to produce their bottle conditioned *Imperial Extra Double Stout* under the label of A. Le Coq. This beer, dating from the end of the eighteenth century, is truly a taste of the past. It is bottled within the brewery after twelve months storage. The company has bottled its own beers, uninterrupted, since the late nineteenth century and local distribution continues to make returnable bottles viable.

An exciting current development of the brewery is the establishment of a five barrel brewing plant. This will take on a multi-faceted role - part museum, part education, part training and part product development. It is situated on the site of the original Georgian brewhouse where Head Brewer Henry Barrett arrived in 1866 "to brew in a small brewery where mashing operations were performed by four men in a very primitive way, mashing with oars."

In 1881 the current tower brewery, designed by William Bradford, replaced the original Georgian brewhouse. It is a beautiful example of a Victorian country brewery in the industrial Gothic tradition.

Within the 'Georgian' micro plant it is intended to reproduce old recipes from long closed Lewes breweries and offer them to the public houses of Lewes to enhance the brewing heritage of the town. God willing, they will

*"send thee good ale enough,
whether it be new or old ..."*

Brewer of the Year

HARVEY'S

Sussex
**BEST
BITTER**
Alc 4.0% Vol

*Local Sustenance
Since 1790*

A Campaign of Two Halves

Campaigning for Pub Goers & Beer Drinkers

CAMRA, the Campaign for Real Ale, is an independent not-for-profit, volunteer-led consumer group. We campaign tirelessly for good-quality real ale and pubs, as well as lobbying government to champion drinkers' rights and promote local pubs as centres of community life. As a CAMRA member you will have the opportunity to campaign to save pubs under threat of closure, for pubs to be free to serve a range of real ales at fair prices and for a reduction in beer duty that will help Britain's brewing industry survive.

Enjoying Real Ale & Pubs

CAMRA has over 130,000 members from all ages and backgrounds, brought together by a common belief in the issues that CAMRA deals with and their love of good quality British beer. From just £20 a year – that's less than a pint a month – you can join CAMRA and enjoy the following benefits:

Subscription to *What's Brewing*, our monthly colour newspaper, and Beer, our quarterly magazine, informing you about beer and pub news and detailing events and beer festivals around the country.

Free or reduced entry to over 160 national, regional and local beer festivals.

Money off many of our publications including the *Good Beer Guide* and the *Good Bottled Beer Guide* and *CAMRA's Great British Pubs*.

Access to a members-only section of our national website, **www.camra.org.uk**, which gives up-to-the-minute news stories and includes a special offer section with regular features.

Special discounts with numerous partner organisations and money off real ale in your participating local pubs as part of our Pubs Discount Scheme.

Log onto **www.camra.org.uk/joinus** for
CAMRA membership information.

CAMPAIGN
FOR
REAL ALE